P9-ARX-893

EMPOWERING CHILDREN

Empowering Children

Children's Rights Education as a Pathway to Citizenship

R. BRIAN HOWE and KATHERINE COVELL

UNIVERSITY OF TORONTO PRESS
Toronto Buffalo London

Property of the Library
Wilfrid Laurier University

DISCARD

Property of WLU
Social Work Library

© University of Toronto Press Incorporated 2005
Toronto Buffalo London
Printed in Canada

ISBN 0-8020-3857-3

Printed on acid-free paper

Library and Archives Canada Cataloguing in Publication

Howe, Robert Brian
Empowering children : children's rights education as a pathway to
citizenship / R. Brian Howe and Katherine Covell.

Includes bibliographical references and index.
ISBN 0-8020-3857-3

1. Children's rights – Study and teaching.   2. Citizenship – Study and
teaching.   I. Covell, Katherine   II. Title.

HQ789.H69 2005   323.3′52′071   C2004-906967-5

This book has been published with the help of a grant from the Canadian
Federation for the Humanities and Social Sciences, through the Aid to Scholarly
Publications Programme, using funds provided by the Social Sciences and
Humanities Research Council of Canada.

University of Toronto Press acknowledges the financial assistance to its
publishing program of the Canada Council for the Arts and the Ontario Arts
Council.

University of Toronto Press acknowledges the financial support for its
publishing activities of the Government of Canada through the Book Publishing
Industry Development Program (BPIDP).

This book is dedicated to the newest citizens in our family:

Alexander, William, Oliver, and Logan

Contents

Acknowledgments

This book is the culmination of research funded by a standard research grant of the Social Sciences and Humanities Research Council of Canada. It has been published with the help of a grant from the Humanities and Social Sciences Federation of Canada, using funds provided by the Social Sciences and Humanities Research Council of Canada. We acknowledge also the anonymous reviewers whose comments were helpful and so very positive, and University of Toronto Press editor Stephen Kotowych, an always pleasant bearer of good news.

EMPOWERING CHILDREN

CHAPTER ONE

Denying Children's Rights

It undermines the integrity of the family and involves children in a political undertaking. There is a gradual erosion of parental authority and this is one more step in that direction.

Abbotsford School Trustee cited in the *Abbotsford News*, British Columbia, 16 September 1999

You might suppose that this Canadian school trustee was referring to some new subversive organization for children and youth. Were children being called to join a radical new political party? Were children being lured into cult membership? No. What this trustee and many parents and adults across Canada were and are worried about is children in schools being informed that they have basic human rights. In celebration of the tenth anniversary of the adoption of the United Nations Convention on the Rights of the Child (hereinafter the Convention), UNICEF Canada and Elections Canada jointly organized an election for schoolchildren to take place in November 1999. A key purpose of the election was to stimulate thinking about children's rights and to educate young people about the rights of the child as described in the Convention. Comparable elections previously had taken place in Belize, Colombia, Mexico, and Mozambique. As in these countries, to raise awareness of children's rights, children in schools across Canada were given the opportunity to discuss and then to vote on the relative importance of children's rights in the general areas of education, family, food and shelter, health, safety, name and nationality, and the expression of opinions.

The election was quite remarkable. It was remarkable, first of all, in the enthusiastic response of the children whose schools and teachers allowed them to participate in the election. Following an intense educational campaign, in which young people learned about the Convention and about the issues of children's rights, three-quarters of a million students in over 1,900 schools across Canada voted on the rights that they thought were most important. In doing so, they expressed a very high level of interest. The election also was remarkable in the vociferous objections it engendered. Strong opposition was expressed by a number of groups including family values organizations, traditional conservative politicians, and parents' groups who actively campaigned against the election, writing letters to educational authorities urging that schools not participate. Consistently, the opposition to the vote reflected a belief that allowing children to know and to discuss their rights was inappropriate because such education would undermine family and adult authority, involve children in undesirable political activity, and invite an undue degree of state intrusion into the family. Link Byfield (1999), for example, writing in the conservative *Alberta Report*, described the vote as 'silly, utterly meaningless' and as a 'pernicious waste of money.' Byfield admonished education authorities to tell the government to 'mind its own knitting.'

Most of all, the election was remarkable in the irony of the results. Many had expected that the students would become overly demanding and defiant and would give priority to their own personal freedoms. Contrary to these expectations, however, the results, announced by UNICEF, showed that the right held to be most important to children and youth was the right to grow up in a family. The right to a family was voted to be the most important of all children's rights by 24 per cent of the participants. This was followed by the right to food and shelter (20 per cent) and the right to health care (11 per cent). The importance of such rights to Canadian children is consistent with patterns that obtain in other countries. Children in Mozambique voted the most important right to be the right to a name, nationality, and family. Those in Belize and in Mexico ranked the right to education as the most important. And children in Colombia voted for the right to a safe environment. In none of these countries did children give priority to personal freedoms.

Other assessments of children's beliefs about the importance of their rights demonstrate similar findings. Children in Yemen, for example, who had been taught about the Convention by child advocates, identified the most important areas of children's rights issues to be those relevant to child labour, school dropout, and street children (Woll, 2000). Australian adolescents, when asked for their views, gave priority to rights related to survival and development, health and medical care, and family (Irving,

2001). In essence, when children are taught about their rights and then given the opportunity to discuss them and to identify the rights that are most important to them, the outcome is often antithetical to that expected. When educated about the rights of the child, children do not become overly demanding and self-centred, giving priority to individual freedom or the right to self-determination. Most often children are concerned about social rights and rights related to family. It is noteworthy that in the years that have passed since the unanimous adoption of the Convention on the Rights of the Child by the General Assembly of the United Nations in 1989, no reports have appeared demonstrating that awareness of rights has led children into defying the authority of parents, religious leaders, or teachers (David, 2002). Nonetheless, determined opposition to teaching children about their rights at school or at home or in the community persists. In fact, in a number of school districts where the UNICEF student elections took place in 1999, parental opposition was so strong that it was effective in blocking children's participation in those elections (*LifeSite Daily News*, 1999).

Rather than understanding the Convention on children's rights as a tool for improving the lives of children, critics have described it as UNICEF propaganda and as an anti-family document that serves only to indoctrinate children into unquestioning acceptance of U.N. policy (e.g., Steel, 1999). In some parts of the non-Western world, such as Vietnam, the Convention has been criticized as being a document so grounded in Western individualism that it is in conflict with traditional family values (Burr, 2002). When asked about educating their students about the rights of the child, teachers often express discomfort with the idea (Arnot, Arujo, Deliyanni-Konintze, Rowe, & Tome, 1996; Covell & Howe, 2000). The underlying concern appears to be mainly the fear that if children are aware of their rights, then teachers, parents and other adults will lose their authority and their ability to control children. To date there is no evidence to support such a concern.

Why Children's Rights Education?

Children's rights education is necessary for reasons of international law. Under the U.N. Convention of the Rights of the Child, ratified by virtually all countries of the world, member countries are obligated to educate children – as well as adults – on the rights of the child that the Convention describes. In the Convention, and in this book, *children* are defined as all young persons under eighteen years of age. Children's rights education is a key to promoting citizenship. As they learn about their rights under the Convention, children also learn about the rights and responsibilities of citizenship. They learn about the values, virtues, and practices of good citizenship. Opponents have little reason to be so fearful of children's rights or of education about children's rights.

Karl Knutsson (1997) argued that there is no reason to suppose that children will become more demanding of rights or more defiant if they learn about their rights. First, it is very unlikely that children will come together and form a widespread rights-demanding movement comparable to that of the American civil rights movement of the 1960s or the women's movement of the 1970s. Knutsson pointed out that the variations in children's socialization and resources make it highly unlikely that there would be enough children together at any one time and any one place who share the sense of purpose and efficacy, or who have the resources to effect the formation of a critical mass. Second, where there is evidence that children have taken action after learning about their rights, such action has been pro-social, and for the most part other-oriented. Children have not demanded more rights for themselves, but have acted in response to the knowledge that the rights of other children are being violated (e.g., Covell & Howe, 1999; Decoene & De Cock, 1996).

A number of children's rights initiatives have shown that teaching children about their rights does not lead to anarchy in the family or school, but has highly beneficial effects. Education about children's rights affects the learner in at least three ways (Tibbits, 1997). First, and most obvious, such education provides basic information about children's rights and responsibilities. Children learn about their rights and responsibilities in a systematic way, and they learn about the underlying principles of human rights more generally. Second, through imparting the attitudes and values upon which the practice of citizenship and democratic living is based, children are taught respect for the rights of others, social responsibility, and to support justice and equality. Third, children's rights education empowers children as citizens and enables them to take positive citizenship action. In this way children can learn the skills and achieve the competence necessary for effective citizenship and for participating in and promoting a democratic and human rights-based culture. Some case studies are illustrative.

Learning about her rights transformed the life of Uchengamma, a fourteen-year-old girl in India, leading her to advocate the rights of children, especially girls. Prior to knowing that she had a right to education, Uchengamma believed she had no choice but to leave school at age eleven, to work in the fields, and to enter an early arranged marriage. But in learning about her rights, Uchengamma was empowered not only to go to school and improve her own life, but also to fight injustices committed against other working children and children denied education. Uchengamma has become well known for the success of her efforts (Shetty & Ratna, 2002). Another example of how awareness of children's rights can promote social action is the story of Canadian Craig Kielburger. At the age of twelve, Kielburger learned that many children do not enjoy the rights he had taken for granted in growing up in Canada. He was particularly struck by the violations of children's rights in countries, such as Pakistan and India, where children are forced into child labour at the expense of their health and education. In his book *Free the Children* (1998), Kielburger described his travels to the sweatshops of South Asia and the profound impact this experience had on his life. He subsequently became engaged in social and political action, mobilizing children and adults throughout the world against the practice of child labour. Such examples abound.

The evidence shows overwhelmingly that children who learn about and experience their rights are children who demonstrate the fundamentals of good citizenship. They gain knowledge not only of their basic rights but also their corresponding social responsibilities. They develop the attitudes and values that are necessary for the promotion and protection of the rights of others, and they acquire the behavioural skills necessary for effective participation in a democratic society.

The purpose of this book is to make the case that we should embrace children's rights education in schools and not fear the prospect of children learning about their rights. Educating children about their rights is important because without doing so, countries will not be able to meet the international legal commitments that they have made in ratifying the U.N. Convention on the Rights of the Child. But meeting legal commitments is not the only reason for children's rights education. Children's rights education recognizes children as persons and worthy citizens rather than as the property of their parents or as small and vulnerable 'not-yets' (Verhellen, 1999). The goal of children's rights education is to provide the knowledge, attitudes, values, and skills that people need if they are going to build, sustain, or rebuild a society that is democratic and respects human rights. A concomitant goal is to promote a society characterized by an appreciation for cultural diversity and the values of tolerance, social equality, peace, and global citizenship. As such, children rights education is important as a pathway to citizenship and to citizenship education and as a vehicle for the development of the values and practices of global citizenship. Not teaching children about their rights is both a violation of their rights and a denial of their status as citizens. Under the Convention, children are not only citizens of the future but also citizens of the present with the right to express themselves in the present and to participate in decisions that affect them now. Knowledge of their rights is fundamental to children's practice of citizenship.

The New Interest in Citizenship Education

Over the past few years, the joint forces of broadening democracy and globalization have led to increased awareness of the need for effective citizenship education (Print, Ornstrom, & Nielsen, 2002). Some type of initiative for democratic reform could be observed in every major region of the world in the years between 1989 and 1993, and throughout the 1990s more societies than ever were trying to establish, re-establish, or maintain democracies (Torney-Purta, Schwille, & Amadeo, 1999). During this same period, engagement with and participation in citizenship decreased significantly and continues to do so in many countries, particularly among young people (Print et al., 2002). Concerns have been expressed that a disengaged and apathetic citizenry threatens the health and sustainability of democracy (Naval, Print, & Veldhuis, 2002; Osler & Starkey, 2002). As a result, educating young people for democratic citizenship has become an almost universal concern (Tiana, 2002), and there is consensus that school students must be provided with the knowledge, competencies, and values to motivate and enable democratic participation globally (Print et al., 2002).

The importance of democracy, and the need to redress the imbalance of resources and the inequities of society, have been brought to the fore by dramatic acts of terrorism such as the suicide bombings in the Middle East and the attacks of 11 September 2001 on the United States (Rouissi, 2002; Nordland, 1996). Terrorism, as seen in the context of the increased consumerism, and the worldwide availability of advanced communications and technology that are all part of globalization, has underscored the importance of education to promote and protect democracy (see Hornberg, 2002). In the report of UNESCO's International Commission on Education (Delors, 1996), it is argued that globalization requires shifts from nationalism to universalism, from prejudice to understanding, and from autocracy to democracy. These shifts, suggests the Commission, are most likely to occur as a result of effective citizenship education. Many others have likewise proposed citizenship education as a primary remedy for overcoming the difficulties associated with globalization, sustaining democracy, national cohesion, and social harmony (Audigier, 1996; Crick, 2000; Print et al., 2002). The challenges of globalization increase the importance of citizenship education that develops children's sense of social responsibility, respect and concern for others, and commitment to inclusiveness and justice (Battistich, Watson, Solomon, Lewis, & Schaps, 1999).

So far, no appropriate action has been taken in response to the calls for such citizenship education and concerns about democracy. In terms of education in practice, it appears that globalization has had a major impact in shifting the focus of education to enable competitiveness in the global marketplace (Anour, 2002; Porter, 1999). This trend of schools giving primacy to technology, with emphasis on economic values and principles, has been observed in many countries (Knutsson, 1997; Majhanovich, 2002; Priestly, 2002). Moreover, there have been recommitments of education budgets from areas such as cultural diversity or human rights to the funding of instruction about the new forms of technology (Synott, 2000). Globalization does not just involve economic changes, but also changes in environmental, cultural, and social consciousness, and it seems that these aspects of globalization are being overlooked entirely. (Synott, 2000).

Recent developments in curricula for schools in the United Kingdom illustrate this emphasis on economic rather than human values. In disregard of the Council of Europe's recommendations to include children's rights in its new compulsory citizenship curricula (Ruxton, 1996; Wyse, 2001), the British government decided to focus on responsibilities – especially economic ones. A major learning objective of the new citizenship education curriculum for all fourteen- to sixteen-year-olds in the United Kingdom is knowledge of how the world economy functions. The rationale is as follows. The capacity to understand various economic perspectives is necessary for the exercise of the rights of citizenship; in fact, it is an understanding of economics that provides the foundation for participation in the democratic process (Davies, Howie, Mangan, & Telhaj, 2002).

The new citizenship education initiative in Great Britain is but one of a proliferation of such education reforms undertaken in response to concerns about citizen disengagement from the democratic process, perceived threats to democracy, and an underlying assumption that education can and should teach citizenship (Audigier, 1996; Rouissi, 2002). Besides programs of civics or citizenship education in general, there have been a variety of innovations in curricula in response to current social conditions. Among these are the following: use of information technology to increase global competitiveness, promotion of the development of occupational skills to improve prospects for employment, sexuality education to discourage an early transition to parenthood, environmental education to slow or reverse the pattern of environmental degradation, and moral education to promote the values of tolerance, peace, and justice (Benavot, 2002). Unfortunately, citizenship and related curricula, generally, do not appear successful in achieving their overarching goals of increasing social or political engagement and participation (Print et al., 2002; Torney-Purta, 2002). The failure of these curricula to engage students in democratic activity stems in part from their failure to take fully into account two essential aspects of democratic citizenship: knowledge of rights and responsibilities on the one hand, and democratic values and behaviours, on the other (Print et al., 2002).

Democratic citizenship requires that citizens have knowledge of their rights and responsibilities. In most existing citizenship education programs, as in the British citizenship curricula, there is little attention to education about rights. Where rights are included, they typically are not the rights of the child as described in the U.N. Convention. Rather, the domestic citizenship rights of adults are what is meant and addressed. In Germany, for example, students are taught about their future (adult) rights with regard to voting, as well as with regard to participation in political parties and interest groups (Handle, Oesterreich, & Trommer, 1999). In Cyprus, the focus of rights education is on Cypriot society – it is a narrow selective focus that disregards children's rights under the Convention and narrowly defines citizenship to be consistent with the adult status quo (Torney-Purta et al., 1999). When denied knowledge of their rights children are implicitly denied citizenship status. Furthermore, children are explicitly denied citizenship status when they are treated as future rather than present citizens.

Democratic citizenship also requires that citizens hold democratic values and have the skills and motivations that underlie democratic behaviour. The development of democratic values and behaviours requires continual experience with democracy at school. How the school and classroom operate have a profound impact on the attitudes, habits, and behaviours of the students (Wraga, 2001). Citizenship education should do more than tell children about democracy. The school and classroom

should be democratic and have respect for rights and democratic principles as modelled by teachers and administrators (Terren, 2002). The call
for democratic schools largely has been met with silence (Torney-Purta et
al., 1999) or failure (Mann & Patrick, 2000). The core practices needed in
the democratic classroom are engaging teaching strategies with systematic provision of opportunities for student participation (Audigier, 1996;
Torney-Purta, 2002). If citizenship education is to meet its goals, children's rights, particularly the provision for age-appropriate participation
in matters that affect the child, must be the guiding principle for educational practice. Yet despite widespread recognition among researchers
and educators of the value of allowing students active participation in
decision-making concerning their education, and despite participation
being the key indicator of the health of democracy (Terren, 2002), participation by schoolchildren in school policymaking is rare. Democratic
classrooms are almost non-existent (Print et al., 2002). On the contrary,
there appears to be a growing tendency to assume that good teaching is
simply transmitting facts to children (Hancock & Mansfield, 2002).

As noted forty years ago by Holt (1964), and eloquently reinforced
more recently by Scardamalia and Bereiter (1996), schools may actually
discourage the skills that are necessary for effective citizenship. Instead,
these authors contend, schools sometimes train more for effective membership in the military rather than participation in a democracy, by providing extensive practice in the fulfilment of meaningless tasks, rote
learning, and unquestioning obedience. School systems tend to reward
students who avoid thinking and instead focus on rote learning (Barrett,
1999). Over the past decade, there appear to have been few changes in
pedagogical approaches to citizenship education. In Toronto, two years
after the U.N. Convention on the Rights of the Child was passed, when
asked what he was learning, a student told the researcher: 'To take notes
off the overhead projector' (Osborne, 1991, p. 10). The same answer
might very well be given today. Recently, when asked to describe how
much participation the class had in decision-making, a child interviewed
in a school in England answered: 'The most choice we ever get is which
felt pen to use' (Wyse, 2001, p. 217).

To date, there appears little recognition in the literature that school
reform or changed pedagogy may be missing some of the ingredients of
effective citizenship education. Instead, the discourse in response to the
observed failure of current citizenship curricula centres on whether it is
appropriate or possible for schools to teach the knowledge, values, and
skills that provide the foundation for democratic citizenship. The Cana-

dian Teachers Federation, for example, is studying whether schools should teach the content and skills necessary for participation in a global democratic society or for participation in a global competitive market-place (Wall, Moll, & Froese-Germaine, 2000). As Majhanovich (2002) has put the question, should the focus be on 'education for life' or 'education to make a living'? Others have focused on the difficulties of teaching values. How do we raise the moral sensitivity of young people enough to teach them values (Audigier, 1996)? How do we know what values we should teach to promote effective citizenship (Sutherland, 2002)? Mortimore (2001, p. 243) contended that we should teach 'the best humanitarian values,' but how are these to be defined? Many educators have come to believe that it is misguided to expect schools to provide education aimed at achieving social values or political goals and unreasonable to expect school curricula to facilitate international understanding and coexistence (e.g., Benavot, 2002). Margaret Sutherland (2002) offered a solution when she submitted that, given the lack of consensus about what values should be taught and given the failure of the various approaches that have been tried, schools should not try to teach citizenship as a separate subject, but rather through teaching history, languages, and political literacy. We disagree.

Students learn from both the formal and the hidden curriculum in schools. Seaton (2002), among many others, reminded us that the hidden curriculum has a profound impact on what students learn. Students are unlikely to learn democratic values and behaviours unless these are present throughout the school. The importance of democratic rights, values, and behaviours must be reflected in both the formal curricula, through explicit teaching, and throughout the hidden curriculum, as embodied in school structures, codes of conduct, mission statements, and classroom interactions that model democracy and respect for the rights of all. Only with these conditions met through school reforms that promote and respect children's rights and participation can we realistically expect the goals of citizenship education to be fully realized. Rights education, based on the U.N. Convention on the Rights of the Child, can and should provide the foundation for values teaching and for democratic citizenship. The use of the Convention as the standard for teaching democratic and citizenship rights overcomes the difficulties of identifying appropriate values, because it reflects a cross-cultural agreement on the rights that all children should have respected. Moreover, the Convention overcomes the dichotomy of education for life versus education for living because, acknowledging their inter-relatedness, it provides for both. Although it is clearly not a panacea for all social ills, we do see children's rights education as a pathway to effective democratic citizenship.

What Is Children's Rights Education?

The U.N. Convention on the Rights of the Child describes an international consensus on what the rights of children are and the corresponding responsibilities for ensuring that the rights of all children are respected. Children's rights education is the explicit teaching of the rights described in the Convention in an environment that itself models and respects those rights.

Priscilla Alderson (1999) discussed five characteristic approaches to rights education as implemented in schools. The most common is the 'not-yet' approach. Children are educated for the roles and responsibilities that they will assume as future citizens and as adult members of their society. Alderson noted that there may be some acknowledgment that children have citizenship rights, but most frequently this is made in a trivial manner, for example, by teaching children that they have a right to a clean environment and therefore a responsibility to pick up litter. This approach does not recognize the citizenship and rights-bearing status of children. Rather it assumes children to be future citizens in need of preparation. It fails to meet any of the specified goals of rights or citizenship education to promote democratic values or behaviours and citizenship engagement.

A second, less commonly used approach is 'constrained rights education.' This gives grudging recognition of the rights of children, while at the same time, it assumes that children generally are insufficiently rational to understand them. Children may be taught that they have rights under an international convention; however, many of their rights will not be respected at the school, and they will not be provided an opportunity to exercise their rights. This approach, too, is unsuccessful in promoting democratic citizenship values and behaviours. On the contrary, it is most likely to promote disengagement and alienation as students detect its inherent hypocrisy.

In the third and equally less commonly used approach, children's rights education is selective and tends to focus narrowly on issues such as how fortunate children are to have the Convention's rights to protection. Alderson called this approach 'limited rights education.' It is unlikely to have an impact on the attitudes or behaviours of most children. It may, however, be argued that children who are not experiencing their rights to protection, who are being sexually, physically, or economically exploited, are children who will be somewhat confused or perhaps dismissive of what they are being taught.

The fourth, again not commonly used approach is essentially 'rights violations education.' Students are taught about developing countries as places that are rife with abuses of children. They learn that there is a convention of rights for children that is supposed to protect children in the developing world, but that it fails to do so (Alderson & Arnold, 1999). If successful in raising students' knowledge of the difficulties faced by many children in developing countries, this approach is perceived to be of little, if any, relevance to the students themselves.

'Full-blown rights education,' the fifth approach, is the least commonly used of all the approaches to rights education. It is, however, the only approach that takes the children's rights under the Convention seriously, and as Alderson (1999, p. 196) has said, 'combines talk with action.' The Convention is taught in a democratic classroom environment, which is characterized by mutual respect among the students and between the teacher and students. Students are given both the knowledge and skills that provide the foundation for effective democratic citizenship. This is a classroom in which children's rights are not just taught, but are recognized, respected, and modelled. It is a classroom that reflects the spirit and the philosophy of the U.N. Convention on the Rights of the Child. This classroom recognizes the child as citizen. This teaching promotes social responsibility and the related values and behaviours of democratic citizenship. This is what we mean by children's rights education: It is at once the most beneficial and the most rare.

Its rarity is seen in the failure of citizenship education programs to promote democratic values or behaviours, as summarized above, and in the pervasive ignorance of the Convention. A number of surveys conducted over the past few years have demonstrated the lack of knowledge of the children's rights Convention among children (as well as adults) living in countries that have ratified it. A lack of knowledge and understanding of children's rights has been found wherever surveys have been taken. Typical findings are those of Alderson. In her survey of over 2,000 British schoolchildren between the ages of seven and seventeen years, in thirty-four focus groups conducted in English schools, Alderson (1999, 2000) found little knowledge of children's rights. Only 5 per cent of the children reported that they had heard about the U.N. Convention on the Rights of the Child 'a lot,' 19 per cent had heard about it 'a bit,' while the majority (76 per cent) had heard about the convention 'not at all.' Similar studies and findings were reported from New Zealand. Only three eleven- to twelve-year-olds out of five classes in Auckland had heard about children's rights (Tapp, 1997), as had only 15 to 16 per cent of schoolchildren surveyed across the country (Gilbert, 1998; Taylor et al., 2001). Studies undertaken in England (Wyse, 2001), Canada (Covell & Howe, 1999; Ruck, Keating, Abramovitch, & Koegl, 1998), and Spain (Ochaita & Espinosa 1997) also revealed little knowledge among children of children's rights under the U.N. Convention. In their comparative study of knowledge about human rights among schoolchildren in Botswana, India, Zimbabwe, and Northern Ireland, Bourne, Gundara, Ratsoma and Rukanda (1997, p. 17) noted that there was 'widespread ignorance of the United Nations Convention on the Rights of the Child.' Each of the countries above has ratified the Convention and accepted the responsibility to spread awareness about children's rights. None is fulfilling its obligations. Efforts to make children aware of their Convention rights have been limited to specific initiatives, rather than the systematic inclusion of children's rights education in school curricula.

The lack of knowledge of the U.N. Convention contributes to the perpetuation of misperceptions about children's rights and thereby the reluctance to teach children's rights. Children who have not been taught their rights, in a rights-respecting environment, tend to personalize the concept of rights and have difficulty in appreciating the rights of others (Dye, 1991). Rather than understanding that responsibilities are inevitable concomitants of rights, and rather than understanding rights as a foundation for democracy, children who have not received children's rights education tend to believe that having rights means being able to do what you want (Covell & Howe, 1999; Melton & Limber, 1992). Thus, a lack of, or avoidance of, rights education may be more likely to promote a culture of personal entitlement rather than a culture of democratic values. Children's understanding of rights frequently is based on their experience of the media. We should not discount the impact of increasing access to misinformation on the world wide web, a place where many of the dot.com generation obtain their knowledge of rights (see Willinsky, 2002).

The U.N. Convention on the Rights of the Child had been ratified by most countries of the world by the mid-1990s. Yet we approach the end of the U.N. Decade for Human Rights Education (1995–2005) with persisting disagreements over the goals of education and with an emphasis on education for global economic competitiveness. We are hopeful that

Tibbits (1997) was right in her expressed belief that there is a growing international consensus that education in and for rights is essential to build and maintain free, just, and peaceful societies. But this must become more than rhetoric.

Overview of This Book

In Chapter 2, we examine the U.N. Convention on the Rights of the Child and the obligations it sets forth for children's rights and children's rights education. We begin with a brief historical review of the evolving status of the child from property and not-yet to person and citizen and the movement towards the Convention. We then analyse the Convention including its categories of children's rights, basic principles, and system of implementation. Our analysis then turns to the educational obligations of 'states parties' to the Convention and to the articles that call for children's rights education. The Convention would be illogical and incoherent if it did not assume that in order for children to exercise their rights, they need to be educated about their rights. We then conduct a search for programs of children's rights education and the degree to which states parties have fulfilled their obligations. What the record shows is that, contrary to their obligations, states parties have generally failed to provide for such education. However, the silver lining is that educational programs have been developed that show promise in pointing the way to a wider consciousness of children's rights.

In Chapter 3, we examine children's rights education as a pathway not only to fulfilling an international obligation, but also to a deeper understanding of citizenship. We begin with a review of the literature about citizenship and discussions of the evolving meaning of citizenship. We find that such discussions are largely 'adultcentric.' On the one hand, the meaning of citizenship has evolved to recognize the importance of responsibilities as well as rights, to recognize the differentiated nature of citizenship, and to appreciate the global dimension of citizenship. On the other hand, there is a failure to recognize children as citizens. We then provide an account of children as citizens on the basis of the Convention and in reference to the developing concept of citizenship, which has evolved to appreciate the importance of social responsibility, differential citizenship, and global citizenship. Finally, we examine schools as settings for educating children in citizenship. We find that schools continue to operate on the basis of outdated and adultcentric understandings of citizens and citizenship. They fail to recognize that children are not only citizens of the future but also citizens of the present.

In Chapter 4, we assess existing approaches to citizenship education and suggest the benefits of an approach based on children's rights. Generally, citizenship education can be categorized into three types that vary with the relative emphasis placed on teaching the values, behaviours, or knowledge that promotes democratic citizenship. We illustrate each type with discussions of character and moral education; anti-racist, environmental, and peace education; and civic education. We assess the successes and limitations of each type with reference to evaluation research data. We then describe how human rights education provides a more comprehensive approach to citizenship and why it also is limited. Unlike the other approaches, human rights education has interrelated goals of empowerment and motivation for social change, and it is contextualized within human rights documents such as the U.N. Universal Declaration of Human Rights. What human rights education (like other approaches) fails to recognize, however, is the current citizenship status of the child; it also fails to provide teachings of salience in and relevance to the child's daily experiences. The benefits of citizenship education that is both contextualized within and informed by the U.N. Convention on the Rights of the Child are explained.

The value of children's rights education is described in Chapter 5. First, we examine the considerations in the design and implementation of children's rights curricula. We then discuss their essential pedagogic components, which include the following: democratic teaching, cooperative learning, and critical thinking. Our discussion of the impact of children's rights education is limited to curricula that include these components and for which evaluation data are available. Such curricula have been designed for and used with children as young as three years and as old as seventeen; they have been used and evaluated in Belgium, Canada, and England. Overall, the evaluation findings converge to suggest that children's rights education has a contagion effect. When children learn about their Convention rights in a democratic classroom in which their rights and citizenship status are respected, they develop attitudes and behaviours that are reflective of respect for the rights of all others. We describe the model of contagion and its link to effective citizenship.

In Chapter 6, we address the issue of implementing children's rights education. Together with the failure to acknowledge children as citizens, and the pervasive myths about the Convention, there are a number of other potential challenges to systematic inclusion of children's rights education in school curricula as called for by the U.N. Committee on the Rights of the Child and as impelled by world conditions. These include the practical difficulties for teachers, such as the hurdles of lack of training in the Convention and the necessary pedagogy. Key is the need to reform schools so that they practise children's rights, so that a culture of children's rights becomes the context for citizenship and rights education.

CHAPTER TWO

Fulfilling an Obligation

The word should not be mistaken for the deed.

Annie Franklin and Bob Franklin (1996)

Children's rights education is important because it is necessary to fulfilling an obligation of international law. During the 1990s, virtually all countries of the world, with the two exceptions of the United States and Somalia, have ratified the U.N. Convention on the Rights of the Child. In ratifying this legally binding document, they committed themselves to the task of not only implementing the rights of the child as defined in the Convention, but also of providing for children's rights education. Under the Convention, it is not enough that a country take measures to secure children's rights. It also is important that it ensure that children know their rights, thus equipping and empowering them to exercise their rights like other members of society. However, this obligation has not been fulfilled. Children still remain largely unaware of and uneducated about their rights, reflecting the continuing lack of action on the part of adult authorities worldwide to take seriously the rights of the child. As suggested in the quote above, the word – that states have committed themselves to implement children's rights education – should not be mistaken for the deed – that they actually are doing so.

We now analyse children's rights education as an international obligation. Our analysis begins with a brief review of the evolving status of children from property to persons and citizens. We then examine the Convention, the general obligations of states that result from their ratification of it, and their specific obligations in the area of education and children's rights education. We conclude with a search for programs of children's rights education that should be in place, if states were committed to fulfilling their educational obligations under the Convention. Although our search ends in disappointment, we also see a silver lining. Small but progressive steps have been taken that may yet lead to a wider and more genuine implementation of children's rights education.

The Evolving Status of Children

Only very recently in human history have children attained the official status of persons with inherent rights. Only with the signing and ratification of the U.N. Convention on the Rights of the Child have countries and adult authorities throughout the world embraced the concept of children as individual and independent persons with rights of their own. Before the Convention, in the not-so distant past, children had low status and were often regarded as the property of their parents. Over the past few hundred years, the status of children improved insofar as they came to be considered a special and vulnerable class of immature beings who are in need of the protective care of society and the state. But with this new status they continued to be seen as 'not-yets' rather than as existing persons (Verhellen, 1999). However, after the Second World War, in an era of expanding consciousness of human rights, the older concepts of children as property and as not-yets gave ground to the new concept of children as persons and bearers of rights. The adoption of the U.N. Declaration on the Rights of the Child in 1959, and then of the U.N. Convention on the Rights of the Child in 1989, gave official global recognition of this new concept and the elevated status of the child.

There is much debate among historians and social scientists about the treatment of children in the historical past (Pollock, 1983). However, most agree that in varying degrees at different times and in different places, many – if not most – children were ill-treated and often regarded as the property of their parents, as was reflected in the law (Freeman, 1983; Hart, 1991; McCoy, 1988; Stone, 1977). In Roman times, under the legal principle of *patria potestas* (power of the father), the father had the absolute power of life and death over his children. As possessions of their father, children were left unprotected by the law, subject to the practice of infanticide, maltreatment, and parental cruelty. In medieval and early modern Europe, although conditions for children were not quite so severe, the property concept continued to apply. Parents continued to have almost unlimited power over their children, and children continued to be subject to abuse, abandonment, and cruelty, unprotected by the state. By the seventeenth and eighteenth centuries, the concept of children as property became relatively more humane, as children were valued for their contribution to family work and their potential financial support of their parents in old age. Increasingly, parents were expected to maintain and protect their children. Still, children had the status of property. They could be cared for in a relatively humane way by their parents, but they were, nevertheless, typically seen as parental possessions and the private domain of their parents.

The belief that children were parental property was reflected in the laws, policies, and practices of the times. Laws developed to protect the interests of children were minimal, in deference to parental rights and parental authority over their children. For example, it was a legal offence for parents to kill or maim their children, but they were permitted to use harsh discipline, punishment, and beatings against their children. Parents were legally required to provide their children with the basic necessities of life, while they also had a relatively free hand in virtually all matters of child rearing. Prior to the nineteenth and twentieth centuries, beyond basic protection in criminal law, there were virtually no protective laws for children whether in the family or in society. Legislation to protect children against abuse or neglect did not exist. There were no policies or laws against the economic or sexual exploitation of children. There was no requirement that children receive education. There was no protective system of juvenile justice. Young offenders were treated harshly and in much the same manner as adult offenders.

From the nineteenth to the mid-twentieth century, the property concept gave ground to a new concept of children as a special and vulnerable class in need of paternalistic state protection (Freeman, 1983; Hart, 1991). Policies and laws still assumed that parents had fundamental authority over their children, but the rights of parents became more circumscribed. Influenced by a rising tide of humanitarianism and sentimentality towards children, and by social problems for children and families arising from industrialization, urbanization, and immigration, the belief gained ground that the state had to do more to protect and advance the interests of children. Not only were children to be protected from excessive cruelty or deprivation, they were also to be provided a nurturing and supportive social environment. Children still were assumed to be the possessions of their parents and the privacy of the family was still assumed to be of major importance. Parental rights were not to be intruded upon by the state except when absolutely necessary. However, it became recognized that society and the state had a responsibility to intervene when parents or other adults were abusive or exploitive and when the interests of children were at stake. The assumption of children as parental property started to give way to the assumption that the state sometimes must intervene when parents could not, or would not, fulfil their responsibilities or when children needed protection from other adults.

These new assumptions were influential in a child-saving era in which a wide number of new protective laws and policies were developed (Flekkoy & Kaufman, 1997). Child protection (or child welfare) legislation was developed in the nineteenth and early twentieth centuries to protect children from abuse or neglect and to provide alternative state care for children. Public education legislation was established requiring parents to send children to schools in the educational interests of their children, as well as in the public interest. Child labour laws were developed to protect children from economic exploitation. Juvenile justice legislation was created; a separate system of juvenile justice was established and youth courts were given authority to youth courts to provide for the paternalistic treatment of youth who were in trouble with the law. In legal proceedings involving children, the principle of *parens patriae* (the state as father) was applied: the state must sometimes substitute for the parent so that the developmental needs and interests of the child are provided for. This principle assumed that while parents still had primary responsibility to meet the needs of their children, there were occasions when the paternalistic state must step in to restrict or override parental control or to compel parents to fulfil their obligations towards their children. However, such intervention was to be done only as a very last resort.

With these new laws and policies of paternalistic state protection, children were given greater social and legal status. They were no longer thought of as simply property. But they were still regarded as objects in need of care either by their parents or by the paternalistic state. Children were still seen as 'not-yets' or as potential persons with a master status of 'not-yet-being,' in need of protection and nourishment, and not as existing persons with their own inherent rights (Verhellen, 1994). Under these laws, parents had duties and obligations towards their children, but children had no rights to claim anything from their parents (Howe, 2001). If parents were to fail to fulfil their obligations, the state must intervene – not on the ground that children had basic rights but because their parents failed to do their duty. The new policy of state paternalism was progressive in that it offered children certain protection from abusive parents and from harmful social and economic conditions. The policy remained limited, however, in that it continued to deny children voice and value as independent persons and bearers of rights of their own.

Finally, in the new era of human rights consciousness that followed the Second World War, the concept of paternalism gave ground to a newly emerging concept of children as independent bearers of rights. There had been hints of such a concept in earlier times. The political philosophy of John Locke shows early recognition of the child as an independent person (Archard, 1993). Locke was the first major thinker to assert that a child is not the property of his or her parents but a person with certain limited rights to protection. In his philosophy of education, Jean Jacques Rousseau promulgated the modern view that the child has value *as an existing child* (Seaford, 2001). In *Emile* (1762), Rousseau argued that children should be recognized and appreciated for who they are in the present, not simply for who they will become – 'Nature wants children to be children before they are men.' Finally, in the early twentieth century, building on the child-friendly positions of Locke and Rousseau, the idea of a new international code of children's rights emerged. British child advocate Eglantyne Jebb argued that children around the world need wider and better protection (Joseph, 1995). Jebb drafted a Code for Children that was adopted by the Save the Child Fund Union (which she founded) in 1922 and by the League of Nations in 1924. This Code became a basis for the U.N. Declaration on the Rights of the Child, adopted in 1959, and the U.N. Convention that followed three decades later.

Consciousness of children's rights became a significant force only after the Second World War. This was the result of a number of trends including the growth of human rights consciousness in general, the advancement of protective legislation for children and the educational effects of this legislation, and the growth and influence of the study of child development as a social science (Flekkoy & Kaufman, 1997). These trends converged to change the view of children as property or not-yets to children as independent subjects and existing persons in the here and now, with dignity and basic rights of their own (Hart, 1991). Under this new concept, children are entitled to have their needs provided for not only because parents have obligations or because government has a paternalistic responsibility for children, but because children themselves have fundamental rights (Howe, 2001). Because children have rights, parents and the state have responsibilities to provide for these rights. Children have claims based not on adult sentiment or the benevolence or duties of adult authorities, but on the basis of their own status as persons with inherent rights.

Prior to the 1970s, children's rights were conceived largely in terms of protection rights. Children had the basic human right to be protected from maltreatment and exploitation and the right to be provided with basic material welfare. This was the view of Jebb and other so-called protectionists. However, according to 'liberationists' such as Robert Ollendorf and Richard Farson, the protectionists show too little appreciation for the child's autonomy and preferences (Freeman, 1996). For protectionists, the child remains too much an object of concern instead of being a person with rights to participation and self-determination. If children are to be fully recognized as persons, their right to wider autonomy and self-determination must be recognized. These were the ideas that informed the children's liberation movement of the 1970s. Although seen as too radical within the wider children's rights movement, they left their mark by raising the issue of children's participation in decision-making. The idea began to take hold that children, at a certain age, should have representation in legal proceedings and input into the decisions that affect them.

Children's rights are being incorporated into new legislation, legal principles, and court decisions (Covell & Howe, 2001a; Freeman, 1983; Schmidt & Reppucci, 2002). This has occurred in varying degrees in different countries. The general pattern is this: In child protection legislation, children are now equipped (in some measure) with legal rights to be parties to proceedings and to have independent legal representation. They also have rights now in state child care systems and adoption proceedings. In health legislation, children now have the right, at a particular age, to consent or withhold consent for medical treatment. In education legislation and regulations, children – as students – have rights now in such areas as suspension and expulsion procedures. In juvenile justice legislation, children have new or stronger legal rights which include the right to legal counsel, the right to be informed of their rights, and the right to be heard in the proceedings. Finally, in family law and in legal proceedings dealing with children, there has been widening recognition of the principle that a child is a person before law and of the principle of the best interests of the child – both of which are principles related to children's rights. In custody disputes and child protection cases, increasingly the best interests of the child have become recognized as the determining principle for judicial decisions and not parental rights or parental interests or other considerations. Legislation and procedures have been adjusted, to some extent, to make room for the child's input into such decisions.

At the international level, the status of children as holders of rights received full recognition in 1989 with the adoption of the U.N. Convention on the Rights of the Child and with ratification of the Convention by virtually all countries of the world during the 1990s. A step in this direction had been taken in 1959, with the adoption of the U.N. Declaration on the Rights of the Child, but, like other international declarations, this one is a statement of broad moral principles, ideals, and aspirations rather than a document that is legally binding. The ratification of a convention or a covenant, however, is quite a different matter. A convention is an expression not only of a moral stand but also of a legal agreement and obligation. By ratifying the U.N. Convention, states parties officially committed themselves to a policy of recognizing and implementing the rights of the child, not merely to aspiring to practise children's rights. Ratification constitutes a legally binding commitment, obligating states parties to bring their laws, policies, and practices into line with the standards set out in the Convention (Cantwell, 1992).

The U.N. Convention on the Rights of the Child

It would be misleading to say that the rights and state obligations as set forth in the Convention were entirely new. Many of them can be found in earlier documents and, in particular, the International Covenant on Civil and Political Rights and the International Covenant on Economic, Social, and Cultural Rights. Both covenants were adopted by the U.N. General Assembly in 1966 and gained the force of international law in 1978. Many of the human rights specified in these documents were assumed to apply to children. But one difficulty with these older documents is that they did not made clear which rights applied to children and which did not (Covell & Howe, 2001a). No general distinction was drawn between children and adults and, thus, whether children had basic rights different from adults. What is significant about the U.N. Convention on the Rights of the Child is that, in addition to the recognition of certain new rights not recognized before, international standards for the rights of the child are given clear and systematic statement. International support for these standards is very strong, as reflected in the fact that the Convention is the most widely ratified and most quickly ratified treaty in world history.

By ratifying and embracing the Convention, countries essentially committed themselves to the principle that children have fundamental rights as individual persons and that parents, adults, and state authorities have obligations for providing for those rights (Freeman, 1996; Verhellen, 1994). This is why the Convention is such a landmark document in the history of childhood and of international law and public policy dealing with children. It officially puts to rest older and lingering assumptions about parental rights and state paternalism in regard to children, and it officially elevates the status of children to rights-bearing persons and citizens. In their relations with children, parents and state authorities are no longer assumed to have fundamental rights. Under the Convention, it now is children who have fundamental rights, and it is parents, adults, and state authorities who have obligations to respect and provide for those rights (Howe, 2001). If parents and adult authorities can be said to have rights, these are rights delegated to them under the Convention and conditional and closely connected to their duties and responsibilities to children. By ratifying the Convention, virtually all countries of the world are obligated to ensure its implementation. States parties have the obligation to make their laws, policies, and practices consistent with the provisions of the Convention, if not immediately, then over time.

One notable exception is the United States. Although the United States signed the Convention in 1995, it has not yet ratified it. Ratification would require the approval of the Senate Foreign Relations Committee and a two-thirds majority vote of the Senate. At this time, then, the United States does not have the same international legal obligation to children as do other countries. The reason for the American failure to ratify the document appears to be related largely to public concerns that the rights of children would override the rights of parents and that the Convention would override American sovereignty (Price, 1996). But despite this failure, the Convention remains an important guide for child advocacy in the United States and for professional practice (Small & Limber, 2002). U.S. states such as Vermont have passed resolutions in support of the Convention and of its ratification, which is important given that so many of the rights of the child are administered at the state level. Furthermore, authorities have used the Convention as a basis for developing child policies and practices at the local, state, and federal levels. Finally, that the United States has signed – although not ratified – the Convention is not unimportant. As a signatory to the Convention, the United States is at least obligated not to adopt policies contrary to it (see Melton, 2002).

Following Thomas Hammarberg (1990), we can divide the substantive rights of the Convention into the 'three Ps': provision, protection, and participation. The first two reflect the influence of the protectionist wing of the children's rights movement. The rights of provision refer to the child's right to be provided with basic economic and social needs. For example, children have the right to survival and development (article 6), basic economic welfare (article 27), basic health care (article 24), and basic education (articles 28 and 29). The rights of protection refer to the child's right to be protected from harmful or exploitive practices. Included here is the right to be protected from abuse or neglect (article 19), economic exploitation (article 32), and sexual exploitation (article 34). Finally, the rights of participation – the third P – reflect the influence of child liberationists, although the Convention's focus is on participation rather than self-determination. The rights of participation refer to the child's right to express opinions in matters affecting the child and to have his or her views heard in judicial and administrative proceedings (article 12). As part of the practice of participation, children have the right to freedom of expression and information (article 13); freedom of thought, conscience, and religion (article 14); and freedom of association and peaceful assembly (article 15). These participation rights give children the status not only of individual persons but also of participants or citizens in society.

The three Ps are rights that apply to all children. But the Convention also describes rights for children in special circumstances. For example, children who are refugees have the right to special assistance (article 22), and children with physical or mental disabilities have the right to special care (article 23), including in the areas of education, health care, rehabilitation services, and preparation for employment. Furthermore, children of minority communities and indigenous populations have the right to enjoy their own culture, practise their own religion, and use their own language (article 30).

The Convention's main guiding principles are the principles of non-discrimination, the best interests of the child, and age-appropriate participation (Flekkoy & Kaufman, 1997; Freeman, 1996; Toope, 1996). The principle of non-discrimination is described in article 2. It requires that states parties 'take all appropriate measures to ensure that the child is protected against all forms of discrimination or punishment.' Apart from article 2, the principle of non-discrimination is given expression throughout the Convention in articles referring to 'every child' or 'the child' without qualification or restriction. The principle of the best interests of the child is described in article 3. It requires that in 'all actions concerning children, whether undertaken by public or private social welfare institutions, courts of law, administrative authorities or legislative bodies, the best interests of the child shall be a primary consideration.' Furthermore, as stated in article 18, the best interests of the child are to be the basic concern of parents as well as other adult authorities. Finally, the principle of participation is given statement in article 12. It requires states parties to take steps to 'assure to the child who is capable of forming his or her views the right to express those views in all matters affecting the child, the views of the child being given due weight in accordance with the age and maturity of the child.' This essentially means that while the views of the capable child need not be decisive in decision-making, they are to be listened to and given more weight with the age and maturity of the child.

The incorporation of the principle of participation is a particularly important feature of the Convention (see John, 1996). It means that children have the status not only of persons but also of democratic participants or citizens of their society, with a right to a voice in matters affecting them. These may be relatively narrow matters within families but they also may be broader public matters within schools or neighbourhoods or broader matters of public policy affecting children. By ratifying the Convention, states parties have committed themselves not only to recognizing that child citizens have the right to a voice but also to listening to children as well. 'They have accepted that they can no longer make assumptions about what children should or do think; children's *own* views and voices have to be heard and taken into account' (John, 1996, pp. 3–4).

The Convention calls for the recognition of the fundamental rights of children but also for the implementation of those rights and for the monitoring of their implementation (Verhellen, 1994). Article 4 directs states parties to 'undertake all appropriate legislative, administrative, and other measures for the implementation of the rights recognized in the present Convention.' Furthermore, according to article 44, implementation is to be monitored through a reporting system in which states parties are required to send reports of their progress every five years to a special expert committee, the U.N. Committee on the Rights of the Child. The Committee is to review each report, along with reports of child advocacy organizations, and provide feedback and recommendations for improvement where needed. As with other international conventions, enforcement of the law is to be accomplished not through international police and courts but through the force of international peer pressure and domestic moral and political pressure. If states parties do not live up to their obligations, they run the risk of having to face sharp criticism and political embarrassment.

The significance of the Convention is that it officially elevates the status of children worldwide to persons and citizens. By agreeing to the Convention, states are agreeing to the principle that children are not simply 'noble causes' but 'worthy citizens' (Knutsson, 1997). The Convention essentially provides a blueprint for the betterment of children by recognizing them not as vulnerable little not-yets in need but as bearers of rights.

Education Obligations

A number of articles in the Convention deal with education and with children's rights education. Following Eugeen Verhellen (1993; 1994), we can divide the Convention's provisions on education along three tracks. First, there is the child's right to education (articles 28 and 23). This includes the right to free primary education, the right to accessible secondary and higher education, and the right of children with disabilities to appropriate education and support. Second, there are rights in education (articles 2, 12, 13, 14, and 15). These include the right to non-discrimination, participation, and the fundamental freedoms of expression, thought, and religion. Third, there are rights through education (articles 29 and 42). This refers to education in which children are able to know their rights and to develop respect for human rights and fundamental freedoms, including the rights and freedoms of children. This third track of education points to the need for effective programs of children's rights education.

The importance of this third track of education has long been understood by the United Nations and its agencies (Hodgson, 1996). It is not surprising that the United Nations would have a major interest in rights education. One of the organization's main purposes as set out in the United Nations Charter is the promotion and encouragement of respect for human rights for all without distinction. Since its creation in 1945, and especially since the 1960s, the United Nations and its various associated agencies have been active in promoting human rights education both as an end in itself and as a means to goals such as international security, peace building, and national development (Andreopoulos, 1997; Dias, 1997; Marks, 1997). Such promotional work has been reflected in the emphasis on education in various international declarations, conventions, resolutions, conferences, and special proclamations. Education was judged to be so important by the United Nations that it proclaimed 1995 to 2005 as the U.N. Decade for Human Rights Education.

Thus, it is no surprise that the U.N. Convention on the Rights of the

Child would give major attention to public education. But the Convention went further than previous treaties and conventions in calling for education (Lanotte & Goedertier, 1996). In previous human rights treaties, although states parties were encouraged to promote human rights awareness, there was no clear and positive duty to do so. However, in the Convention on the Rights of the Child, there is such a duty and it is explicit. This makes the Convention unique and original. Under article 42, states parties are required – not simply encouraged – to inform children as well as adults of the rights of children under the Convention. The architects of the Convention assumed quite logically that the exercise of rights by children presupposed that children have basic knowledge of their rights. They believed that the dissemination of knowledge was so important that there should be a dissemination duty built into the Convention. Thus, they made children's rights education an obligation, not simply a worthy objective to be pursued.

Children's rights education is called for directly in two articles of the Convention. First, under article 29, states parties agree that 'the education of the child shall be directed to the development of respect for human rights and fundamental freedoms, and for the principles enshrined in the Charter of the United Nations.' The development of respect for human rights and freedoms presupposes that the child possesses a basic understanding of human rights and freedoms, including the human rights and freedoms of children. A prerequisite to such understanding is knowledge gained through education. Thus, when states parties agree that a primary aim of education is to cultivate respect among children for human rights, they are agreeing that a primary aim of education is to teach children about human rights. This means educating children about human rights in general, as expressed in a country's constitutional documents, human rights laws, official policies, and history. But it also means educating children specifically about the human rights of children as described in the Convention, officially recognized and affirmed by its signatories.

Second, under article 42, states parties agree 'to undertake to make the principles of the Convention widely known, by appropriate and active means, to adults and children alike.' (In addition, under article 44, states parties are to make their reports widely known to the public, thus also contributing to public education.) Article 42 is unique and original in that it represents a duty of dissemination not present in previous human rights treaties (Lanotte & Goedertier, 1996). There is a clear obligation under this article for states to disseminate information and to educate children – as well as adults – about the rights of the child and to provide education 'by appropriate and active means.' Usage of the phrase 'appropriate and active means' assumes that it is inadequate merely to send out informational brochures or copies of the Convention to the public or copies of a state's report to the U.N. Committee on the Rights of the Child. It also is inadequate merely to construct a web site containing children's rights information, or to arrange a special day such as a national child day to publicize the Convention. Article 42 calls not for passive and sporadic informational programs but for active and robust programs that will reach children and adults in an effective way.

Children's rights education also is called for indirectly on the basis of the Convention's provisions regarding participation. If children are to participate in the decisions that affect them, and to exercise their rights to freedom of expression, freedom of thought and religion, and freedom of association and assembly, it is vital that they know that they have the fundamental right to do so. Otherwise, by keeping children in the dark or providing them with limited information, participation is not going to take place or is going to be tokenistic or so heavily controlled that the participation is not meaningful. It is perhaps arguable that protection and provision rights can be provided for without much knowledge or awareness of rights on the part of the child. However, this would be a return to paternalistic assumptions of an earlier era in which children – despite being cared for – would have no sense of themselves as rights-bearing persons with dignity. But in the case of participation rights, there is little argument. It is inconceivable that these rights can be exercised in a meaningful way without knowledge of the right to participate. Failure to provide children's rights education is to disempower children and inhibit their exercise of their rights.

Even if the Convention were silent on the question of children's rights education, it would be incoherent and illogical without the underlying understanding and requirement that children – as well as adults – should be educated about the rights of the child. If children have basic rights, they should be able to know and to exercise them. It is inconceivable that in agreeing to recognize and implement the rights of the child, states parties would be permitted by the Convention to hide or withhold information from their citizens about those rights. In short, the Convention calls upon the state to provide for not only children's rights but also children's rights education.

Educating children in their rights is also important as part of the system of monitoring and implementing the Convention. The Convention is designed to be enforced through moral and political pressure (Doek,

1992). It is to be implemented through a pressure-based process of states reporting to the U.N. Committee on the Rights of the Child every five years and through the monitoring of reports and state action, or inaction, by citizens and non-governmental organizations (NGOs). Pressure is to be generated on the basis of monitoring and criticism so that states will be spurred forward to improve their performance and ensure fuller implementation of the Convention. Pressure on the state will come from the U.N. Committee. It will also come from NGOs and child advocacy groups who are authorized under article 44 to provide supplementary and critical information to the committee (Verhellen, 1994). Monitoring organizations, will in turn, receive input from concerned groups and citizens. It was the intention of the framers of the Convention that input would also come from children. This was a reason for the dissemination duty described in article 42 (Van Bueren, 1995). Article 42 recognizes the importance of children's rights education in creating a trickle-down effect and pressure for fuller implementation of the Convention. It assumes that children will be educated in their rights and, thus, be in a position to be contributors and participants in the monitoring and implementation process.

For example, child and youth organizations representing children in state care would be able to provide input into the monitoring of policies and laws dealing with child protection and alternative child care. Student organizations or associations of student councils would be able to do the same in the area of educational policies. Organizations representing children with disabilities would be able to do the same in the area of legal and policy developments dealing with the issue of children's disabilities. This would be in line with both the system of monitoring and the participation provisions of the Convention.

The Convention assumes the importance of children's rights education as a vehicle for empowering children to participate as active citizens in the decisions that affect them and in the advancement of their rights. Such empowering effects may be better understood with a look first at two basic functions of rights. One basic function of rights is 'to provide some minimum protection against utter helplessness to those too weak to protect themselves' (Shue, 1980, p. 18). Rights function as a protective shield for the defenceless and as a restraint upon economic, political, and other forces that could otherwise harm the weak and powerless. Basic rights, argues Shue, 'specify the line beneath which no one is to be allowed to sink.' To ensure that people do not sink and to protect them against the powerful, rights need to be established in the law, policies, and practices of individual countries and in international conventions in which countries are bound to provide for these rights. But this is not enough. As emphasized in various U.N. declarations and conventions, 'familiarity with human rights is the best protection against infringement' (Verhellen, 1994, p. 100). Citizens need to know about their rights, if their rights are to have effect. If citizens are not aware of their basic rights, they are not in a position to exercise them, to apply pressure on governments to ensure that their rights are present in domestic laws and policies, or to apply pressure on the international community to ensure the implementation of their rights under international human rights standards. Education is required to empower citizens so that they may take steps to protect and secure their rights. Through human rights education, citizens are enabled to begin the process of acquiring the knowledge and critical awareness necessary to understand and question oppression and the denial of their rights (Meintjes, 1997).

These points apply to all citizens, but especially to children and their advocates. Children are widely recognized to be among the most vulnerable, weakest, and defenceless members of society. More than most others, they require basic rights as a protective device to shield them against forces that could harm them. Children cannot depend simply on sentiment or feelings of benevolence or a sense of duty among adults towards children. This is not sufficient. To rely on a sense of duty is to idealize adult-child relations and to ignore the too numerous cases of child maltreatment, exploitation, and denial of expression and voice. As with adults, it is vital that children and youth not only have basic rights but also know that they have basic rights. With such knowledge, children and child advocates are empowered to act. They are in a better position to raise issues and to apply pressure on authorities to ensure that the rights of the child are properly provided for. With awareness of their rights, children and youth are better able to voice concerns when their rights of provision, protection, and participation are violated or ignored. They are more able to resist those who would violate their rights and to raise concerns or lodge complaints with appropriate authorities. They also are more able to work with child advocates and provide input about the adequacy of child-related laws and policies, the enforcement of these laws and policies, and the implementation of the U.N. Convention on the Rights of the Child.

A second basic function of rights is a means for building human dignity or a sense of self-esteem. Philosopher Joel Feinberg (1970, 1973) has noted that the possession of rights is closely associated with the development of a sense of value. Rights, according to Feinberg, 'are not mere gifts or favors, motivated by love or pity, for which gratitude is the sole fitting response. A right is something that can be demanded or insisted upon without embarrassment or shame' (1973, pp. 58–59). A right is one's due. It says to bearers of rights that they are dignified persons worthy of respect. It conveys a sense of value and, in doing so, instills a sense of confidence or efficacy and empowers people to act as equal and valued citizens who exercise their rights. Feinberg's analysis of the linkage between rights and the sense of value may be applied to children. Children are entitled to certain things not out of pity or love or benevolence but because they have rights. It is their due. The possession of rights means that in their own eyes, as well as in the eyes of others, children are dignified persons worthy of respect. Rights equip children with a sense of value as individual persons, apart from their relation to their parents or adult authorities. Children are not parental property or dependents or objects of paternalistic concern. Rather, they are individual persons with rights and with value. With inherent value, children are empowered to hold their heads up high and to participate as citizens in their community. At the same time, in a community in which adults recognize the basic rights of children, children are further empowered because 'rights flow downhill' (Federle, 1994). In adult-child relations, because rights and power flow downhill to children, and because adults treat children less as powerless beings to do with as they please and more as persons with rights, children's sense of control is increased. Such treatment, in turn, has empowering effects.

Clearly, it is important that children know that they have basic rights. Children's rights education is at once an obligation of states parties to the Convention and a vehicle for the empowerment of children. Those who opposed the national student election on children's rights in Canada and other countries in 1999 had no solid ground to stand on. They certainly had the right to criticize the principle of children's rights and Canada's ratification of the Convention. But the fact is that Canada and virtually all countries of the world did ratify the Convention and in doing so agreed to implement the rights of the child and 'to make the principles and provisions of the Convention widely known, by appropriate and active means, to adults and children alike.' The Convention is part of international law and states parties are bound by international law to implement the rights of the child, certainly over time. Under the Convention, states parties are directed under article 4 to 'undertake all appropriate legislative, administrative, and other measures for the implementation of the rights recognized in the present Convention.' In short, countries have the obligation to bring their laws, policies, and practices into conformity with the standards of the Convention. Thus, although opponents of Canada's national student election can criticize the Convention and Canada's agreement to it, they cannot deny that Canada and other countries have the obligation to implement not only children's rights but also children's rights education.

In Search of Children's Rights Education

As indicated previously, studies reveal that the vast majority of children lack knowledge of their fundamental rights under the Convention or have a distorted or incomplete view of them. This is not unexpected. Despite the dissemination duty prescribed by the Convention, virtually all countries have failed to develop comprehensive and effective programs of children's rights education. Such failure is indicated both in reviews by researchers of international educational developments during the 1990s and in inspections by the U.N. Committee on the Rights of the Child of state reports on compliance with the Convention. Concerned by the lack of children's rights education, the Committee recommended to states parties that they advance children's rights education through incorporating it into regular school curricula. However, this recommendation has yet to be carried out.

Judith Torney-Purta and her colleagues (1999) have published a comprehensive academic study of the state of civic education (or citizenship education) in twenty-four countries. Examining developments in the 1990s, this study was an update and expansion of an earlier cross-national study of civic education done in the 1970s. The study was in part a review of curricula, pedagogy, and policies with respect to the teaching of citizenship, democracy, and human rights. Absent in the findings of the study was reference to the teaching of the rights of the child and the Convention. Reference was made to the teaching of citizenship rights and responsibilities and to human rights – with an adult focus – but not to the systematic teaching of children's rights. One exception was civic education in Bulgaria, where reference was made to the translation of the Convention into native languages and to the circulation of the Convention in schools in order to provide information for new teaching materials. But missing even in this example was children's rights education as part of the regular school curricula and teacher training.

Similar findings came out during a review of educational developments in the member countries of the International Save the Children
Agency, also done during the late 1990s (Muscroft, 1999). Implementation of the Convention was assessed in the areas not only of education,
but also sexual exploitation, juvenile justice, and the displacement of
children. The essential aim of the study was to determine whether reality matched rhetoric. Apart from a few pilot projects and efforts in a few
schools and regions, the review found a general absence of children's
rights education and failure in the countries studied to incorporate education on the Convention into the regular school curricula. Some
progress had been made in the area of rights to education and rights in
education, but very little in the area of rights through education. This
was reflected in the fact that while there was a certain degree of rights
awareness by professionals working with or on behalf of children, there
was little children's rights consciousness among children themselves
and in the general populations of the twenty-six countries studied. In
making its recommendations, Save the Children urged that the rights of
the child should become an 'essential feature of all education curricula'
and that failure to do so would be a 'fundamental contradiction' of the
Convention (Muscroft, 1999).

Reviews undertaken on a smaller scale had similar findings. A study of
human rights education in four countries of the British Commonwealth
– Botswana, India, Zimbabwe, and Northern Ireland – revealed a
remarkably low level of awareness of children's rights among school children reflecting the scant attention given to children's rights and to the
Convention in education curricula, teacher education, and school texts
and materials (Bourne, Gundara, Ratsoma & Rukunda, 1997). Only in
India was there a reasonable reflection of human rights principles
embodied in the school curricula. Even in India, however, there was no
specific and systematic teaching of children's rights. In another study, a
review of educational developments in Europe showed that, although
the Council of Europe had urged the inclusion of education on the
rights of the child at all levels of the curricula, so far very little actual
progress had been made in this respect (Ruxton, 1996). Much had been
done to encourage children in the broad values of democracy and
human rights in some countries, for example, Sweden. The specific
incorporation of children's rights into the school curricula, however,
was conspicuously absent. Finally, in their review of human rights education in three transitional European democracies – Romania, Slovakia,
and Albania – Neacsu-Hendry, Turek, Kviecinska, Kati, and Orlin (1997)

noted that some problems were associated with the new programs of civic education that had been designed to help prevent a return to total-itarian rule. On the one hand, progress had been made in incorporating into these programs information on the principles of democracy and human rights and on international human rights treaties, including the U.N. Convention on the Rights of the Child. But on the other hand, problems had emerged in Slovakia, for example, because teachers there were inadequately trained in human rights and did not put the pro-grams into full use.

This general lack of children's rights education came to the attention of the U.N. Committee on the Child, as it examined the first round of country reports that it received in the early to mid-1990s. In its assess-ment process, the Committee realized that little was being done on the third track of education – rights through education. The efforts of states parties were being directed mainly to the distribution of informational material about children's rights (and mostly in response to requests for such information), the construction of web sites, and periodic publicity through special events such as national child days, student parliaments, and student elections on children's rights. Little was being undertaken to reach children on a comprehensive and systematic basis and to edu-cate them seriously about their rights. The Committee saw this as a major problem. In failing to discharge their duty of dissemination, what states parties were doing, in effect, was to disempower children and restrict or deny their participation in the exercise and implementation of their rights.

The Committee took the dissemination duty very seriously as it began its work in the early 1990s (Hodgkin & Newell, 1998; Raadi-Azarakhchi, 1997). The Committee incorporated a guideline for children's rights education into its general instructions to member countries for prepar-ing their initial reports. This guideline asked states parties 'to describe the measures that have been taken or are foreseen, pursuant to article 42 of the Convention, to make the principles and provisions of the Con-vention widely known, by appropriate and active means, to adults and children alike' (U.N. Committee on the Rights of the Child, 1991). Reporting countries were instructed to describe the specific measures that they were undertaking, for example, in the areas of translating and distributing the Convention, educating children in schools, educating parents, educating professionals, and spreading awareness of children's rights through the media (Hodgkin & Newell, 1998). The Committee was determined that children would be made aware of their Convention rights and that countries would be prodded to fulfil their responsibilities under the Convention.

Thus, on receiving the first round of reports, the Committee was both disappointed and concerned by the general failure of states parties to make a serious start in implementing the Convention. The Committee made the following general points and recommendations. First, countries need to do more than to sponsor awareness-raising campaigns and the provision of informational material. They need to intensify their efforts and develop robust programs of children's rights education that would reach children and adults in more effective ways. Second, countries need to give particular attention to the development of professional education programs so that those who work with children – teachers, child-care providers, social workers, justice officials, lawyers, and judges – are educated on the rights of the child. These programs would educate not only adults in positions of authority, but also, through spreading awareness to these professionals they would educate children and future adults. Third, and of key importance, countries need to take steps to incorporate children's rights education into the regular school curricula. Only in doing this can children be reached in a comprehensive and systematic way. For children, this was the true meaning of 'appropriate and active' children's rights education.

It was logical for the Committee to give schools special attention. Strong programs in schools are the means of reaching children directly, and thereby systematically increasing their awareness of the Convention, overcoming their sometimes confused understanding of the nature of rights, and deepening their understanding and appreciation of their basic rights and responsibilities. Over time, as children became adults, schools would thus become a pathway to the development of a global children's rights culture, leading to further advances and implementation of the Convention.

The Committee's call for more serious children's rights education did not mean that it was totally unimpressed with state efforts (see the Committee's various country reports in U.N. Committee on the Rights of the Child, 1999 and 2003). It commended a number of countries for undertaking important measures. It noted, for example, that Sweden (1993), Costa Rica (1993), and Poland (1995) had done a great deal to promote awareness of children's rights through publishing and widely distributing significant educational materials; organizing workshops, seminars, and conferences; and funding NGOs for the purpose of publicizing the Convention. Poland and Costa Rica had taken the important step of giving training in children's rights to professionals who work with children. Norway (1994), Iceland (1996), and Austria (1999) had spread awareness through the programs and educational efforts of special children's ombudsman offices. Both Austria and France (1994) had advanced children's awareness of their participation rights as described in the Convention through the development of structures for the practice of participation. Austria had established a comprehensive system of student representation in schools. France had established a system of special youth councils to give youth a greater voice not only in schools but also in local communities. All of this was a start. But even in these relatively progressive countries, the Committee urged that educational efforts be intensified. It was vitally important, said the Committee, that each country develop a 'comprehensive strategy' for the dissemination of knowledge about children's rights (Hodgkin & Newell, 1998). Such a strategy required not only more extensive public awareness campaigns but also serious professional and teacher education programs and serious school-based children's rights education.

In the second round of country reports – ones that were due five years after the first round – the Committee found that while educational efforts had improved they still fell short of the comprehensive strategies that had been called for earlier. On the positive side, an examination of the second reports showed that most countries did, indeed, carry out more extensive public awareness campaigns and programs than they had in the first years reported on. Sweden, Costa Rica, Ethiopia, Finland, Russia and Iceland had undertaken such activities as the translation and distribution of the Convention and booklets about the Convention; the organization of children's rights workshops, seminars, and conferences; support for NGOs in publicizing and popularizing the Convention; and the promotional work of special agencies such as a children's ombudsman. Sweden (1998) and Iceland (2003), for example, highlighted the extensive informational programs that their children's ombudsman offices had carried out. Russia (1998) reported the large-scale publication of the text of the Convention and reference materials and the important support it had given to children's organizations in promoting awareness. Canada (2001) also reported the large-scale publication and distribution of materials as well as to the establishment of SchoolNet, whereby all public schools and public libraries were connected to the Internet, thereby allowing children to access information on their rights. Costa Rica (1998) reported its highly successful governmental campaign to publicize the rights of the child through the media, pamphlets, conferences, and workshops. Consciousness of children's rights was raised on a wider scale than before.

Progress was reported in the area of professional training and teacher education. Poland (2002), for example, had established a training program about children's rights for judges, legal guardians, and juvenile justice officials. Sweden and Denmark (2000) were training police officials about children's rights. In Egypt (1999) and Ethiopia (2000) NGOs and governmental bodies were offering training programs on children's rights to civil servants and those working with children. In the important area of teacher training, Sweden, Iceland, Poland, Russia, Honduras (1998), and the Czech Republic (2001) all reported the development – in varying degrees – of programs to educate teachers, school heads, teacher aides, and auxiliary staff on human rights, including on the Convention and the rights of the child. In addition, Poland now had teacher training programs in which teachers learned not only about the rights of the child but also about the educational and psychological consequences of violating children's rights. Sweden and Iceland had supplied schools and teachers with materials and resources about children's rights and ensured that the Convention is incorporated into school texts. In the Czech Republic measures had been undertaken not only to educate teachers but also to require schools to use the Convention as a standard for school life and to respect the Convention in day-to-day activities.

What is conspicuously absent in the second round of reports, however, is children's rights education as part of the regular school curricula, as well as full education on the rights of the child, as had been called for by the Committee. Although certain progress had been made in training professionals and teachers, countries had still failed to fulfil their educational commitments to children more than a decade after beginning to implement the Convention. Without children's rights in the school curricula and without educating children directly, there is no assurance that meaningful and effective children's rights education is taking place for children. Respect for children means educating children themselves about their rights. This generally has yet to be done.

The Silver Lining

Generally, countries have failed to provide children's rights education for children. However, there has been a silver lining in their disappointing performance. As already indicated, in the second round of country reports, it was apparent that steps had been taken in a few countries to develop education programs for children. Costa Rica (1998) had put the rights and duties of children into its school curricula of formal education. Russia (1998) and Ukraine (2001) reported that the study of the Convention was now included in their school curricula. Canada (2001) had developed new programs of children's rights education in the provinces of Nova Scotia (Grade 6) and Prince Edward Island (Grade 9). In the Czech Republic (2002) information on human rights and children's rights is now included in the social science section of standards for elementary education and in basic teaching material for academic secondary education and occupational education. However, to the extent that they exist, a major drawback to these programs is that they generally are limited to providing children with some basic descriptive information on the Convention and the rights of the child as a small part of a wider program of education on human rights and documents on human rights. Information generally is provided without the in-depth study, lessons, and activities that enable children to fully learn, digest, and appreciate their rights and responsibilities.

There is a silver lining within the silver lining. Initiatives have been undertaken with respect to children's rights curricula. For example, curriculum resource materials have been developed for individual teachers and schools by UNICEF that provide not only information on the rights of the child but also educational exercises and activities. UNICEF has long been critical of countries for failing to fulfil their obligations under the Convention in the area of children's rights education (Willemot, 1997). To remedy this situation UNICEF has developed a special education for development program, which provides resources and educational materials – directly and through the Internet – for teaching children's rights. Through its national offices and education officers worldwide, UNICEF has been applying pressure on various countries to get the program incorporated into their school curricula. But in the absence of the agreement of a country to do so, UNICEF has made educational material – informational booklets, lessons, activities, videos, and interactive CD-ROMS – available for teachers and schools on an individual basis. The result has been the use – albeit scattered use – of the material by many individual teachers and schools worldwide.

Particularly promising are children's rights curricula developed in some parts of Canada. Since its establishment in 1995, the Children's Rights Centre at the University College of Cape Breton in Nova Scotia has been working on programs for assessing and instituting children's rights education at the Grade 6 and Grade 8 levels. Implemented first in local

Cape Breton schools in the late 1990s, the programs are now being incorporated into the Nova Scotia elementary school curricula. As of 2002 one of these programs has been incorporated into a province-wide Health and Social Studies curriculum for Kindergarden to Grade 6. Another is to be used in the Personal Development and Relationships part of the Grade 8 curriculum. The Cape Breton programs have been favourably evaluated and reviewed (Levine, 2000). They are designed to provide children with factual information about the Convention and their rights and to educate children experientially through role-playing exercises, class discussions, games, case studies, and independent writing.

Such education is rare. Nevertheless, it does represent a silver lining in an otherwise generally dismal international record so far of providing for 'active and appropriate' children's rights education, as called for by article 42 of the U.N. Convention on the Rights of the Child.

CHAPTER THREE

Recognizing Children as Citizens

It is widely accepted that a basic task of schooling is to prepare each new generation for their responsibilities as citizens.

Will Kymlicka (2001)

Children's rights education is not just a requirement of international law. It also is important to the recognition of children as citizens with rights. As the above quote indicates, even leading international writers on citizenship such as Will Kymlicka (2001) assume that children are future rather than existing citizens. The commonly held assumption is that children are not-yets or potential citizens of the future and that schools therefore, have the function of preparing these not-yets for their future status as adult citizens. This is an adultcentric and narrow understanding. But children already are citizens in their own right, not pre-citizens who are being prepared by schools to become citizens. The value of children's rights education is that it provides children, as well as adults, with a fuller and more inclusive understanding of citizenship where children are recognized and valued as citizens of the present as well as of the future.

We now examine the linkage between children's rights education and citizenship. We begin with a review of the modern meaning of citizenship, looking first at the classic work of T.H. Marshall and then at more recent work that expands this meaning. We then show that the recent expansion of the concept of citizenship has been progressive, but there remains a problem of adultcentrism and the neglect of children. We point to the need for a fuller understanding of citizenship that includes children as citizens. Finally, we examine the function of schools in promoting citizenship. Our conclusion is that, as in the literature on citizenship, schools operate on the faulty adultcentric assumption that children are future citizens to be moulded rather than citizens of the present to be respected. Children's rights education is a necessary corrective and a means to arriving at an understanding of citizenship in which children are recognized not only as 'becoming' citizens but also as 'being' citizens with rights and responsibilities of citizenship.

The Modern Meaning of Citizenship

Citizenship is both a legal and a normative concept. In law, its meaning is relatively straightforward. Citizenship simply refers to the status of being a citizen or participating member of a political community (Gabriel, 2001; Kaplan, 1993). Associated with this status are certain rights and responsibilities that define the relationship of individuals with each other and with the state. Citizens are legal 'insiders' within a state in contrast to legal 'outsiders' such as foreigners, resident aliens, and guest workers. Such outsiders may have certain defined legal rights, but they do not possess the full rights of citizenship. Citizens also stand in contrast to people living under authoritarian regimes. They may be members of a state and recipients of that state's protection, but they do not have the status of effective participating members in a political community with the rights and responsibilities of true citizenship. They may be called citizens, as indeed they are in totalitarian states, but their participation rather than being autonomous is mobilized by state authorities (Heater, 1990).

Citizens have legal status in a country usually on the basis of that country's domestic law. A country may confer citizenship on the basis of birthplace, descent, or naturalization, which are the three most common methods of doing so (Kaplan, 1993). But a country may also confer citizenship on the basis of international law and an obligation under an international treaty. For example, the 1961 U.N. Convention on the Reduction of Statelessness requires states parties to confer nationality (or citizenship) on persons born in their territory who would otherwise be stateless. The legal definition of citizenship may be either socially exclusive or inclusive. The historical trend has been towards inclusion (Heater, 1990; Pocock, 1995). In Ancient Athens, however, citizenship was restricted to a small elite of males who were warriors and slave-owners; they were granted the privileges and obligations of self-government. In Ancient Rome, as the boundaries of the Republic and the Empire were enlarged, citizenship was extended to include conquered peoples, which had not been the case in Ancient Greece, although citizenship remained the preserve of a small property-owning elite. In Europe and North America, at the time of French and American revolutions, citizenship became more broadly defined on the basis of common equality and natural rights. Influenced by the political philosophy of John Locke and others, citizenship was understood to belong to the free and equal members of a country who all had equal natural rights which the government was obligated to protect. Equality was defined narrowly to apply only to those with property and social status. Citizens, therefore, were an exclusive association of white, male, property-owners. Nevertheless, the idea of citizenship based on common equality had emancipatory power. During the past two centuries, with the movement towards greater democracy and with the growing recognition of human rights, the legal meaning of citizenship was broadened to include people with little or no property, members of minorities, and women.

But beyond its legal meaning, citizenship as a normative concept – a concept of the desirable features and practices of citizenship – is less straightforward. This is because the conceptual meaning of citizenship is contested and the subject of conflicting philosophical and political perspectives. Since the Second World War, however, what may be called the prevailing view of citizenship, and the starting point for analysis of citizenship issues, has been the view associated with the work of British sociologist T.H. Marshall (1950). In the citizenship literature this is sometimes referred to as the 'postwar orthodoxy' (Kymlicka & Norman, 1995, p. 285). Marshall was interested in developing an account of citizenship that would overcome social class differences in England, promote social integration, and welcome members of the working class as full and equal citizens (Heater, 1990; Kymlicka & Norman, 1995). He took the position that citizenship should be understood to mean not only legal membership in a state but also a sense of membership. Citizens are people who not only belong to a state but also feel that they belong. For citizens to be able to feel that they belong, argued Marshall, it is important for them to have rights and to know that they have rights. That they have rights is the message society sends people that proves to them that they are true members of society. Thus, for Marshall, at the heart of the meaning of citizenship is the sense of membership in a political community based on a sense of having rights.

Marshall examined the development of three types of citizenship rights in modern democratic societies which have helped to promote the sense of social membership. The first is civil rights. Emerging in the eighteenth century, these include the freedom of speech, the legal rights of due process, and the right to own property. These rights give citizens a certain sense of membership in their society because in that society they have personal freedoms and the protection of the law. The second category is political rights. Emerging in the nineteenth and twentieth centuries, these encompass the right to vote and the right to run for political office. These rights give citizens a fuller sense of membership in their society because in that society they are able to participate politically and offer input into the making of the law and public policy. Finally, the third category is social rights. These provide for 'social citizenship,' which has been associated with the development of the social welfare state in the twentieth century. Social rights include entitlements to health care, public education, and old-age pensions. They give citizens a yet fuller sense of membership in their society because in that society they have the assurance that their basic needs will be provided for by the state. All of these rights are necessary to the feeling of belonging.

As these rights were evolving, noted Marshall, the status of citizen was becoming more socially inclusive. Initially limited to white men who owned property, over time citizens came also to include non-white working-class men – and women. Thus, by the middle of the twentieth century, not only did citizens enjoy a wide range of rights but also a wide range of social groups enjoyed the status of citizen. What this double expansion did was promote a wider sense of membership in society, and in doing so it advanced citizenship. For Marshall, the fullest expression of citizenship required that citizens have civil, political, and social rights and that these citizenship rights are accessible to a wide range of people including members of the working class. The key to citizenship is having rights so that citizens feel that they are genuine and worthy members of a political community, and the key to having rights is a liberal democratic welfare state that provides for these rights.

Marshall's rights-based account of citizenship has been criticized in recent decades for failing to appreciate the importance of the responsibilities of citizenship, for giving inadequate attention to the issue of social and cultural differences in citizenship, and for ignoring the dimension of global citizenship. There is much validity to these criticisms. The rights-based conception does, however, represent a major contribution to our modern understanding of citizenship. Responsibilities may be important to the practice of citizenship. But it is the rights of citizenship that must hold a central place in countries that embrace the values of democracy and human rights. To put responsibilities and duties above rights would be to live in countries different from those that have ratified international conventions on human rights and that have incorporated rights and freedoms into their constitutions and basic laws. Citizenship must mean more than simply membership in a democratic society. Citizenship must mean, as Marshall pointed out so emphatically, a quality of membership that gives citizens a sense of genuine value and belonging as they practise their citizenship.

Recent Modifications

In the citizenship literature, Marshall's rights-based conception of citizenship has been criticized for inadequacies on three major fronts. This does not mean that the conception has been replaced by an alternative. Critics remain divided among themselves about what should constitute the most desirable features of citizenship. But it does mean that critics have been successful in bringing about a general acceptance of the view that citizenship needs to be understood more broadly than in the way Marshall understood it.

Recognizing a Place for Responsibilities

According to critics, a first shortcoming of the rights-based conception is that it fails to appreciate the importance of responsibilities, duties, and civic virtues in the practice of citizenship (Gabriel, 2001; Kymlicka & Norman, 1995). A more adequate understanding of citizenship must accommodate the need for a proper balance between rights and responsibilities.

The problem, they say, is this. Too much focus on rights promotes passivity among citizens and inordinate attention to the private rather than the public sphere of life. It fosters an entitlement culture and self-regarding consciousness where citizens give their primary attention to the private life of the consumer, careerist, worker, and family member, without much thought to their broader social responsibilities and duties as citizens. In a self-centred entitlement culture there is a lack of public-spiritedness and a lack of desire among citizens to be active participants and contributing members of their society. Citizens are passive in their practise of citizenship, content to periodically vote and take a passing interest in community and public affairs. They do not feel an obligation to take responsibility and play a more active part in the public life of their society. Apathy and lack of citizen participation is the result. The root of the problem, according to critics, is a strong and misplaced focus on the rights of citizenship, when citizenship should be understood to include responsibilities and obligations as well as rights. Rights need not be supplanted, but they need to be afforded less attention. The focus should be less on the passive possession of rights and more on the active exercise of the duties and responsibilities of citizenship. Together with more emphasis on responsibilities, there needs to be more emphasis on the values, qualities, and civic virtues of responsible citizens.

What these critics mean by upgrading the importance of responsibilities and duties varies with their political philosophy. Will Kymlicka and Wayne Norman (1995) described a number of positions including those of the new right and the new left. For critics on the new right, a key problem in the rights-based conception is the social rights of citizenship as highlighted by Marshall. Civil and political rights are a valuable part of citizenship, but the welfare state and social rights are seen as a negative force that promotes dependency and passivity among citizens (e.g., Mead, 1986). Citizens are encouraged to see themselves as passive recipients of social benefits rather than as active contributors to their society. Citizenship should not be understood to include social rights. Rather, it should mean that citizens have a social obligation to work, contribute, and be economically self-supporting. Citizenship should mean being economically responsible and self-sufficient. But for critics on the new left, the problem is quite different. For them, it is less to do with the welfare state than with the lack of opportunities (Mulgan, 1991). To increase opportunities for economic participation, public policy needs to be directed at achieving full employment and expanding worker training programs and educational opportunities. To increase opportunities for political participation, more effort needs to be made in decentralizing and democratizing the state. More points of access to decision-making and more opportunities for democratic input will empower citizens to participate. Through participation citizens will develop a greater sense of responsibility, respect, and tolerance for others, and thereby become even more active in their participation.

Kymlicka and Norman (1995) considered the inadequacies of both these positions. On the one hand, the new right's perspective is too narrow, focusing primarily on economic life. The responsibilities of citizenship must mean more than economic duties for workers and corporate executives. There must be a prominent place for a political obligation to participate in the broader public life of communities and the state, an obligation given little attention by the new right. On the other hand, the new left does not fully address the issue of responsibility. Because opportunities for empowerment and wider participation are increased, it does not necessarily follow that citizens will act out of a sense of responsibility and participate on a wider scale than before. The position of the new left assumes that citizen participation has an educative function in teaching people greater social responsibility, tolerance, and respect. It also assumes that acts of participation will broaden the mind, familiarize people with broader social interests rather than narrow ones, and lead people to wider social responsibility. However, experience has shown that it is not automatic that empowerment and participation in themselves result in responsible social action. Empowerment can have its dark side (Chisholm, 2001). Skinheads, for example, may be empowered to participate but not in a socially responsible and respectful direction (Hilden, 2001). Responsible citizenship requires not only that citizens participate but that they internalize the values of respect and social responsibility and that they learn and possess the qualities and virtues of democratic citizens.

As Kymlicka and Norman pointed out, it is important that responsible citizenship be informed by citizen virtues and values consistent with the development and maintenance of a democratic society. Useful in the identification of citizen virtues is the 'liberal virtue theory' developed by William Galston (1991). Galston divided the virtues of citizenship into four groups: general virtues such as law-abidingness and loyalty, social virtues such as independence and open-mindedness, economic virtues such as the capacity to delay self-gratification, and political virtues such as tolerance and respect for the rights of others, the ability to evaluate the performance of those in office, and the willingness to engage in public discourse. The first three kinds of virtues make contributions to responsible citizenship. The political virtues, however, are particularly important to life in a society that is democratic and has respect for human rights. Unlike skinheads, politically virtuous citizens appreciate the values of tolerance, civility, and respect for the rights of others. They also have the democratic ability to question authority and to participate in public debate. These qualities are critical to a well-functioning democracy where citizens get along with each other, provide input into political decision-making, and hold elected representatives accountable for their actions.

Thus, in the current citizenship literature, there is appreciation for the social responsibilities and civic virtues of citizens that did not exist in Marshall's rights-based conception. Analysts may disagree as to the exact meaning of social responsibility and civic virtue. But there is wide agreement that the possession of rights is insufficient for citizenship. It is correctly concluded that room must be made for responsibilities and civic virtues. Nevertheless, it would be quite wrong to suggest that in a society that prizes democracy and basic human rights, responsibilities should come before rights and that the exercise of rights should depend on the fulfilment of responsibilities. Unlike responsibilities, fundamental rights are inherent. They do not depend on something else. Most countries have ratified international conventions on human rights, agreeing to recognize and implement fundamental rights. By doing so, they have agreed to endorse these rights as fundamental rights of citizenship within their borders. These countries have not ratified international conventions on responsibilities and duties. By not doing so, they acknowledge that what is most fundamental are not responsibilities but rights. That said, responsibilities are important and flow from the meaning of rights. As often pointed out in rights literature, with rights are correlative duties and responsibilities (e.g., Shue, 1980). The ability to exercise a right means a responsibility on the part of society, and on the part of the state acting for society, to ensure that the right can be exercised. But it is not only a responsibility of the state. It is also a responsibility of the individual citizen to recognize and respect the rights of other individual citizens and to support governments in taking responsible measures protective of rights.

The importance of citizenship responsibilities may be further appreciated when considering the successful functioning of a society that values democracy and rights. Such a society rests on the willingness of citizens to cooperate in fulfilling their responsibilities so that their society and its values may endure. Laws need to be obeyed if social order is to be preserved. The physical environment needs to be respected if human health is to be maintained. Work needs to be done if the economy is to function. Votes need to be cast if elections are to be the basis for democratic government. These needs cannot be fulfilled simply through police forces and coercion by the state. Society depends on citizens who appreciate that they have social obligations and who act accordingly. If citizens are content merely to claim their rights, if they demand entitlements but do not assume social responsibilities, the society that provides them with rights and democracy is surely to fall into decay and disorder. The practise of citizenship in a democratic and rights-based society requires the exercise of social responsibility.

As part of social responsibility, citizenship calls for active citizen participation, which may range from the discussion of public issues, to voting, to membership in interest groups and political parties, and to running for public office. Participation is a right of citizens – which includes a right not to participate – but it also is a responsibility. The successful functioning of modern democracy depends in some degree on citizen involvement. Theorists of democracy may disagree on the requisite extent and intensity of citizen participation, but they do agree on the necessity of participation at some level (Pateman, 1970). Should large numbers of citizens choose to exercise their right not to participate in a democratic community, to focus instead only on their family and economic lives, that democracy will be in trouble. Thus, participation must be seen not only as a right but also as a responsibility. This does not have to mean a legal responsibility, as in a legal obligation to vote. But it does have to mean a moral responsibility and a social expectation. Certainly, it does not have to involve the intensity and depth of participation as existed in Ancient Greece, where political life was regarded as superior to private life. Contrary to modern-day 'civic republicans' who share the Ancient Greek belief in the superiority of political participation, participation should be encouraged but not at the expense of other activities (Kymlicka & Norman, 1995). Understandably, many people find their greatest happiness not in citizen participation but in their family life or work or religion. It is unreasonable to expect from them intense civic involvement. That said, in the interests of viable democracy, it is reasonable to encourage citizen participation and to characterize participation as an important social responsibility.

Recognizing the Need to Affirm Differences

A second shortcoming identified in Marshall's conception of citizenship is that it fails to recognize pluralism and to affirm group differences (Gabriel, 2001; Kymlicka & Norman, 1995). What is required is not the group-denying unitary or universal citizenship as prescribed by Marshall but the recognition of pluralistic or 'differentiated citizenship' as suggested by Iris Young (1989).

For Young (1989) and for Kymlicka and Norman (1995), the issue is this. Marshall's intention was to advance a concept of universal citizenship – where all citizens would have equal status and rights – which would function to integrate previously excluded groups within British society and provide a means of shared identity and a source of national unity. His particular intention was to integrate the working classes through a universal citizenship that would provide them with equal rights, including equal social rights, and thus bring to them a sense of belonging. The working classes in Britain had long been excluded from the 'common culture' because of their lack of socioeconomic resources and education. But with the development of the welfare state and with social rights, they would have equal rights of citizenship and thus feel themselves to be a genuine part of the common culture. For Marshall, if social inequalities could be significantly reduced through the welfare state, and if citizens – including working-class citizens – had social rights, everyone would have universal status, exercise common rights of citizenship, and feel a sense of belonging in a more unified society. Social and cultural exclusion would no longer be a problem.

But the problem of exclusion and the feeling of exclusion persists. Even in the welfare state, and with expanded social rights, many groups of people continue to feel culturally and socially excluded and unable to identify fully with the values and institutions of their society. Despite having the universal status and common rights of citizenship that Marshall celebrated, ethnocultural minorities, aboriginal peoples, women, people with disabilities, and gays and lesbians still are without a sense of genuine belonging, and they do not fully participate in their society as valued citizens. The problem with the universal approach is that formal equality in rights and the reduction of social inequalities do not in themselves translate into inclusive citizenship where citizens feel themselves to be members of their society. The common citizenship approach ignores or even denies important cultural and social differences among citizens and does not recognize and affirm these differences. As a result many members of disadvantaged or marginalized groups do not feel welcome as full and equal citizens, which is contrary to Marshall's definition of citizenship as a sense of belonging. Indeed, the strict pursuit of a universal conception of citizenship may be unjust because it marginalizes or oppresses historically excluded groups (Young, 1989; Pateman, 1989). In providing individuals only with formal equality and universal rights, and in ignoring the historical disadvantages and special needs of particular groups, it reinforces previously existing inequalities and works against substantive equality and social justice.

The better approach is to recognize differences and to conceptualize citizenship as 'differentiated citizenship.' This does not mean the abandonment of the individual rights and responsibilities of citizenship. It does mean incorporating into the political community members of historically disadvantaged or marginalized groups not only as individuals but also through their group membership. It means affirming and embracing group differences rather than ignoring or denying them. It means recognizing that particular groups face disadvantages and barriers, and they are in need of special measures to protect their interests. It also means recognizing that particular groups have distinctive needs that require group-differentiated policies and laws including policies of special support for persons with disabilities, traditional hunting and fishing rights for aboriginal peoples, reproductive rights for women, publicly funded schools for religious minorities, and language rights for ethnocultural minorities.

Differentiated citizenship means that citizens have rights not only as individuals, but also as members of groups. Kymlicka and Norman (1995) identified three different kinds of group rights. First are special representation rights for historically disadvantaged or marginalized groups including visible minorities, women, persons with disabilities, and gays and lesbians. These groups are entitled to special attention in the political process (e.g., guaranteed representation in political bodies) and in public policies (e.g., affirmative action) until disadvantages and barriers are removed. Second are multicultural rights for immigrant communities, ethnocultural minorities, and religious minorities. These groups are entitled to preserve their cultural heritage, traditions, and languages either with state assistance (as in Canada) or through largely private means (as in the United States). Third are self-government rights, as claimed by many aboriginal peoples and by national minorities such as the Scots and Québécois. These groups claim the right to govern themselves in matters critical to the survival and well-being of their group. Thus, on the basis of differentiated citizenship, in Australia a minority person with a disability would have the universal citizenship right to due process of law as an individual but also the collective right to special assistance and cultural recognition as a member of a group. The aboriginal person in Canada would have the right to vote as an individual but also the right to self-government as the member of a group.

The concept of differentiated citizenship is certainly not without opposition (Glazer, 1983). The main concern is that groups will be encouraged to focus on their differences rather than their commonalities, thus undermining shared identity, social cohesion, and national unity. Nevertheless, differentiated citizenship and group rights are now recognized to varying degrees in virtually all modern democracies, which reflects an appreciation of genuine group differences (Kymlicka & Norman, 1995). For the most part, groups want to be included in the larger society and they want to be part of the mainstream. Recognition and accommodation of their differences is an important means of making them feel welcome and giving them the sense of belonging that Marshall so desired. Self-government rights do raise deep problems for shared identity and national unity. But it is also true that demands for self-government by national minorities pose problems for advocates of universal and differentiated citizenship alike. The attempt to assimilate national minorities in the name of common citizenship does not work any better in promoting unity than does differentiated citizenship. But the special case of self-government rights aside, differentiated citizenship is a welcome reality that fosters belongingness by recognizing differences.

Recognizing the Global Dimension of Citizenship

Finally, a third problem for critics of Marshall's understanding of citizenship is the failure to appreciate its global dimension (Gabriel, 2001; Held, 1995). Like previous conceptions of citizenship, Marshall's dwells on the practice of citizenship at the level of the state. But, given the reality and effects of globalization, it is more appropriate now to think of the global community as the most important setting for the practise of citizenship (see Heater, 1993).

David Held (1995) has analysed this issue as follows. Various forms of globalization – or increasing worldwide economic, financial, technological, and environmental interconnectedness – have eroded the capacity for meaningful democratic citizenship at the level of the nation-state. Although nation-states are not becoming obsolete, they have increasingly less room for manoeuvre in autonomously enacting legislation and setting public policy. Nation-states are becoming 'decision-takers' as much as 'decision-makers.' In setting economic policy, for example, government policies are significantly constrained through pressures from international financial markets, decisions of the World Bank and International Monetary Fund, and the power of large multinational corporations. Options in the domestic development of social, labour, and environmental policy are narrowed by the decisions or threats of corporations to invest or move elsewhere. Given the growing need for international cooperation and international standards in the areas of trade, labour regulations, social legislation, and the environment, international organizations, agreements, and laws continue to be developed to provide for cross-national standards. But this, too, is a problem for meaningful democratic citizenship at the level of the state as states are subject to standards that they are obligated to follow. As states become decision-takers, state citizenship and the participation of citizens in making domestic decisions becomes less meaningful. The real action is at the international level.

Given this new global reality, citizenship needs to be reconceptualized to allow that citizens have multiple citizenships (Held, 1995). Citizenship needs to be understood more broadly where people are citizens not only of nation-states but also of larger regions (e.g., the European Union) and the wider global order. Citizens not only have state citizenship but also global or cosmopolitan citizenship. For cosmopolitan citizenship to be made a more positive reality, one that is in accordance with the principles of human rights and democracy, certain changes are necessary. First, the system of international standards and enforcement of human rights needs to be strengthened. With such strengthening, global citizens will see themselves more clearly as having not only the human rights of cosmopolitan citizenship but also responsibilities for respecting the rights of fellow global citizens and for supporting a global order that upholds human rights. Mindful of such global consciousness, countries will become more committed to fulfilling their obligations in upholding and enforcing international laws and standards on human rights. Second, in accordance with the principle of democracy, international organizations and processes need to be altered so that global citizens can participate in meaningful ways in making the decisions that affect them. This means creating more avenues for their input into international decisions and the development of means for making global decision-makers more accountable. This is a major challenge, of course, but is necessary for the practise of global citizenship.

Critics point to a number of problems with the concept of global or world citizenship (Heater, 1993). First, since there is no world state, there is no civic relationship at the global level. Citizenship pertains only to the relationship between individual citizens and a sovereign state, but since there does not yet exist a world state, there is no such thing as world citizenship. Furthermore, even if a world state should exist, it would be highly undesirable, given its concentration of power and capacity to restrict or deny human rights and freedoms. Second, only within the framework of the state can the rights of citizenship and the practise of citizen participation take place. Only states can enact laws to protect the rights of their citizens. International law deals only with the conduct of countries and their relations with each other. Only the regimes of individual countries can provide opportunities for voting and other meaningful forms of citizen participation. Finally, only within a particular country can citizens feel loyalty and have affective bonds based on common experience, traditions, and culture. The notion of a common humanity is far too amorphous to command the kind of emotional attachment and sentiments that the concrete and shared identity of citizenship requires.

Derek Heater (1993) has offered a balanced and persuasive response to these criticisms. First, Heater contends that it is wrong to say that in the absence of a world state, the nation-state is the sole and sovereign political community. Even if analysts such as Held have overstated the extent of globalization, few can deny that there has been a major growth of global interdependence and that individual countries have less independent ability to set policy in many areas than they did before. To deny the importance of entities such as the European Union and the United Nations, and to claim that the individual state has a monopoly on its citizens' sense of political identity, is unreasonable in the modern world. Heater's second point is that it is misleading to say that only a country provides the framework for the legal exercise of rights and the practice of participation. We are seeing the beginnings of an international system where individuals have legal rights and obligations beyond the borders of their own particular countries. For example, in most of the member countries of the Council of Europe, citizens can claim their legal rights before the European Court of Human Rights. Under international law, individuals can be held accountable for committing crimes against humanity. We are also seeing the growth of avenues for citizen participation at the global level through, for example, interest group and NGO activity. To deny the possibility of cosmopolitan citizenship because citizens cannot vote for representatives in global assemblies is an extremely narrow interpretation of citizenship. Finally, Heater argues that it is not true that citizens can only identify with and have an affective bond with their nation-state. Just as within countries citizens can feel affection for both a part of their country, for example, Texas or Alberta, and for the country as a whole, the United States or Canada in these cases, they can feel a bond with their particular country and with the world community. Affection or loyalty may not be as intense for the world community, but it can develop nevertheless. This development is now more possible with globalization, a growing sense of the common concerns of humanity as a whole, and a growing awareness of the essential similarities among different peoples or groups of people.

Understanding Children as Citizens

Our current understanding of the meaning of citizenship, beginning with the work of T.H. Marshall which held that citizenship is based on the possession of rights, has evolved to a conception of citizenship that rec-ognizes the importance of responsibilities as well as rights, that appreci-ates differentiated as well as common citizenship, and that acknowledges global as well as state citizenship. Strong debate continues about the par-ticular features and purposes of citizenship, as well as about the correct balance between rights and obligations. Nevertheless, there is general agreement about the basic contours as being those described above. Today, there is widespread acceptance that citizenship involves the active exercise of rights and social responsibilities; appreciation for the citizen-ship virtues and values of tolerance, civility, and critical democratic think-ing; the recognition of differentiated citizenship; and identification with the global community as well as with a particular state. Furthermore, there is widespread agreement that the underlying aim of such a wide understanding of the concept of citizenship is to foster a sense of genuine belonging among citizens and to encourage their active and meaningful participation in society.

A major shortcoming persists in the citizenship literature. Children, generally, have been ignored or downgraded as citizens. When children are mentioned at all, they usually are referred to as future citizens in dis-cussions about citizenship education. It is ironic, therefore, that in the concern among analysts to be socially inclusive and to enhance participa-tion and the sense of belonging, they should allow for the exclusion and disempowerment of a large segment of society. When the problem of social exclusion is discussed, examples usually are given of ethnocultural minorities, women, gays and lesbians, and persons with disabilities. Rarely are children referred to. This is all the more troubling when con-sidering that a common theme in much of the writing on the experiences and rights of children is the deep sense of exclusion and powerlessness felt by children and young people (Lansdown, 1995). Analysts either need to provide an account of citizenship that includes children as citi-zens or, if they want to reject children, provide good reasons for doing so.

One possible reason for exclusion is that children have not been accepted as legal citizens of a state, reflecting the democratic will of adult citizens not to confer the rights of citizenship to children. This might be done in the name of the child's best interests or the best inter-ests of society. However, the fact is that like women and minorities, chil-dren now are legal members of modern democratic states (and even of authoritarian states). In virtually every country today, children have been assigned the legal status of citizenship. Canada is typical. Under its Citizenship Act, citizens are all persons born in Canada; persons born abroad who have at least one parent who is a Canadian citizen; or persons who have immigrated to Canada, applied for citizenship after meeting conditions, and then been naturalized as Canadian citizens. Said conditions include a minimum age of eighteen, a three-year period of residency, an ability to communicate in either English or French, and knowledge of Canada's geography, political system, and the rights and responsibilities of Canadian citizenship. The vast majority of children in Canada are legally Canadian citizens. A similar kind of legal situation exists in most other countries. Even in countries such as France and Germany, which have long traditions of citizenship based on descent, laws recently have been amended to confer citizenship on children born there but of foreign parents.

Another possible reason for rejecting children as citizens is the assumption that children lack the capacities and competence to exercise the rights and responsibilities of citizenship (Kulynych, 2001; Roche, 1999). This is part of the general argument against children's rights (e.g., Purdy, 1992). According to the argument, although children may be citizens in the narrow legal sense of membership, they are not and should not be citizens in the wider political sense of full and equal citizens, involved in such activities as voting, running for office, and serving on juries. At best, they are partial citizens of the present, awaiting the political status of full citizenship once they reach adulthood (Roche, 1999). A key argument offered for why children are not and should not be full citizens is that they lack economic independence, and they lack the capacity for reasoning and for making decisions in their own best long-term interests and in the best interests of society. Such independence and reasoning capacity are necessary for the appropriate exercise of rights and responsibilities. Unlike adults, children are economically dependent on their parents and, therefore, not in a position to form views and make decisions independently of their parents. Unlike adults, children do not yet have sufficient reasoning capacity because they do not have the necessary cognitive development, the accumulated background knowledge, experience, and self-control. It is in the best interests of children that children not to be given the burden of the rights and responsibilities of citizenship. Rather, it is in their best interests to have their freedoms limited during childhood to enable them to acquire the self-control and virtues necessary for successful adult life and responsible citizenship (Purdy, 1992). Childhood is a time not for citizenship activity but for protection, nourishment, and preparation so that children become properly equipped to handle the rights, responsibilities, and participation activities of adult citizenship.

There are a number of flaws in this argument. First, if accepted, the argument of economic dependency could be used against many groups who make claims for inclusion in citizenship. For example, it could have been used against women who were economically dependent while responsible for managing the household and children (Kulynych, 2001). Today, it could be used against many dependent citizens including stay-at-home mothers, househusbands, seniors, young adults whose disabilities prevent their economic independence, and young adults who are attending university or professional schools with the financial help of their parents or others. Obviously, there are dangers in making economic independence a requirement for citizenship (Coles, 1995). While economic dependence may influence the way some people form their views or make decisions related to the practice of citizenship, economic dependence does not mean a complete inability to exercise rights and responsibilities or make a contribution as a participating member of society.

Second, from the perspective of developmental psychology and neuroscience, and apart from the issue of economic dependency, it is both simplistic and misleading to draw such a sharp distinction between childhood and adulthood (Flekkoy & Kaufman, 1997). It is true that there are important and obvious differences between children and adults in terms of their neurological development, experience, and maturity. It is also true, however, that there is no magic moment when a child suddenly becomes an adult. Development takes place across childhood and across the lifespan. Rather than characterizing children as having a limited capacity for responsible decision-making, it is more accurate to describe children as having 'evolving capacities,' using the language of the U.N. Convention on the Rights of the Child (Flekkoy & Kaufman, 1997). These evolving capacities are related not only to intellectual development but also to social interaction, emotional development, and the development of empathy. It is important to appreciate that adults, too, have evolving capacities as they undergo new experiences and as they grow older. In many areas, while the capacities of adults may increase with age, they also diminish in very old age. Although, in general, the reasoning capacities develop through neurological maturation in childhood and adolescence, and therefore, adult-like reasoning is unlikely in earlier childhood, there are some older children who have greater capacity for reasoning and empathy and for the making of rational decisions than some adults (Roche, 1999). Moreover, widespread evidence suggests that the competence of children increases when they are treated with respect and assumed to be capable and responsible (Alderson, 1992). Thus, the sharp distinction between incapable children and capable adults is misleading.

Third, while childhood is a period for protection and preparation, as well as a period for age-appropriate learning and activities to enable a successful transition to adult life. To prepare children for adulthood by denying them the opportunity to exercise certain rights and responsibilities is a recipe for denying them successful entry into the life of adult citizenship. The successful practice of adult citizen participation and the exercise of rights and responsibilities does not arise out of thin air. These are learned through experience and in childhood and adolescence (Flekkoy & Kaufman, 1997). The prospects for democratic citizenship are enhanced when democracy is practised in primary social institutions, such as families and schools, and when children and adolescents are given age-appropriate opportunities for participation and the exercise of rights and responsibilities. In virtually all modern democratic countries, whether through domestic law, the country's constitution, or its ratification of the U.N. Convention on the Rights of the Child, children have basic rights and responsibilities. At the very least, they have rights such as the right to freedom of expression and due process of law, and they have responsibilities such as to obey the law and respect the rights of others. The question is whether children are given ample opportunities to exercise their rights and responsibilities. To the extent that children are given these opportunities and given a democratic social environment, the prospects for the practice of adult democratic citizenship are enhanced.

Finally, to exclude children from citizenship is contradictory to the modern meaning of citizenship. In the tradition of T.H. Marshall, at the heart of the meaning of citizenship is the construction of a sense of membership in a political community. It is belittling of children to say that they are not genuine citizens or that they are partial citizens or future citizens. It is disrespectful to portray children as economically dependent and incompetent not-yets and to not recognize children as valued members of their political community. To equate citizens with voters and to equate citizenship with the full possession of political rights is a very narrow and adultcentric interpretation of citizenship. Citizenship is not about voting but about participation, and children have much to offer. Like all members of society, children need a sense of belonging if they are to be able to identify with the society and participate in its institutions, in accordance with their own evolving capacities. To request that they be included in citizenship should not be to ask for a passport of full rationality but to ask, as Jeremy Roche put it, 'that children be seen as members of society too, with a legitimate and valuable voice and perspective' (1999, p. 479).

The better approach is to recognize that children are, indeed, citizens. Such recognition is consistent with the modern concept of citizenship which has evolved to incorporate an appreciation for differentiated citizenship. People may be citizens as individuals. Differentiated citizenship means that people may also be citizens on the basis of their membership in a group. This concept applies to children as well as to adults. With the signing and ratification of the U.N. Convention on the Rights of the Child, children are widely recognized to be a special and vulnerable group within their own country and in the global community. Children are recognized to be a special collectivity with certain adultlike rights but also certain group-differentiated rights that are appropriate to them. Under the Convention, children have many civil and social rights and certain political rights, although they do not have the full range of political rights that adults possess. For example, children have the right to participate in making decisions that affect them, including political decisions that affect them, although they do not have the right to vote in elections for political office. Participation rather than voting, is at the heart of the meaning of citizenship.

The Convention affirms children not only as persons with rights but also as citizens with rights (Miljeteig-Olssen, 1992; Verhellen, 1999). It was the intention of the drafters of the Convention that children be 'active, participating citizens, playing a role in governance 'according to their age and maturity,' rather than simply being passively governed' (Stasiulis, 2002). This intention is reflected in article 12, a unique and quite remarkable part of the Convention, which equips children with rights of expression and participation to be exercised in accordance with their age and level of maturity. Like the principle of the best interests of the child, the principle of participation was put forward as a key principle of the Convention. The drafters might have chosen to limit or qualify participation in the name of the best interests of the child, but they chose not to do so (Marshall, 1997). Instead, participation was made an integral part of the best interests principle. Providing opportunities for participation and listening to children are important components of providing for the best interests of the child. The Convention promotes this position. Denying children a voice in the name of their best interests is a problem in that it may mean denying decision-makers with valuable input into their deliberations about the child's best interests. Children's participation and input are of central importance. Participation is important at both the individual level of the best interests of the child and at the level of the political community as a whole. In a political community based on democracy and respect for rights, decision-makers should hear the voices of children and children should have opportunities to be heard. In embracing children as citizens, the U.N. Convention affirms a democratic process respectful of children.

Under the Convention, children are seen as future adult citizens but, and importantly, also as existing citizens in their own right. The Convention recognizes children to be in a condition not only of 'becoming' but also of 'being' (Hart and Pavlovic, 1991). As becoming-persons, or persons in the process of development, children are entitled to rights that are subject to parental and adult direction and in relation to their evolving capacities. Thus, in accordance with article 5, although parents do not have proxy rights, they do have the responsibility to guide children in the exercise of their rights, as consistent with their (the children's) evolving capacities. As being-persons, children have rights in the here and now, irrespective of guidance. Under article 27, for example, every child has the right to an adequate standard of living. Parents may guide children in the way that they eat, but every child of whatever age or level of maturity has the right to food. Similarly, children are in a condition both of 'becoming' citizens and of 'being' citizens. As becoming-citizens, child citizens have rights of participation that are subject to guidance and the children's evolving capacities. Article 12 states that children have the right to be listened to and, by rights, their views are to be given weight in accordance with their age and maturity. Article 29 gives children the right to education to prepare them for responsible life – including the responsible life of the citizen – in a free society. As being-citizens, children also have citizenship rights in the here and now. Thus, article 12 also states that, like adult citizens who are capable of forming their own views, child citizens who are similarly capable have the right to express views freely in all matters that affect them. The views of children may not be decisive, but children do have the right as citizens to express their views.

If citizenship is to be understood inclusively and mean participation for the purpose of bringing about a sense of belonging, children are citizens – of the present as well as of the future. Children are being-citizens as well as becoming-citizens.

The Nature of Child Citizenship

How is child citizenship to be understood? To address this question, we need to recall the main features of citizenship as understood in the current citizenship literature and to describe child citizenship in terms of these features. This involves a discussion of children's rights and responsibilities, child participation, differentiated child citizenship, and global child citizenship. The discussion is informed by the principles of the U.N. Convention on the Rights of the Child, with which current practices of child citizenship are consistent only in part.

The Exercise of Rights and Responsibilities

The enjoyment of rights is basic to citizenship. Like adult citizens, child citizens enjoy certain basic rights as recognized in their country's domestic legislation or constitution or through its ratification of the U.N. Convention on the Rights of the Child. The Convention rights of the child citizen – provision, protection, and participation rights – are in some ways more limited than the citizenship rights of adults. Children, for example, do not have the full range of political rights such as voting. In some areas children have more extensive rights than do adults because of their special vulnerability. In the area of protection rights, children have the rights to not be abused, neglected, or sexually exploited, and these rights do not apply in the same ways to adults. In in the area of provision rights, which are mainly the social rights highlighted by Marshall, children have a wider range of rights and rights that are less contentious than the social rights of adults. The main point is that child citizens, like all citizens, do enjoy certain fundamental rights.

Child citizens enjoy the Convention rights of participation including the rights to be heard, to freedom of thought, freedom of expression, freedom of association, and freedom of assembly. These rights are to be enjoyed not only in social institutions such as the family and school, and in legal and administrative proceedings relevant to children, but also in local communities and in the wider political community. They are of particular importance to the practice of citizenship. Under article 12, child citizens have the right to express opinions in all matters affecting the child, including political decisions at the municipal, provincial (or state), and national levels. As with other rights in the Convention, the exercise of participation rights is subject the guidance of parents and other adults. Article 5 emphasizes that such guidance is to be provided in a manner consistent with the 'evolving capacities' of the child. Guidance must not be arbitrary or overly controlling. It must be appropriate to the age and level of maturity of the child, and more autonomy must be given to the child with the child's increasing age and maturity. Upon becoming capable of forming an opinion, a child has the right – with age-appropriate guidance – to express her or his opinions freely. Whether on family, educational, or broader political issues, a child's opinion is to be given due weight by adult authorities in accordance with that child's age and maturity.

A child's exercise of participation rights, like an adult's, is subject to limits. An adult citizen does not have the right to yell 'Fire!' in a crowded theatre or other confined space, neither does a child citizen. Article 13 limits the child citizen's right to freedom of expression by restrictions such as those that are necessary for the protection of public order, national security, public health, and the rights and reputations of others. Article 14 limits the child's right to freedom of religion and belief similarly, so as not to be in conflict with the requirements for public safety, order, health, morals, or other citizens' fundamental rights and freedoms. Article 15 similarly limits the child's right to freedom of association and peaceful assembly. These restrictions on participation are not different from the restrictions on adult rights, and the burden of proof rests with those who want to restrict rights – whether of the adult or of the child.

Providing for child participation rights is consistent with a commitment to the basic principles of democracy (Flekkoy & Kaufman, 1997). One such basic principle is that citizens who are to express opinions and engage in political participation require, in addition to the right to participate, access to relevant information and the free exchange of ideas. Article 13 provides child citizens with the right to receive and impart information as a requirement for informed opinions and decisions. As noted by Flekkoy and Kaufman (1997), secrecy and censorship are opposed as firmly for child citizens as they are under international treaties pertaining to adults. Another basic principle of democracy is that citizens who are to express themselves freely require freedom of thought and conscience. Child citizens have these vital freedoms under article 14. Parents and guardians have a duty to provide the child with direction in exercising these freedoms. Their duty is 'to provide direction' rather than 'to determine' outcomes and to provide such direction in relation to the evolving capacities of the child. Democracy also rests on the principle that for political participation citizens need to be able to meet one another and gather in groups for the purposes of sharing information and making their views known. Article 15 assures child citizens the right to association and peaceful assembly.

Finally, democracy broadly conceived as participatory democracy involves the belief that practising participatory decision-making during childhood and adolescence is basic to citizen participation during adulthood (Pateman, 1970). Adult citizens are more likely to be engaged in the political process if they have had prior participatory practice in their families and schools. In providing child participation rights, the Convention provides the building blocks for democracy. In providing for them as being-citizens, the Convention provides for children as becoming-citizens. Article 5 recognizes that children have the right to participate in accordance with their evolving capacities. Thus, parents and other adult authorities are to allow for and encourage the participation of the child and provide guidance in proportion to the child's age and maturity. Once children are capable of forming opinions, they have a right to participate in decisions that affect them. But with their increasing age and maturity, the scope of their participation and degree of autonomy increase. Promoting the practice of age-appropriate participation among child citizens is consistent with the principle of participatory democracy.

Assuming and carrying out responsibilities is also basic to citizenship. Like adult citizens, child citizens have certain responsibilities and obligations. These include moral responsibilities appropriate for younger children, as well as legal and moral responsibilities appropriate for and applicable to older children. Very little explicit mention of the responsibilities of children appears in the U.N. Convention on the Right of the Child. The framers of the Convention correctly assumed the primary importance of rights because, unlike responsibilities, the rights of the child are inherent. Just as in the case of adults, children's enjoyment of rights does not depend on their fulfilment of responsibilities. Just as an adult is not required to do anything in particular to enjoy a right against discrimination, say, it is not required of a child to do particular things in order to have the right against abuse and neglect. Inherent rights are not contingent. When the Convention does deal with duties and responsibilities, it is in relation to parents, other adult authorities, and the state. Parents have a responsibility to provide for the best interests of their children and to guide their children in exercising their (the children's) rights. The state has a responsibility to provide conditions for child citizens that enable them to exercise their rights, as well as a responsibility to assist parents in fulfilling their obligations to their children.

It is understood in the concept of rights and in the Convention that children also have responsibilities. In articles 37 and 40, dealing with the legal rights of youth in conflict with the law, it is understood that older children have a responsibility, as well as a legal obligation to obey the law. These articles assume the presence and desirability of a juvenile justice system where young persons from a certain age – in Canada, for example, from age twelve – can be held accountable should they break the law. Juvenile justice systems, in turn, are based on the assumption that although they do not have the same social responsibility to obey the law as adults do, older children are to be held responsible to some level. Very young children have no or very little responsibility to obey the law; at best, they may have a moral responsibility. Older children, usually teenagers, have a legal and a moral obligation. They can be held legally accountable, although not to the same degree as adults. In the separate system of juvenile justice, minors do not face the same sentences as adults, but they do face sentences. That older children have some level of criminal responsibility recognizes the position that children have some capacity to assume responsibility, and this position is reflected in the Convention.

The concept of rights generally implies correlative duties or corresponding responsibilities. If someone is entitled to exercise a right, someone else must have the duty or responsibility to ensure that the right can be exercised. Otherwise, to say that one has a right is meaningless. Henry Shue (1980) has submitted that for every basic right there are three types of corresponding responsibilities. First, there is the very basic duty to avoid depriving others of their rights. Second, there is the duty to protect those whose rights are being deprived or threatened. Third, there is the obligation to assist those whose rights are being deprived or threatened. Applied to the situation of children and bullying, for example, if a child has the right to not be bullied in the schoolyard or on the street; other children, especially older ones, have the responsibility to ensure that the right to not be bullied can be exercised. It is important to recognize at the outset that major responsibility resides with school and adult authorities to ensure a safe school and neighbourhood environment where bullying does not take place, or if it does, where there is preventive or remedial action. As immature persons, children – even older children – do not yet have full responsibility. Nevertheless, older children do have some measure of responsibility. At the most basic level, they have a responsibility to avoid depriving another child of a right, for example, they have a responsibility to not be a bully. Second, they have a duty to protect others against bullying through alerting authorities or standing between the bully and the victim. Third, if necessary, they have a duty to assist the victim by taking direct action against the bully or giving support to authorities.

Children understand, at some age and at some level, that with a right goes a responsibility (Flekkoy & Kaufman, 1997). It is misleading, however, to say that rights and responsibilities are always two sides of the same coin or that 'the exercise of the right must be matched by the exercise of responsibility within the same person' (Lansdown, 1995b, pp. 24–5). To take an extreme example to illustrate the point, it does not follow that while an infant has the right to food and the right not to be abused, an infant has the corresponding responsibility to ensure that others have food or that others are not abused. An infant obviously is not in a position to exercise responsibility and has not the capacity or the understanding to do so. Responsibility here must completely lie with parents and other adult authorities. However, to return to the bullying example, teenagers in a high school setting do have the capacity and understanding to assume some measure of responsibility for ensuring the right of others to not be bullied. To deny that teenagers have any level of responsibility is to deny that they have any ability to understand and to connect with others.

What these examples indicate is that like with the exercise of rights, it is necessary to see the exercise of social responsibilities in relation to the 'evolving capacities' of the child. Child citizens have responsibilities that are in relation to their age and level of maturity. To specify with precision what degree of responsibility children should be expected to assume at a given age is difficult because it is difficult to specify individual capacities and levels of understanding and competence. The law attempts to provide an approximate answer to the question of capacities through designating ages of consent or rules to govern the determination of competence or decision-making authority. But, as found in social science research, there are often mismatches between the actual capacities of children and the capacities assumed in the law (Schmidt & Reppucci, 2002). Sometimes the actual capacities are more and sometimes less than those designated, or assumed. Generally speaking, however, according to principle of evolving capacities, infants can be assumed to have no capacity for the exercise of responsibility, young children have some degree of such capacity, and older children have a greater capacity, although it is not at the level of adults. Where the lines are drawn for purposes of the law must be based on the best social science evidence available and a willingness to modify the law in line with new evidence.

Age-appropriate exercise of social responsibility is an important part of child citizenship. Like adult citizens, child citizens have responsibilities corresponding to their rights, responsibilities that are necessary to building and maintaining a democratic and rights-based society. Such a society could not be sustained without the cooperation and willingness of its citizens to accept social responsibility. Taking responsibility does not come out of thin air. Rather, it is learned through experience. In a step-by-step process, through the age-appropriate exercise of responsibilities as being-citizens, child citizens learn to take responsibility as becoming-citizens. In doing so, they are more able to assume responsibilities as future adult citizens.

The Practice of Participation

The active and age-appropriate participation of child citizens is important. Child participation is both a right and a social responsibility, and it is both part of democracy and a foundation for democracy. As being-citizens, children – in the here and now – exercise their rights of participation and assume responsibilities in a democratic society. As becoming-citizens, their participation contributes to the foundation and building blocks of democracy.

Child participation is more easily understood and appreciated when democracy is conceived in its broader sense as participatory and deliberative. This is in contrast to an earlier and narrower interpretation of democracy meaning simply a method by which adult citizens choose leaders through free and periodic elections, without much citizen participation beyond voting. Participatory democracy embraces widespread participation not only in the formal political system but also in society. As discussed by Carole Pateman, (1970) drawing on the classical democratic theories of Jean-Jacques Rousseau, John Stuart Mill, and G.D.H. Cole, democracy requires not only elections and representation in formal political institutions but also a participatory society. Participation in social and economic institutions is necessary in order to provide citizens with the experience, confidence, and training needed for effective and widespread participation in formal political institutions. Participation in society and at earlier ages – the participation of child citizens in families and schools – over time, helps create the confidence and sense of efficacy that empowers people to participate in the political system. Participation also provides the practical learning and experience that enables people to effectively share in the making of political decisions, assess the performance of their representatives, and hold their representatives accountable. Thus, the social participation of child citizens in families and schools – their involvement as becoming-citizens – is a means to building participatory democracy.

The concept of deliberative democracy has recently been developed as part of the meaning of participatory democracy. According to Iris Young (1997), democracy should not be seen only as a method for choosing leaders or a procedure for regulating political competition among different interests but as a deliberative process of discussion, debate, and decision-making in solving collective problems. For Young, voting is just one part of the larger democratic process. To have democratic legitimacy, the process must involve opportunities for different interest groups in society to express their views and paricipate in decision-making, which must be based on full discussion and deliberation of these various and varying views. In promoting their own interests, participants must justify their case, while also taking the interests and perspectives of others into account. Participants' commitment must not simply be to promote their own interests but also to cooperate and to seek the solution that is most just. Decisions should be arrived at through careful listening to all perspectives and through deliberation that reflects not only narrow self-interest or arbitrary wants but the considered will and common good of all citizens. If the process is to be legitimate, and the decisions both informed and justified, all interests and social perspectives must be represented (Kulynych, 2001). This is not the case when only the most powerful interests are represented and other interests are kept silent or marginalized.

Deliberation and decision-making based on carefully listening to the voices of all groups of citizens includes the voices of child citizens. Child citizens are able to express their views on matters that affect them and they have much to offer. The particular social positions, understandings, and perspectives of children can provide adult decision-makers with valuable input. To some extent, of course, adults may have a sense of the child's perspective through their memories of what it was like to be a child themselves. But adults do not have complete recall and even if they did, the childhood experiences of adults would not be identical to the experiences of children today. Exposure to the perspectives of child citizens gives decision-makers more knowledge and understanding of how different decisions, policies, and laws may affect children. Decisions may or may not be based on what child citizens want to see happen, but their input may be valuable in any case. Excluding children from participation is to exclude a social perspective that can provide a valuable contribution to deliberation on the best interests of children, as well as on the common good of all citizens. Thus, the participation of children as being-citizens is important for a deliberative democracy.

Child participation is a part of genuine democracy and a part of the U.N. Convention on the Rights of the Child. Child citizens should participate in matters that affect them, and it is their right under the Convention to do so. The main settings for children's participation include the family, school, local community, and the wider political community. Families and schools are of primary importance. They are social and educational institutions. They are also political or politically relevant institutions because within them are the politically relevant practices of authority, learning, and participation that have implications for the wider political community. At their best, families are what Flekkoy and Kaufman (1997) referred to as the world's 'smallest democracy.' Consistent with the Convention, democratic families are ones that allow for and promote age-appropriate participation. They are 'characterized by mutual respect, sharing, integrity, autonomy and equality in the sense that each member, while not identical, has equal value as a human being' (1997, p. 61). With mutual respect and the integrity of each member of the family as a given, democratic parents are sensitive to the developmental stages and evolving capacities of their children. Democratic parents allow for the increasing exercise of rights and responsibilities and for age-appropriate participation in family decision-making. Similarly, a democratic school functions as a 'workshop for democracy' (Flekkoy & Kaufman, 1997, p. 109). Democratic schools are characterized by their provision of opportunities for participation – such as through student councils – and by their democratic teaching styles that allow for and encourage age-appropriate participation in the classroom (Covell & Howe, 2001a). Democratic participation in families and schools, equips and empowers child citizens to participate in the world outside these settings and in the wider political system.

Roger Hart (1992) has described the evolving participation of child citizens in terms of a ladder. At the lowest three rungs are kinds of involvement that are neither authentic forms of participation nor consistent with the Convention. The bottom rung represents 'manipulation,' where perhaps children are used as consultants for some adult purpose, but they are given no feedback and support. An example would be giving pre-school children political placards on which support for some adult cause is expressed, even though the children have no understanding of the cause and its issues. The adults, for their own political objectives, would pretend that the event is child-inspired. The second rung represents 'decoration,' where using the same example, the children are dressed in T-shirts that illustrate the adults' cause, but they have no understanding of what the message on the T-shirts is all about or why they are wearing them. The difference, however, is that the adults do not pretend that wearing the T-shirts (or some other decorative event) is child-inspired. The third rung is 'tokenism,' whereby children appear to be given a voice, but they have little or no choice regarding the subject and little or no opportunity to formulate their own views on it. For example, children are sometimes used on conference panels as a means by which adults attempt to demonstrate that they have consulted with children and made their deliberations on the basis of listening to them. However, the children are not actually given any opportunity to prepare their statements or to meet with the peers that they are supposed to represent. This participation is inauthentic.

The next five rungs on Hart's ladder are forms of participation that are both authentic and generally consistent with the Convention. Here child involvement moves from tokenism to citizenship. The lowest of these rungs represents 'assigned but informed' participation. Although an activity or project is selected and planned for by adults, children are reasonably well informed about it, understand the issues, and have a meaningful role in the activity or project. An example is a meeting or conference planned by adults, but with the informed and meaningful involvement of children. Next up is 'consulted and informed' involvement where, while a project is designed and run by adults, children have a good understanding of the issues, and their views are taken more seriously than at the rung below. Up a rung further is participation called 'adult-initiated, shared decisions with children.' While adults initiate a project or activity, children's views are taken more seriously still, and the decision-making process is actually shared with child citizens. With 'child-initiated and directed' participation, the next rung up, adults provide supportive conditions for child involvement, but it is largely children who conceive and carry out the project. Finally, the highest rung of the ladder represents participation called 'child-initiated, shared decisions with adults.' Here, adults provide encouragement and support, but it is children who design the project. The difference from the lower rung is that adults are included in the project only at the initiative of children, and children share their decisions with adults.

One problem with Hart's ladder is that no clear distinction is made between participation and self-determination. In accordance with the Convention, what is required at the highest rungs is not complete autonomy but age-appropriate input and listening. Overall, however, the ladder is generally consistent with the spirit of the Convention and the principle of the evolving capacities of the child citizen. In relation to their age and maturity, as child citizens move up the ladder, their views are given more weight and increasing room is made for their self-direction and initiative. Hart's focus was on children's involvement in particular projects and activities. But deliberative and participatory democracy, and the U.N. Convention, holds that the participation of child citizens is also necessary in the wider democratic process beyond particular projects. For example, in proposals to modify or develop new laws or policies affecting children, it is appropriate that decision-makers consult with relevant groups of child citizens and deliberate on the basis of their input as well as other input. Similarly, in reviews of laws or of a country's implementation of the Convention, child citizens should be consulted and allowed a voice, and their views should be given increasing weight with their evolving capacity. For instance, child and youth organizations that represent children in alternative state care may have something important to say about laws and policies that deal with child protection and state care. Student councils may have something important to say about educational practices and policies. Groups representing children with disabilities may have something important to say about policies and laws dealing with disabilities.

Admittedly, to seek and provide for the input of children on a regular basis and over a wide range of areas may be a major challenge for decision-makers. It would be a significant departure from current practices. Nevertheless, the active participation of children is part of child citizenship and part of authentic democracy.

Differentiated Child Citizenship

Citizenship is differentiated rather than uniform. This applies to adult citizens and to child citizens as well. It is important to recognize that, while adults and children share some common rights and obligations of citizenship, there are also differentiated rights and obligations. It also is important to recognize that in addition to child citizenship being differentiated from adult citizenship, within child citizenship there is differentiation on the basis of age categories and other sub-groups of children.

First, child citizenship is differentiated from adult citizenship. Various international human rights conventions, including the U.N. Convention on the Rights of the Child, have recognized that adults and children have certain basic human rights in common. These include the following: subsistence rights (food, clothing, shelter); the right to basic health care; the right to due process of law; and the rights to freedom of expression, freedom of association, and freedom of assembly. By ratifying such human rights conventions and incorporating these rights into their domestic laws, countries recognize some of the common rights of citizenship. Adult citizens also have certain rights of citizenship not enjoyed by children. The political right to vote is but one example. But children, too, have certain citizenship rights not enjoyed by adults. For example, under the Convention, while children in conflict with the law have similar rights to due process as adults – for instance, the right to legal representation and to the presumption of innocence – they also have special legal rights appropriate to children. Children have special rights to contact with their family, to be separated from adult offenders, to have their privacy protected, and to not be subject to the death penalty or a sentence of life imprisonment (Howe & Covell, 2001a). Similarly, child citizens have group-differentiated responsibilities of citizenship. For example, like adults, children have the same general obligation to obey the criminal law. But, given their lower age and level of maturity, children are recognized to have a lesser degree of responsibility than adults.

Second, child citizenship is differentiated on the basis of age categories. Children have evolving capacities. Therefore, their ability to engage in participation and to exercise their rights and responsibilities differs at different stages of their development (Flekkoy & Kaufman, 1997). This becomes complicated when childhood is being considered all the way from infancy to adolescence and in different participatory settings ranging from the family and sandbox democracy to participation in schools and in legal proceedings. The citizenship of younger children is quite different from that of older children (or youth). In the area of participation rights, for example, younger children have the right under the Convention to express their views, but they do not have the right that their views be given weight in the same way that older children's views are. As another example, younger children have the right – under the Convention's Optional Protocol on Child Soldiers – to not become child soldiers, whereas older children (from age sixteen) can be recruited into the military and into armed conflict. Finally, as another example, older children (juveniles) have the right to due process in the legal system, but that right does not apply to younger children – on the assumption that the level of responsibility and degree of criminal culpability are greater with older children. Younger children have some level of moral responsibility for their actions, but they have no legal responsibility and are, therefore, not subjectable to a juvenile justice system and, therefore, have no need for the right to due process. These are but some examples that illustrate child citizenship as differentiated by age group.

Third, child citizenship is differentiated on the basis of different sub-groups of children. All children have the right to enjoy the Convention rights of provision, protection, and participation. Some children also have group-differentiated rights of citizenship. One such group is children with disabilities. A child citizen with a physical or mental disability has rights as an individual and special rights, under article 23 of the Convention – as a member of a collectivity – to special care, assistance, and education. The state has the obligation to provide assistance and ensure that a child with a disability has effective access to opportunities and social services. Other groups are ethnic, religious, and linguistic minorities. Minority child citizens have special rights, under article 30, to enjoy their own culture, practise their own religion, and use their own language. The state has the obligation to ensure that these special rights are not denied. Aboriginal or indigenous peoples are a sub-group of citizens. Aboriginal children have special rights, also under article 30, to enjoy their own culture, religion, and language, although not necessarily in the same ways as minority children. Refugee children have special rights, although because they are not citizens of the new country, these are not the rights of citizenship. Under article 22 of the Convention, refugee children are entitled to special protection and assistance, including, in the event of separation from their family, assistance in being reunified with their family.

Differentiated citizenship requires that child citizens, like adult citizens, recognize and accept group differences and that they display the citizenship qualities and virtues of tolerance, civility, and mutual respect. Intolerance, disrespect, and prejudice against groups who are different from the mainstream are common problems or potential problems in virtually all societies. Sometimes these problems are amplified by the awareness that special rights are claimed by and provided to these groups. Resentments can build against members of groups provided with group-differentiated rights and policies. Thus, in the interests of social peace and cohesion, it is important that child citizens as well as adult citizens understand the circumstances and needs of different groups in their society and accept, if not embrace, social and cultural diversity.

Global Child Citizenship

Child citizens should identify with the political community in which they practice their citizenship. The active practise of participation and the exercise of rights and responsibilities is much more possible when child citizens, like adult citizens, identify and have a bond with their community. In the absence of this identification, child citizens are more likely not to be involved or to be only passively involved or to be negatively involved with their community. This can be seen, for example, in the activities of skinheads or other groups that disrespect people's rights.

Since the time of the French Revolution, the main object of identification and affection has been the nation-state. With globalization and the increasing awareness of the interconnectedness and international dimensions of social problems, there has been increasing identification with larger regions beyond the state (e.g., the European Union) and with the 'global village' as a whole. Obviously, this does not mean that the state has become obsolete or unimportant in the minds and hearts of adult and child citizens. In varying degrees, most citizens have feelings of patriotism and affection for their country. Some people have feelings of nationalism where there is not just affection but deep attachment and intense loyalty to their country. Many child and adult citizens also identify with the global community, and they see themselves as citizens not only of a particular country but also of the world. This spells an evolution in the meaning of citizenship – from state citizenship to 'multiple citizenship' (Heater, 1993). It is now recognized that citizens have multiple citizenships and that, within these, global citizenship has an important place.

What is the particular meaning of global citizenship as it applies to child citizens of the world? To begin with, it means that child citizens identify with the global community and, thus, with other global citizens. This identification is developed on the basis of awareness of people other than themselves and their needs and problems, of the interconnectedness of people and our global environment, and of the essential human sameness of people everywhere. These child citizens are aware that many problems and issues are global in nature and require global approaches and solutions. They are particularly aware of serious problems such as degradation of the environment, poverty, and the effects of war, and they identify with the problems and suffering of other global citizens. This does not mean that global child citizens have no attachment to their own country. Like their adult counterparts, these children have feelings of patriotism, although not of nationalism. It is important to note a key difference between patriotism and nationalism (Heiman, 1966). With patriotism, citizens have feelings of affection for their homeland that are informed by reason. Patriotism is not deep and blind attachment that excludes other loyalties. Patriotism, therefore, can coexist with a cosmopolitan attachment to the global community. With nationalism, citizens have feelings of deep loyalty to the nation-state that can be so intense that identification with other countries and with the international community is impossible. Nationalistic thinking is inward and guided by the principle of 'my country, right or wrong.' Global child citizens are patriotic, but not nationalistic.

With global identification, child citizens practise their global citizenship: they enjoy the basic international rights of the child; respect and support the rights of others all over the world, including other people's group-differentiated rights; participate in global decision-making about issues that affect children; and take social responsibility for the well-being of our planet. The rights that these children enjoy are the global citizenship rights as described in the U.N. Convention, and these rights exist apart from their endorsement by nation-states. Global child citizens exercise these rights in a manner consistent with their evolving capacities. They engage in age-appropriate participation in international decisions that affect children through involvement in national decision-making, international meetings and conferences, and the activities of NGOs, both domestic and international. These children are active in addressing international issues such as child labour, child prostitution, and the recruitment and use of children in the military. Finally, as part of their participation, global child citizens take age-appropriate social responsibility for the well-being of the global village. This means a general willingness to support national and international efforts to ensure that the global citizenship rights of others are provided for and to promote a global order aimed at peace, a healthy environment, democracy, and human rights. As a model of global child citizenship, Daiva Stasiulis (2002) points to the example of Canadian teenager Craig Kielburger (see Chapter 1) and the youth organization he founded in 1995, when he was twelve years old. Free the Children has campaigned intensively against child labour and child poverty and for children's rights and education. Involving over 100,000 youth in more than thirty-five countries and achieving tangible results on behalf of children, members of this organization epitomize the features of global child citizenship.

This is a picture of the practice of global child citizenship that, of course, is not in place. But it is a picture that is consistent with a conception of citizenship that recognizes the child as citizen and the global community as an important part of the citizen's community.

Promoting Citizenship

At least since the time of the Ancient Greek city-states, it has been widely assumed that the state should play a leading role in promoting the practice of citizenship. Furthermore, it has been widely assumed that the means by which the state should promote citizenship is schools. In Ancient Athens, education in citizenship was traditionally the responsibility of the family (Heater, 2002). Wealthy families were given the responsibility to employ tutors for training their sons in civic virtue. However, as Athens became a democratic city-state, and as the need for education grew, schools were founded. One of their primary objectives was the advancement of citizenship. In European and world history, the concept of school-based education about citizenship never disappeared, although it periodically went into eclipse. With the French and the American revolutions, this concept was resurrected as a means of building national unity, democracy, and a sense of common identity within nation-states. The need to ensure unity and social cohesion and to educate citizens for democracy gave modern schools the responsibility of promoting citizenship.

It is logical that schools – public schools (or common schools) but also state-regulated private schools – should have this responsibility. It could be left with the family. But parents have many and differing views on the content and importance of citizenship. Many have authoritarian parenting styles that are at odds with democratic participation. It is, therefore, not logical that the family be given the responsibility to promote citizenship (Frimannsson, 2001). Moreover, because the family is often considered – although wrongly – to be part of the private rather than public sphere, it would be difficult for state authorities to obtain consensus on the duty of parents to educate their children in citizenship. This would be seen as overly intrusive. Responsibility to promote citizenship could be delegated to associations of civil society such as churches, charities, unions, ethnic minority groups, cooperatives, environmental groups, and neighbourhood organizations. It is arguable that, because participants within these associations learn the virtues of mutual obligation and internalize the idea of personal and social responsibility, these associations would be a seedbed of civic virtue and citizenship education: people who participate in the voluntary associations would be educated in citizenship and would more likely be good citizens. Thus, the state should promote voluntarism and voluntary associations. However, there is little empirical evidence to support this argument (Kymlicka & Norman, 1995). Associations may or may not promote the practice of citizenship in the wider political community. It may be the case that rather than fostering citizenship, some churches teach the supreme value of inward religious life, or that some ethnic associations teach prejudice, or that some neighbourhood groups teach the principle of not in my backyard (NIMBY; see Kymlicka & Norman, 1995). Since there is not necessarily a linkage between what is learned within these associations and what is educationally required for democratic citizenship, these associations – like the family – are not to be depended on to promote education for citizenship.

The key institutional setting for citizenship education and promotion should be the school. Clearly, schools are institutions that are in the public sphere and subject to state control and regulation. They are where the overwhelming majority of children (and future adults) can be reached and educated, systematically and comprehensively. School is where participatory learning can take place for democratic citizenship and where the citizenship values and civic virtues of tolerance, mutual obligation, and critical reasoning can be taught (Galston, 1991). If people are to be active, attentive, responsible, and critically minded citizens, it is important to reach and educate them early in the course of their social, moral, and cognitive development: school is the natural and obvious place to do this. Some traditionalists say that giving schools such a citizenship education function is dangerous because then schools would be teaching children to question tradition and all authority, which would include parental and religious authority, as well as political authority (Kymlicka & Norman, 1995). But it is not necessarily the case that children who learn to question political authority will go on to question the traditions of their parents and religion. It is not necessarily the case that children who rebel against parental and religious authority do so out of a sceptical attitude that they learn in schools. Pluralism and respect for cultural and religious diversity are highly important values, and tradition should not be used as a roadblock to democratic citizenship. The practice of democratic citizenship requires critical reasoning and the willingness to question authority. Schools, therefore, should provide citizenship education. This would be in the broad interests of a liberal democratic and rights-based society.

There is widespread agreement that citizenship education plays a vital role in sustaining a liberal democratic society. Political and education philosophers do not, however, agree about the nature or the moral basis of such education (Callan, 2001). Eamonn Callan (2001) has concluded that citizenship and political education in a liberal democratic society faces the philosophical problem of being self-defeating. Citizenship education through schools is necessary to instill the values and virtues that are required to sustain liberal democratic society. But such education must be restrained: it must respect the freedom of citizens to develop and express their own particular values and make autonomous choices. One solution to the problem, noted Callan, is the minimalist political education advocated by John Rawls. According to this approach, citizenship education must be based not on comprehensive moral, religious, or philosophical commitments but on minimum civic assumptions. A key one is recognition of the need for reciprocity and social cooperation in human relationships. To go further than limited education on basic rights, freedoms, and obligations would be to enter the terrain of invasive and illiberal education, which is counter to the values of freedom, pluralism, and tolerance. But as Callan persuasively argued, this is inadequate. Sound citizenship education requires grounding not only in a self-interested appreciation for reciprocity but in deep moral commitment to liberal democratic values and a strong belief in the importance of mutual respect. Thus, citizenship education in schools must have moral content and be aimed at 'the cultivation of robust attitudes of mutual respect among future citizens' (Callan, 2001, p. 96).

On the basis of the assumption that schools are the key institutions for promoting citizenship, since early in the nineteenth century, it has been the responsibility of schools to provide citizenship education (or civic education) as well as education to serve the needs of the economy and of individuals. Indeed, training for citizenship was one of the central reasons for the creation of modern public school systems and for the establishment of compulsory public education. Two powerful forces were behind these developments (Heater, 2002). One was the spread of democracy and with it the steady expansion of voting rights. Education for citizenship was deemed necessary for there to be knowledgeable voters and responsible democratic citizens. The second was the widespread feeling of nationhood and with it the building of new nation-states. Citizenship education, with a focus on patriotism, duty, and shared identity, was considered important as a means to obtain national unity and social cohesion, especially in countries with significant ethnic and cultural diversity and/or large immigrant populations.

In the period following the Second World War, a number of other forces can be cited to account for the development or refashioning of citizenship education (Heater, 1993, 2002). First, postcolonial states in Africa and Asia looked to citizenship education as a vehicle for binding their people together and overcoming the new countries' deep problems such as poverty and instability. Second, with the demise of Communist and other authoritarian states, new transitional democracies in Eastern Europe and Latin America saw citizenship education as necessary to building or rebuilding democratic societies. Third, with the resurgence of ethnic nationalism in countries such as Great Britain (with Scottish nationalism) and Canada (with Quebec nationalism), policymakers looked to citizenship education as a possible glue that would preserve unity. Fourth, mindful of globalization and the importance of global issues, an educational movement has arisen that seeks to revise citizenship education to advance an appreciation for global citizenship. Finally, the concept of citizenship itself has evolved, especially to embrace differentiated and inclusive citizenship, and this has forced policymakers to consider refashioning citizenship education accordingly (Hebert, 2002).

These various forces led to programs of citizenship education through specialized classes in 'civics' but, more importantly, also through various other subjects and approaches throughout the educational system. Thus, education for citizenship was established not as 'an isolated subset of the curriculum' but as 'one of the ordering goals or principles which shapes the entire curriculum' (Kymlicka 2001, p. 293). Citizenship education developed differently and to different degrees in different countries. In France, citizenship education initially was inhibited by the authoritarian influences of the Roman Catholic Church and the state, but beginning in the 1880s it was implemented in a serious and relatively comprehensive way (Heater, 2002). This was done through a mandatory program of 'civic instruction' focusing on civic duties and morality and, from the 1970s, through an updated program of 'civic education.' In England, citizenship education remained a relatively weak and scattered program for a much longer period. This can be explained by such factors as a traditional suspicion of political (partisan) education, a decentralized system of education, a differentiated social system based on class, and pride in empire and commonwealth (Heater, 2001, 2002). In Britain, a national and mandatory program of citizenship education was put into place only in 2002. The influence of pressure groups and think tanks, concerns about Scottish nationalism, the European Union and its culture of human rights, and a commitment to educational reform by the Blair government can take credit for this development (Smith, 2002). To develop a sense of social responsibility, a major part of the British program is the requirement for community service within schools or in the local community.

In the United States, 'civic education' was implemented early and vigorously (Heater, 2002; Marquette and Mineshima, 2002). American educators and politicians in the early 1800s expressed concern about immorality in the growing urban areas and the need to incorporate the increasing numbers of immigrants into American culture. This led to the idea of 'common schools' where, through civic education, students would be trained to be good democratic citizens, of good moral character, who appreciate their rights and obligations and have a sense of committed patriotism. This was to be done mainly through the subjects of history, civics, and social studies, but also through school practices such as the pledge of allegiance. In order to incorporate minority and new immigrant children the American educational approach became one mainly of 'acculturation' rather than assimilation, where the focus was on adding new values while retaining – rather than eliminating – elements of one's older identity (Marquette & Mineshima, 2002). Black children, however, remained outside the mainstream in segregated schools until after the Second World War.

In Canada, the development of citizenship education was similar to that in the United States, but with some important differences. In much of English-speaking Canada, it was similar in that in response to democratization, immigration, and the need for nation-building, there was an early focus on 'civic education' to promote patriotism, unity, moral character, and a sense of duty (Manzer, 1994). But it was different in that patriotism – outside Quebec – for a long time was connected to mother Britain and the British Empire. Furthermore, the building of a strong sense of unity and shared identity has been undercut by the provincial control of education, Quebec nationalism, and Quebec's desire to be recognized as a distinct society if not a separate nation. The development in Canada was different, too, in that after an early attempt to assimilate minorities and impose Anglo-conformity, the approach shifted (especially since the 1960s) to one of embracing multiculturalism and the principle of unity in difference (Osborne, 2000; Sears, Clarke, & Hughes, 1999). Canadian multiculturalism goes much further than does the American approach of acculturation in recognizing and endorsing differentiated citizenship.

But despite its varied historical evolution, citizenship education is now widely understood to have certain common core objectives: children are to be educated about the rights and responsibilities of citizenship; the importance of citizen participation; the values and virtues of tolerance, civility, and mutual respect; and the merits of differentiated citizenship and global citizenship. This understanding reflects the evolution of the concept of citizenship itself. However, in recent decades, serious questions have been raised about citizenship education. One problem is that many of the objectives have not been realized. Critics point to a number of major shortcomings in the practice of democratic citizenship. These include a significant level of citizen disengagement from the political process, especially among youth; a decline in voter turnout; the absence of a widespread sense of social responsibility; a preoccupation with personal rights; and the development of a culture of separation where citizens have become excessively focused on their own personal lives and uninterested in their society and political community (Berman, 1997).

But there is another problem, which is related to the first one. The currently prevailing conception of citizenship education is flawed because children are not generally recognized as citizens in their own right. As in the citizenship literature, schools hold onto an adultcentric and exclusionary conception of citizenship in which children are seen as future or becoming-citizens rather than as present or being-citizens. As will be discussed in the next chapter, citizenship education fails because it is not grounded in children's rights education such that children are recognized and respected as citizens of the present and empowered to learn and act as child citizens.

CHAPTER FOUR

Educating for Citizenship

All truth passes through three stages. First it is ridiculed, second it is violently opposed, third it is accepted as being self-evident.

Arthur Schopenhauer (1788–1860)

The truth is that children are citizens and they do have the rights and responsibilities of citizenship. Difficulty accepting this has, in part, been responsible for the opposition to children's rights education and to its exclusion from citizenship education in schools. We are optimistic that the imperative of children's rights education will become self-evident.

Schools are the first social institution with which children have experience, and schools are like political systems (Flanagan, Bowes, Jonsson, Csapo, & Sheblanova, 1998). In schools, children explore what it means to be a member of a group other than family and they learn to negotiate disagreements among peers. Schools are the institutions in which children first develop their ideas about the rights and responsibilities of citizenship.

Historically, schools have accepted the responsibility for inculcating values and teaching children what is expected of them as adult citizens of their society. With societal questioning and repudiation of traditional values in the 1960s, and with the number of transitional democracies through the 1990s, how schools address education for citizenship has come under sharp focus. It has been found wanting. Citizenship education has been shown to have little impact on the democratic values and behaviours of students. And citizenship education continues to disregard the citizenship status of the child.

The essential goal of citizenship education is to produce the good citizen. Schools aim to develop knowledgeable active citizens whose support for democratic values and engagement can promote and maintain inclusive democracy (Naval, Print, & Veldhuis, 2002). Although there is agreement on this goal of citizenship education, its practice varies widely. Citizenship education is something of an umbrella term. As well as describing traditional civic education, it has been used to describe a wide array of programs aimed at developing the good citizen. These include moral or character education, anti-racist education, peace education, environmental education, and human rights education. Citizenship education has been used to describe specific teachings in the formal curriculum, and it has been used to describe school processes and the hidden curriculum.

The various approaches to citizenship education generally can be categorized into three strands of teaching. Bernard Crick (1998), author of the well-received report on citizenship education in England, has described these strands as (1) social and moral responsibility, (2) community involvement, and (3) political literacy. Others (e.g., Menezes, Xavier, Cibele, Amaro, & Campos, 1999; Tibbits, 1997) have used the comparable terms, values and attitudes, action or behaviour, and knowledge. We combine these terms and use the following to categorize the orientation of the citizenship education programs: (1) citizenship values, (2) citizenship behaviours, and (3) citizenship knowledge. There is, of course, overlap among the three categories in every program, but the term denotes a program's emphasis.

In this chapter we examine the major means through which citizenship education has been taught in the formal and hidden or informal curricula in these three categories. Since there are major published works in each of these areas, the descriptions here are intended to be illustrative rather than comprehensive. We then assess where and why existing approaches fall short of their goals to increase the skills, knowledge, and dispositions that promote active citizenship. We end this chapter with a discussion of the value of a children's rights-based approach for citizenship education.

Teaching Citizenship Values

As many have noted, from Dewey (1933) on (e.g., Noddings, 1997; Schubert, 1997), all curricula shape character, the overt and the hidden curricula. Many social, moral, and political messages are transmitted through what is taught, how teachers behave, and how the school is organized and run. The explicit teaching of values, however, has been given consider-able emphasis since the 1960s, particularly by those who saw the youth cul-ture of the time as reflective of values confusion (Leming, 1997). The values strand of citizenship education has been taught through a variety of character or moral education programs. The assumption throughout is that since values guide behaviours, developing attitudes supportive of democratic citizenship will result in more socially responsible citizenship behaviours.

Values Clarification

One popular, albeit short-lived, approach to developing positive values or virtues in children was that of values clarification (Raths, Harmin, & Simon, 1966). Reflecting the social trends and individualistic spirit of the 1960s, and designed to avoid the imposition of traditional values on the student, schools attempted to promote the personal growth of stu-dents by helping students discover their own values (Battistich, Schaps, Solomon, & Watson, 1991). Students engaged in exercises designed to reveal their values and to stimulate them to examine and evaluate their values. We follow Benninga (1988) in providing the following exemplifi-cation of the approach.

Students are provided a moral dilemma in which they are to role-play a government decision-maker when the Third World War breaks out. They have control of a fallout shelter that contains space and provisions for six people who they must choose from among ten who wish to be admitted. The ten comprise the following: a sixteen-year-old pregnant high school dropout, a police officer with a gun and a record of brutality, a seventy-five-year-old clergyman, a thirty-six-year-old female physician who is a known racist, a forty-six-year-old male violinist who has served seven years for drug offences, a twenty-year-old black militant with no special skills, a thirty-nine-year-old female ex-prostitute, a forty-year-old homosexual architect, a twenty-six-year-old law student, and the law stu-dent's twenty-five-year-old wife who has spent the last nine months in a mental hospital and is still heavily sedated. The law student and his wife refuse to be separated. The students have thirty minutes to decide whom they will admit. There are no right or wrong answers and more impor-tantly no right or wrong justifications. The use of racism or homophobia as a criterion of selection, for example, was to be considered as valid as any other as long as it was the student's own value. Classroom discussions did not address the merits of particular values, nor attempt to reach consensus on any ethical issues. Any and all values were to be considered equally valid as long as they arose from personal conviction. In essence, values were to be clarified in a valueless vacuum.

Such extreme moral relativism fails to teach anything of value or about values. There is no distinction between personal preferences, whims, or biases, which have a self-focus, and moral or social values that subsume an obligation to others (Lickona, 1993). The accepted values of a community might be undermined, and validation given to values which are antipathetic to democracy and respect for the rights of others. This was moral relativism *reductio ad absurdum*. After repeated values clarification programs were notably unsuccessful in improving students' personal or school-related values, attitudes, or behaviours, the approach fell into such disregard that 'some administrators ... would rather be accused of having asbestos in their ceiling than of using values clarification in their classrooms' (Howard Kirschenbaum, cited in Leming, 1997, p. 38).

Character Education

The antithetical position to the values clarification approach is the moral absolutist program of character education. Character education programs teach specific virtues. Like other forms of citizenship education, the goals of character education are to instill in children respect, responsibility, and the values of democratic citizenship. As reflected in curricular materials, however, the path to achieving these goals is through exhortations and inducements designed to make children obedient and industrious through a pedagogy best described as indoctrination (Kohn, 1997). There are two basic approaches.

One approach of character education is the reading of virtue stories. The assumption is that by reading virtue stories, children will want to emulate the protagonists. A strong advocate of this approach was Thomas Lickona (1997a, 1997b), who lamented the loss of the McGuffey Readers. Replacing the use of the Bible in the early part of the twentieth century, the McGuffey Readers provided what were intended to be inspiring stories and poems about honesty, industriousness, thriftiness, kindness, courage, and patriotism. For example, as Lickona described, children learned about Susie Sunbeam, who helped a less fortunate child by giving her one of her own dresses and pair of shoes; and they learned about Henry, who returned a lost wallet and used the reward money to start a shoe-shine business and used the profits from it to support his sick mother and his little sister. It is easy to dismiss such virtue stories as old-fashioned or laughable in today's culture, but would updated versions be effective agents of citizenship values? Would children who read about Susie or Henry want to behave like them? The current theories and research in the research literature on reading suggest that they would not. As demonstrated in a series of studies by Narvaez (2002), readers interpret stories within the context of their prior knowledge, or schema. Like adults, children are not passive assimilators of story content, but they actively construct meaning through their existing schema. Thus, as Narvaez concluded from her research, there is no valid reason to suppose children will extract the intended moral lesson from the story. They may interpret the theme of the Henry story as the importance of running a business or the benefits of shining shoes. There also is neither theoretical nor empirical justification to suppose that children will want to emulate story characters regardless of their interpretation of the story.

In the other approach, students are drilled in specific behaviours through behaviourist techniques, and then they are materially rewarded for the unquestioning adoption of the prescribed values (Nucci, 2001). The approach lacks a cognitive component and does not allow for critical thinking. In essence, children are taught that it is important to exhibit prescribed pro-social behaviours in order to obtain rewards. Unfortunately, the use of reward in this way erodes the child's intrinsic motivation and leads to external attributions of pro-social behaviours. The child learns to help a peer not because she or he values helpfulness or perceives the self as a helpful person, but to obtain the 'helping' reward. In fact, the research data consistently demonstrate that children who receive rewards for caring, helping, and sharing are less likely than their peers who are not rewarded to continue to behave pro-socially (e.g., Grusec, 1991). Moreover, as Kohn (1997) has pointed out, character education programs typically reward a limited number of children: the ones who are identified as the most virtuous. This, of course, engenders competitiveness rather than cooperation, and in turn, competitiveness breeds aggression and a focus on self rather than community. In summary, the character education goals of teaching respect, responsibility, and citizenship are unlikely to be realized. Effectively, these terms are euphemisms for uncritical deference to authority, which together with the behaviourist methodology used is likely to promote values antithetical to those of socially responsible citizenship.

Moral Education

The main competing approach through the same era was Lawrence Kohlberg's cognitive development approach (Leming, 1997), which reflects something of a middle point between the two extremes described above. Kohlberg realized that teachers must be allowed to advocate for certain values, but that their power should be limited and that structure was needed to protect against indoctrination (Higgins, 1991). His solution was to contextualize values education within a participatory democracy – the just community school. However, prior to that were attempts to teach democratic values through the discussion of hypothetical moral dilemmas.

Through peer discussion it was expected that children would be exposed to levels of moral reasoning different from their own. The underlying assumption of the cognitive development approach is that frequent exposure to peer levels of moral reasoning, especially when they are slightly above the child's existing level, would promote growth in democratic values. In Kohlberg's theory of moral development, progressive stages denote ethical reasoning more consistent with democratic ideals. In the early stages what is good is understood in reference to self. By stage 3, obedience and conformity are valued. By post-conventional levels, stages 5 and 6, values are based on universal principles of justice and human rights such as Kant's categorical imperative, or the golden rule.

Kohlberg's first attempt at values education through advancing moral reasoning was to use weekly classroom discussions of hypothetical moral dilemmas with Grade 9 students in their civic classes. Evaluation research showed that these discussions were somewhat effective in raising the students' levels of moral reasoning. However, the major finding was that students and teachers found the weekly discussions to be very boring and did not want to continue with them. In addition, teachers noted that there were no changes in classroom interactions (Higgins, 1991). The limitations of this approach led Kohlberg away from the formal curriculum to the hidden curriculum and to the development of the just community school.

The just community school is organized as direct participatory democracy. It is a community in which all members – teachers and students – make and enforce the governance policies and procedures. The goal of the just community school is to develop in students a commitment to the values of democracy. The idea of school as a democratic community is not, of course, new. As a general approach to education, it was described by John Dewey in 1916. However, Kohlberg's model goes beyond earlier approaches, particularly in the role of the teacher. For Dewey, the teacher was to be a facilitator of democracy. For Kohlberg (1980), the teacher was to be an explicit and strong advocate of democratic values. The Cluster School was developed in 1974, when Kohlberg was involved in the founding of an alternative high school in Cambridge, Massachusetts; it was the first model of a just community school. It was organized as follows. The school was designed to be run democratically with equal votes for staff and students. Community meetings were to be held weekly for the whole school. At these meetings issues of governance and any emerging problems were to be discussed. To enhance the spirit of community, there was to be cooperative work between students and staff (Kohlberg, 1980, 1985).

The reality of the Cluster School was at odds with the ideal. An immediate problem was the distrust of students for staff. Students acted out this distrust by using their voting majority to vote for inappropriate school procedures such as early school dismissal. It took a year for there to be true democratic decision-making (Reimer, Paolitto, & Hersh, 1983). A second difficulty also emerged quickly. Students were often uninterested in self-governance, especially when the discussions at the community meetings become enmeshed in details. Their response, one with which any adult who has spent time in board meetings will sympathize, was to curtail discussion and hold a quick vote. As Reimer et al. (1983) pointed out, quick resolution of issues precludes the type of reflective discussion needed to advance ethical reasoning. A third, perhaps more surprising problem, was that despite being involved in the creation of school rules, the students did not always adhere to them. Generally, it has been found that students' participation in the development of school rules and procedures is an effective route to compliance (e.g., Power, 1997). The difference may be that, unlike most schools where student input is very limited, in the Cluster School students were involved in the making of all the rules of the school. It is unlikely that such pervasive participation would be meaningful to the students. As well as difficulties with meaningful participation, another major challenge was posed by the lack of a clear administrative structure for the daily functioning of the school (Reimer et al., 1983). One factor limiting the success of the school may have been that students had not been taught values on which to base their participation and decision-making. Rather, it was assumed that the experience with democratic participation itself would promote the development of democratic values. Difficulties continued throughout the four years of the operation of the Cluster School.

Overall, the evaluations of the Cluster School and subsequent just community schools report that they did not meet expectations. There was some indication of increases in moral judgment scores and some impact on increasing students' democratic values, but the gains were modest and not found at all schools (Power, Higgins, & Kohlberg, 1989). It may be that the hidden curriculum is a necessary but not sufficient context for the development of democratic values. Explicit teachings and classroom discussions on social and justice issues are also necessary, it seems.

A similar pattern of evaluation data emerges from learner-centred schools, an alternative school model developed in schools that belong to the Center for Collaborative Education, which is based in New York. Like the just community schools, learner-centred schools have among their core principles student participation and training for democratic citizenship (Lieberman, Falk, & Alexander, 1995). The essential philosophy of learner-centred schools is that the school environment should be one that promotes the development of the whole child, within a democratic and supportive community. The school aims to be a 'living democracy' (p. 118). In support of this, the classroom environment is characterized by active involvement of students with curriculum materials, governance procedures, and peer interaction. Classes are heterogeneous with regard to student age, ethnocultural and socioeconomic status, and learning capacity. There is significant emphasis on the value of cultural diversity as well as diversity of learning styles and capacities, and students are encouraged to cooperate on projects blending their skills and perspectives. Teachers, who also act as administrators, function as facilitators of child-centred learning, rather than as transmitters of information.

Like the just community schools, the learner-centred schools have experienced a number of challenges that threaten their continuation. Teachers find their joint roles very demanding, and they report many daily experiences that lead them to question their values, commitment, and competence. A seemingly irresolvable problem is the clash between the teaching and assessment practices within the school, and the school district's mandated curricula and standardized testing which teachers are required to complete. Difficulties for teachers have been exacerbated by a gap between the resources and supports they need and the reality of what has been available. Not surprisingly, many teachers and students' families have had conflicts over the fundamental values and approaches of the schools. Of most relevance to the present discussion, however is that although there is some evidence that such democratically run schools contribute to students' sense of responsibility, there is little evidence of their ability to evoke a generalized change in democratic values or behaviour (e.g., Power, 1997).

Teaching Citizenship Behaviours

There has been a proliferation of programs over the past twenty years designed to teach children to behave as good citizens are expected to behave, with the obvious omission of age-irrelevant citizenship behaviours such as voting. Here we look at education programs whose focus is anti-racism, the environment, and peace as examples of behaviour-based approaches to citizenship education. Each is of particular salience to global citizenship, and each has been impelled by the social and ecological challenges of today's society.

Anti-racist Education

Anti-racist education has the goal of reducing stereotype-based and discriminatory behaviours. There has been a new emphasis on anti-racist education recently in response to the anti-Muslim sentiments that followed upon the terrorist attacks of 11 September 2001 in the United States; the ongoing ethnic divisiveness of war in the Middle East; and, in Europe, a significant resurgence of racism, xenophobia, and anti-Semitism (Brown and Davies, 1998). Educators and policymakers also have been impelled to place more emphasis on anti-racist education in light of findings such as those from Sweden, where a survey of twelve- to eighteen-year-olds indicated that one-third of them deny that the Nazi extermination of Jews occurred, 11 per cent believe that mixing races is 'a crime against nature,' and 10 per cent believe that it is wrong for people of different races to have children together (Brown & Davies, 1998). Moving away from the more narrow and traditional approaches of 'class and color' (Carrington & Short, 1997), anti-racist education has broadened out to examine the impact of stereotyping and racism at the societal level. The current situation in the United Kingdom is informative.

In an attempt to reduce incidents of racist behaviours, and to promote behaviours consistent with democratic citizenship, the national curriculum in England and Wales, since 1995, has mandated the teaching of the Holocaust in history classes (Carrington & Short, 1997). Holocaust denial has been such a problem in Britain that there have been discussions about its criminalization – a suggestion that was supported by Prime Minister Tony Blair (Cesarani, 1997). In response, many teachers have chosen to extend Holocaust teachings beyond what is mandated in order to reduce the incidence of racist behaviours among their students (Brown & Davies, 1998). However, overall evaluations of the impact of Holocaust education have been disappointing. Evidence demonstrated that at best there has been some decline in anti-Semitic behaviour but even that decline has been very short-lived. Moreover, what is learned about the Holocaust has not been generalized to other ethnocultural minority groups (Brown & Davies, 1998). Two evaluation studies shed light on why these programs have not been more effective.

Brown and Davies (1998) interviewed teachers and identified a number of relevant factors. First, despite the statutory requirement, Holocaust education was given little attention by many teachers. Some discussed the Holocaust for as little as two fifty-minute periods in the school year. By way of justification, these teachers argued that neither Holocaust denial nor anti-Semitic behaviours were problems and that there were many other historical events of equal significance. Among the latter were cited the actions taken by William the Conqueror after the invasion of 1066, the massacre at Drogheda by Cromwell, the Vietnam War, and the genocide in Rwanda. A second major finding was that many teachers were uncomfortable teaching about the Holocaust. They expressed concern that providing information about the Holocaust may generate emotional responses among students that, in turn, may result in classroom management problems. The third, and perhaps most important finding was that teachers were treating Holocaust education as they did other history topics. Discussion and open debate, necessary for real learning to occur, were not allowed. Discussion should be an integral component of Holocaust education (Carrington & Short, 1997). Overall, the Holocaust education curriculum was not being implemented as planned or as necessary for it to have real impact on the students.

If teachers were not always providing adequate or appropriate Holocaust education, what were students learning? This was revealed in a study by Carrington and Short (1997) of forty-three fourteen- to sixteen-year-olds who, within the previous year, had taken a history course that included the Holocaust curriculum. They were interviewed to determine whether learning about the Holocaust had developed within them an understanding of the dangers of stereotyping and discriminatory behaviour. In fact, few students had learned the intended messages. Some actually said that they had learned nothing about racism from the Holocaust education, and others said – incorrectly – that Jews were oppressed because of their religious beliefs. Thus, not surprisingly, few of the students had made any links between what they were told about the Holocaust and contemporary problems for ethnocultural minorities. They believed that no such event could recur and that there was no problem of racism in England. These data support the contention that, without open debate and discussion, students extract themes consistent with their existing schema. As evidence of this interpretation were the replies that the students gave in response to the question, 'What has the Holocaust taught you about being a good citizen?' The theme of personal choice and responsibility was evident in the answers of at least six of the students. What they had learned was the importance of making up your own mind on issues.

A much more effective approach to anti-racism has been the Facing History and Ourselves curriculum (FHAO), which was developed in the United States (Strom & Parsons, 1982). FHAO was designed primarily to reduce racism, but also to improve moral decision-making and behaviour among junior high school students (Schultz, Barr, & Selman, 2001). The duration of the program is between eight and ten weeks. FHAO has been more effective than the Holocaust education initiative in Great Britain because of four factors.

First, the content of the FHAO curriculum is broader. The program explores group membership and responsibility to others by examining the Armenian genocide, the Nazi Holocaust, and the history of eugenics in the United States. In not limiting the content to one event, however significant, the possibility of disengaging from it is reduced by precluding the perception that the event was aberrant, unique, and unlikely to recur. Looking at more than one event also facilitates examination of the underlying factors of genocide, rather than specific historical events only, and makes generalization to other contexts more likely. Second, rather than avoiding the difficult issues and emotions that must be part of such learning, the FHAO curriculum was designed to evoke them. The event is personalized through the use not only of primary documents, but also accounts of Nazi supporters and Holocaust survivors. These emotionally powerful materials confront students with the banality of evil (this phrase was coined by Hannah Arendt, philosopher and Holocaust survivor) and sensitize them to the realities of injustice and the violation of fundamental human rights. Third, and this is in sharp contrast to British Holocaust education, debate and discussion are core components of the FHAO curriculum. Students are required to reflect critically on many central issues and discuss them, for example, how genocide can become state policy. Journal-keeping is compulsory. In their journals students are to confront and examine their prejudices, feelings, and values. Fourth, rather than assuming that students will extract the intended message from the curriculum on their own, in the classroom explicit links are made between past genocides and current sociopolitical issues. FHAO students are stimulated to think about any possible connections between these historical atrocities and their own experiences.

Evaluation studies of FHAO have shown that the program was successful in increasing students' understanding of other people (Barbidge, 1981, 1988; Lieberman, 1981, 1986, 1991). Lieberman (1981, 1991) evaluated the curriculum in a number of diverse classrooms, over four years, and demonstrated the effectiveness of the FHAO curriculum in improving students' perspective-taking and social reasoning skills. Barbidge (1981, 1988) analysed the journal entries of students in two Grade 8 classes and found that, overall, these entries indicated that the students had become more sensitive to prejudice, less quick to judge others, and aware of the consequences of both their action and their inaction. Unfortunately, other evaluations have made it apparent that any such awareness and sensitivity have not produced higher levels of ethical reasoning ability (Glynn, Bock, & Cohn, 1982; Schultz, Barr, & Selman, 2001) or affected beliefs about civic responsibilities or involvement with social activism (Schultz et al., 2001). The lack of impact may well have resulted from the short duration of the program, or perhaps students did not fully comprehend the links between what they were learning through the FHAO curriculum and their daily experiences. Thus, one shortcoming of the FHAO program was that it did not address issues of high salience in the lives of the children; an improvement in the program would be to reorient it towards issues of more direct concern to the children (Schultz et al., 2001). The FHAO stands as one of the most successful curricula in anti-racist education, but it, too, falls short of its goals.

In general, much anti-racist education has been of limited impact because it was not directly linked with the students' experience of daily life (Brabeck & Rogers, 2000). Instead, the most commonly employed approach to anti-racist education has been to focus on historical examples. During black history month, in Canada it may be that school children learn about the 'underground railroad' travelled by slaves in escaping from the United States, while in the United States they may learn about Martin Luther King Jr and the civil rights movement. But only rarely are the implications of these historical dramatic events to the daily realities of the children made explicit (Brabeck & Rogers, 2000).

Environmental Education

In most developed countries at this time there is some form of environmental education aimed at promoting 'green citizenship.' Environmental education is expressly concerned with influencing, even changing, students' behaviours (Scott & Oulton, 1998). Its aim is to help students to develop behaviours that reflect a respect for the inter-relatedness of the natural world, as well as to encourage students' active involvement in resolving environmental problems. How this is to be achieved is the subject of considerable controversy, as the earlier behaviourist approaches are being replaced with a focus on sustainable development. In essence, environmental education is wrestling with the same issues of indoctrination versus values clarification that have been so problematic in character education.

The earlier approach was one of indoctrination in which children were rewarded for behaviours such as picking up litter or recycling and taught, either through school policy or formal curricula, the benefits of conservationism, the problems of acid rain, and so forth. In effect, students were taught to become 'green citizens' (see Stewart, 1991). Since the U.N. Conference on Environment and Development in Rio (UNCED,1992), conceptualizations of environmental education have shifted towards a general consensus on the need to focus on sustainable development. Attempts at implementation, however, have revealed conceptual, pedagogical, and practical problems making the field of environmental education as great a quagmire as is the environment with which it is concerned.

The difficulty of conceptualizing sustainable development has led many to suggest that there can be no global definition of environmentally sound behaviour. The use of the environment depends on different interests, and environmental and sustainable development issues are socially constructed and context dependent (e.g., Rauch, 2002). Thus, science alone cannot inform practice, and teaching should not be doctrinaire. The corollary is that students must be taught, through critical reflection and personal investigation, to appreciate what is needed for sustainable development; and they must develop the motivation and sense of personal efficacy that impel action (Rauch, 2002). A number of programs are based on these assumptions. The Royal Danish School of Educational Studies, for example, has created a program that uses critical thinking to develop 'action competence' in students (Schnack, 1998). Action competence denotes the ability, and presumably motivation, to cooperate in responsible environmental action. In Switzerland, the environmental education curriculum has been designed so that students are expected to develop an appreciation of what is needed for sustainable development and become motivated to act accordingly through engaging in the processes of critical thinking and personal analyses (Kyburz-

Graber, Rigendinger, Hirsch-Hadorn, & Werner-Zentner, 1977, cited in Rauch, 2002). The social constructivist model of environmental education avoids the difficulties associated with confronting issues that are inherently complex, as well as potentially controversial. As a reincarnation of the values clarification approach, with specific focus on environmental values, however, it also poses pedagogical challenges.

Successful teaching of sustainable development requires teachers to provoke a fundamental shift in students' values towards a more global and more future-oriented perspective. Without imposing values or defining appropriate behaviours, teachers are expected to guide their students to appreciate that sustainable development requires the use of resources in ways that do not jeopardize the long-term health of our planet or the health and well-being of those in other parts of the world. And they should act on that. Environmental education is to be environmental values education that is taught in a value-free manner.

An example of this approach is seen in the curriculum *Industry and the Environment – Friend or Foe?* (Barry, Fiehn, & Miller, 1992). It provides workbooks that contain a variety of exercises with reference to environmental issues involving industry. Through role-play, simulation activities, and discussion of conflicting perspectives, students are expected to reach a full understanding of the issues and to clarify their environmental values in ways that are consistent with sustainable development. The fundamental pedagogy is to present a balanced view of the issues (Scott & Oulton, 1998). This means presenting and examining all sides of environmental issues, from those of environmental activists to those of capitalist industrialists. Teachers must assume that their students will independently reach conclusions that lead to adopting values and behaviours that are 'right,' that is, consistent with sustainable development. The belief that this is possible reflects a wonderful conception of human nature and how children learn, but one that hardly seems realistic. We do not subscribe to a Hobbesian view of human nature, but we do believe that positive attitudes and behaviours towards sustainable development are often obstructed by Marxist (Groucho, not Karl) concerns about 'what has the future ever done for me?' We agree with Scott and Oulton's (1998) analysis that this values-clarification approach to environmental education reflects a lack of true commitment to education for sustainable development and that it is unlikely to achieve its desired goals.

The practical challenge is that education for sustainable development would appear to be most effective if, rather than pedagogical changes, there are changes to the entire educational system, both in teacher training and school functioning (Posch, 1999; Rauch, 2002; Scott & Oulton, 1998; Verhagen, 2002). The Earth Community School (ECS; Verhagen, 2002) provides a model of the type of innovations called for. The ECS was impelled by the social and ecological challenges of today's global society, and has the following core goals: (1) to contribute to the developing of just and participatory communities and societies, (2) to help children develop values that can guide problem-solving with regard to social and ecological challenges, and (3) to provide a principle upon which a school or subject can be organized. The ECS makes explicit recognition of the inter-relatedness of the natural environment and the social world and of the peace movement and the environment. Consistent with the schools' goals, the curricula incorporate issues of social justice, non-violence, and equity, and its processes incorporate participatory decision-making. The ECS, and similar schools, would appear to be reincarnations of Kohlberg's just community schools. But may well be more successful; however, as yet there are no evaluation data. It is interesting to note that, as new approaches appear, there first seems to be tension between pedagogies that impose values and those that are value-free. As these extremes are demonstrated to be ineffective in achieving their goals, there is an evolution to whole school innovation. This was the pattern with character and moral education. Some thirty years later, environmental education is following the same pattern.

Peace Education

The emphasis in peace education, generally, has shifted from teaching children about peace at the societal or global level to teaching them personal behaviours that are non-violent. Most peace education prior to the late 1980s was about arms reduction and the cessation of war (Reardon, 1988). Peace conceived as the absence of war has come to be called 'negative peace.' This rather narrow conception of peace has broadened to a conception of peace as tolerance, knowledge, and understanding of others. Within this conception, often referred to as 'positive peace,' the issues used include understanding of racism, sexism, the environment, poverty, and social justice (Burns & Aspelagh, 1996; Reardon, 1988). The underlying values – preserving the ecosystem, respecting rights, and so forth – were to be pursued individually and societally through democratic citizenship behaviours. The emphasis has shifted recently towards conceptions of 'personal peace,' which embodies the realization that peace at the personal level is a prerequisite to peace at the societal or global level (Burns & Aspelagh, 1996). In schools, peace education nowadays most often means programs for the prevention of violence, with the explicit aim of reducing incidence of violent interactions among school children (Harris, 2002).

Peer-mediation programs are a commonly used approach to teaching non-violent behaviours. They are grounded on the assumption that learning to communicate, accept, and understand differences is the foundation for peace (Carter, 2002). Peer mediators are trained to communicate with disputing children and to resolve interpersonal problems among them in positive ways. These mediators must take into account the differing perspectives of the parties to the conflict and reach a solution to the conflict that is fair and acceptable to both, or all, the disputants. Those with ample opportunity to practise mediation improve their skills in solving interpersonal problems; however, there is little evidence that peer-mediation programs reduce aggression in schools (Bickmore, 2002; Harris, 2002). Candice Carter (2002) identified a problem that may not only help explain the lack of general impact of these programs but also suggests that peer mediation actually may function to support at least one behaviour that it is intended to eliminate, racism.

Peer mediation is inherently difficult in multicultural societies, such as North America, where it is common. Some reasons for this are the presence of cultural differences in styles and goals of conflict resolution and differential feelings of power among students of different ethnocultural origins. Carter found that where there were cultural differences minority students would accept unjust mediation agreements as in the case of students who had been the targets of racism agreeing to ignore further incidents in their schools. In addition, Carter noted that a common outcome of mediation has been 'avoidance resolutions,' where students agree to stay away from targeted others. Avoidance, of course, does nothing to solve problems, although it may delay them. Teaching victims of aggression to ignore further incidents or to avoid particular students is not an effective way to improve interpersonal understanding, social problem-solving skills, or social justice. On the contrary, these have the potential to escalate tensions. Moreover, they are likely to perpetuate existing inequalities and social stratification in the classroom and school (Carter, 2002).

A more effective way of promoting non-violent interpersonal relations is to involve the whole student body in a comprehensive and pro-active intervention program. Such a program would focus on preventing violent behaviours and interpersonal conflicts through promoting social competence. Extensive evaluation data are available on one pro-active intervention program, the Resolving Conflict Creatively Program (RCCP).

The RCCP's goal is to teach students positive styles of interpersonal interaction and strategies for resolving conflicts. The curriculum, which includes a peer mediation component, has several versions so that it can be used with children ages six through eighteen years. Activities are designed to make children aware of the different choices available in conflict situations, to help them develop skills for making these choices, to promote their respect for all cultures, to teach them how to identify and oppose prejudice, and to make them aware of their role in creating a peaceful world (Ba & Hawkins, 1996). The curriculum requires a democratic pedagogy, and the teacher, therefore, receives training in how to be a facilitator and promote student participation.

The evaluation of the RCCP was based on data from fifteen schools in New York City, involving almost 400 teachers and 8,000 children from grades 1 through 6. RCCP and other programs were compared in a general evaluation of school-based programs for the prevention of violence completed by Henrich, Brown, and Aber (1999). Here we summarize the essential findings. An initial cluster analysis revealed three distinct profiles of the RCCP that varied according to the amount of teacher training experienced, the extent to which the RCCP curriculum was actually used, and the number of peer mediators in the classroom relative to the overall number of students. Labels were assigned on the basis of curriculum usage. The 'high lessons' profile described teachers with a moderate level of training, the greatest use of the RCCP curriculum, and the lowest percentage of peer mediators in the classroom. The 'low lessons' profile described teachers with the most training and little use of the RCCP curriculum, but the highest percentage of peer mediators. The 'no lessons' profile described teachers with no training, no use of the RCCP curriculum, and some peer mediators. Subsequent comparisons demonstrated positive outcomes among the 'high lessons' group. Students in 'high lessons' classrooms showed increases in pro-social and academic behaviours as well as fewer incidents of aggression. The most noteworthy finding, however, may be that the 'low lessons' group did worse than the 'no lessons' group on measures of positive outcomes. Henrich et al. (1999) suggested that these findings may reflect teacher variables such as burnout or inadequate experience. However, as they also note, analyses revealed no teacher differences among the three profiles other than the amount of training received and amount of curriculum used. It is unfortunate that the role of peer mediation was not addressed. Recall that the 'low lessons' teachers had the highest percentage of peer mediators in their classrooms. Consistent with Carter's (2002) findings, we might consider that the peer mediators had a detrimental effect on the other students and may even have been an obstacle to achieving the goals of the RCCP. This may be particularly likely if the teachers in this group depended on peer mediation for the impact expected through the use of the curriculum. Nonetheless, overall, the RCCP has shown that children can be taught to behave in more peaceful ways when to do so they are taught in a democratic manner through an age-appropriate curriculum.

Although the emphasis in peace education is on the resolution of interpersonal conflicts, some very interesting new work has appeared on peace education for inter-group peace (Salomon, 2002, 2003, 2004). In the peace education programs described above, children are expected to learn how to take the other person's perspective. Gavriel Salomon has extended this to the level of the group. He has described an approach to peace education that aims to change perceptions, attitudes, and feelings about the collective other; it deals with relations between groups rather than between individuals. Salomon was particularly interested in the potential of such peace education to be effective in the context of intractable conflicts. As seen in the Middle East, for example, intractable conflicts are those that are violent, total, resistant to change, and accompanied by stress and strong adherence to the collective narrative of the groups in conflict (Salomon, 2004). In his comprehensive assessment of peace education in the Israeli-Palestinian context, Salomon identified approaches that were successful in evoking changed attitudes and beliefs. We summarize two such approaches here. In one (Lustig, 2002, cited in Salomon, 2003), Grade 12 students studied a similar conflict that had happened elsewhere, in this case Northern Ireland. Although no explicit comparisons were made between the students' situation and that of Northern Ireland, the program did promote understanding of the Israeli-Palestinian conflict. A second approach that Salomon found effective is bringing together students from both sides of a conflict to engage in joint activities during which the conflict is discussed. Compared with non-participants, students who had taken part in such programs expressed a greater willingness for social contact with those from the other side, a greater trust of them, and greater agreement with their perspective. Interestingly, the activities also affected the students' understanding of peace, altering it from a negative to a positive concept. Meanwhile, students who had not participated in the program, which was conducted during the Intifadah, demonstrated intensified hatred for the other side. These data are very encouraging. At this time, however, there are no reports of the program's impact on students' behaviours.

Teaching Citizenship Knowledge

Civic Education

In light of the perceived threats to established and embryonic democracies through the 1990s, there were calls for social studies teachers to refocus their classrooms on the teaching of civic virtues and to promote in their students a commitment to the common good (Lickona, 1991a). By the late 1990s, there was consensus on the importance of civic education, but no such consensus on the appropriate approach. Civic education, for the most part, continues to be taught as part of the social studies curriculum, with emphasis on the political literacy or knowledge strand of citizenship education. Most frequently what is taught are the history, structures, and processes of government, and adult citizenship rights.

The extensive international studies of Judith Torney-Purta and her colleagues (Torney-Purta, 2002; Torney-Purta, Schwille, & Amadeo, 1999, Torney-Purta, Lehmann, Oswald, & Schultz, 2001; Schwille & Amadeo, 2002) illustrate well the successes and limitations of civic education. The International Association for the Evaluation of Educational Achievement (IEA), which is an independent international consortium of researchers, undertook a cross-national comparison of the outcomes of civic education among students in twenty-eight democratic countries. In 1999, they assessed the civic knowledge and attitudes towards democracy of 90,000 students. The overall success of civic education was reflected in students' ability to recognize the important aspects of democracy (such as the necessity of free elections) and that citizenship includes the obligation to vote and to obey the law. However, the knowledge acquired by most of the students was superficial and unconnected to daily life. Learning had not been generalized beyond what might be expected with rote learning. Students were unable to interpret simple electoral pamphlets, and they were not able to understand that there are connections between civic knowledge and everyday behaviours. There was no evidence of any impact of civic education on students' political motivation or engagement: Students continued to show little interest in forms of political activity such as writing letters to newspapers, joining a political party, or being a candidate for political office. Evidently, these students had learned aspects of democracy as they learn trigonometric functions. The IEA study is a demonstration of the serious limitations of civic education that is without concomitant classroom discussions and opportunities for democratic participation (Tiana, 2000; see also, Gordon et al., 2000, and Hahn, 1998). The latter is rare. In the twenty-eight countries studied by the IEA, only 16 per cent of students reported that their teachers *sometimes* encouraged discussion on issues. In assessing the implications of the IEA study findings, Schwille and Amadeo (2002) concluded that providing knowledge of democracy is a necessary but not sufficient path to active citizenship and that civic education must occur within schools that model democracy by providing experiences with democratic processes for their students.

In recognition of the limitations of facts-based civic education, some jurisdictions have broadened the definition or goals of civic education to include opportunities for experiential learning. The assumption is that if students actually experience democracy through participation in school structures or community action, they will learn better the structures and processes of democratic citizenship.

It has become quite common, particularly in Europe and North America, for schools to use student councils as a means of civic education. School student councils are intended to provide both direct experience with democracy and modelling of the democratic process. Typically, such student councils comprise teachers, administrators, and one or two representatives from each class in the school. Unfortunately, it is also the case that, typically, the councils function to constrain rather than promote the meaningful democratic participation of students (Bickmore, 1999; Holden, 1998) Student participation in decision-making is usually tokenistic with issues to be addressed at council meetings being restricted to those deemed a priori, in the absence of students, to be safe. School staff are comfortable having students' voices heard on mundane issues such as those regarding the use of washrooms, but not on issues of real concern to students (Holden, 1998). Issues such as students' relationships with teachers, curriculum-related issues, and sexual or racial harassment issues are not on the table. Yet, if school councils are to contribute to citizenship education, students must be allowed to exercise their rights and responsibilities in a truly democratic context. Open expression and discussion of views should be encouraged, and students must be able to perceive that their input into decision-making is taken seriously. Otherwise councils are demonstrating hypocrisy rather than democracy. Moreover, school councils are typically composed of elite students, those with high grades, or those selected by school staff as known cooperators (Bickmore, 1999). Thus, few students even have the very limited opportunity of experiencing direct democracy through participation in school governance.

An attempt towards greater student involvement in experiential civic education can be seen in the increasingly widespread community action, or service, projects. In the United States the proportion of high schools offering community service projects to students has risen dramatically from 27 per cent in 1984 to 83 per cent in 1999 (Kielsmeier, 2000). Although not always compulsory, across the United States there is a growing trend towards high school graduation requirements that stipulate the completion of some specific number of community service hours. Similar patterns are evident elsewhere. For example, to graduate students in Ireland are now required to participate in some form of civic, social, or political action in their school or community (Kerr, McCarthy, & Smith, 2002). Cynics may suggest this provides free labour to communities. The expressed hope, however, is that undertaking a community service project will motivate and empower young people towards political engagement and civic participation and function as an antidote to political apathy. There is little evidence that such goals are realized. At best there would appear to be some short-term impact on students' civic attitudes, but there is no evidence that community service projects in schools have lasting impact on civic engagement (Melchior, 1999). This lack of real impact probably results, in large part, from the types of projects the students most frequently complete.

Participating in community action can be an effective means of providing experience with democracy and civic engagement if that action is student initiated and if students' participation is meaningful. Case studies are illustrative. In one, Grade 5 students worked together to solve a community problem of priority to them – vandalism in their playground (Nagel, 2001). They designed and conducted survey research, identified what changes might decrease the vandalism, and found ways to include their community in revitalizing the playground. In a second example, a group of Grade 8 students on a tour of a historic cemetery identified gaps in information in the gravestones and noted the deplorable state of the area reserved for African Americans (Kielsmeier, 2000). These students initiated and led the restoration of the cemetery raising enough support to replace or repair 166 headstones. They also succeeded in persuading the state of Alabama to place an official registry sign at the cemetery. Furthermore, the students extensively researched the history of those involved, and developed curriculum materials that now are the basis of a

Grade 3 social studies unit. In each of these three cases, real civic learning took place. The community action projects were meaningful, important to and initiated and directed by students. And in each case, the students' actions had a very positive effect on their community. Too often, however, community action projects do not provide such opportunities for civic education. More commonly, community action is limited to helping behaviours such as working in soup kitchens or hospitals (Bickmore, 1999). Undoubtedly, such helping experiences are of significant value to the development of a child, but they are lacking in the provision of socio-political or civic knowledge. Moreover, students are more invested in their learning when they perceive their community service to be substantial and real, rather than an act of charity (Boyt & Skelton, 1997). Lawson's (2001) discussion of the implementation of community service projects highlights their overall ineffectiveness as a means to promote active citizenship. The typical nature of these projects, students' attitudes towards them, and teachers' rejection of them combine to provide support to those teachers, and others, who argue that community service projects are little more than a waste of time.

Calls for reformed civic education in Portugal underscore the general inadequacies of the political literacy, or knowledge, strand of civic education. Menezes and her colleagues (1999) argued for a synthesis of existing approaches. Civic education, they said, should include relevant contemporary themes such as environmental issues and human rights, and also moral and character education. Its aim should not be limited to the provision of information about governance structures and adult citizenship rights. Instead, civic education should facilitate the development of values, reasoning skills, perspective taking, and empathy. Such an approach would also address another major criticism of civic education. The focus has been on adult domestic civic rights and responsibilities, with emphasis therefore on national citizenship. This emphasis stands in contradiction to the need for a more global citizenship identity.

Global Citizenship Education

Global citizenship education does not preclude or deny national citizenship or its attendant rights and responsibilities. Rather, it broadens the scope of citizenship education to include education that aims to develop intercultural empathy, concern for global problems, and motivation to act for justice and peace and that opposes discrimination and inequities (LeRoux, 2001). In essence, global education has as its core goal teachings for understanding humanity, diversity, and human rights and for the appreciation of global ecological and economic interdependence. It is global political literacy in the broadest definition. LeRoux (2001) echoes the conclusions of Torney-Purta and her colleagues (1999). In light of the importance of establishing or maintaining democracies in the countries studied, and in light of the observed ineffectiveness of civic education to promote democratic support, they emphasize that civic education should be taught across disciplines, take into account the diversity of global cultures, be related to the lives of the students, and be taught in a democratic manner. What these critics of citizenship education are calling for is an expanded version of citizenship education that brings into focus human rights issues. Current conditions have highlighted the need for such education, although advocates have been recommending it for some time. For example, in her 1988 publication Betty Reardon emphasized the imperative of a rights-based approach to global citizenship education in her cogent observation that the denial of rights is the major source of conflict and the major obstacle to peace. Reardon's observation remains true at both the interpersonal and societal level. The lack of a rights focus is a key problem with global education resources.

Various curricula resources enable global citizenship education. Seminal among them are those developed by Graham Pike and David Selby (1991, 1999, 2000). But, although there is inclusion of rights in these curricula they are not rights-based. Instead, they remain broadly focused, with a range of topics that look at environmental, economic, health, mass media, multicultural, peace, and technology education issues. In their diversity of content, these resources reflect well the current status of global citizenship education: it appears to be in a state of identity confusion. Although approaches to global citizenship education have the common goal of promoting concern for other people and other species, a comprehensive approach to achieving this has yet to be identified. Pike (2000) has described four areas in which there is significant disagreement among advocates of global citizenship education: its moral purpose, the interests of its constituency, its role in advocating change, and its stance on questions of citizenship. In fact, the fundamental question of whether global education should empower students to improve their competitiveness in global markets or whether global education should empower students to resolve global issues remains unresolved (Pike, 2000). This disagreement poses an obstacle that might be overcome with a coherent rights-based approach.

Human Rights Education

Human rights education involves educating children for citizenship by teaching them about universal human rights and by instilling in them the values that promote social justice (Brabeck & Rogers, 2000). The goal of human rights education is to develop citizens who will partici-pate in creating and sustaining societies in which the social, political, and economic rights of all peoples are promoted and protected. What differentiates human rights education from other forms of citizenship education is twofold.

First are its interrelated goals of personal empowerment and social change – change to bring about conditions that promote and respect rights. To achieve these goals, human rights education overlaps with other forms of citizenship education. It addresses global concerns such as sexism, racism, poverty, and environmental degradation, thus providing students with knowledge about global interdependencies (Lohrenscheit, 2002). But it also addresses values and behaviours. Human rights educa-tion generally is designed to challenge students to reflect on, care about, and act in accordance with the values of freedom, tolerance, justice, and respect for all peoples. A major route to promoting these essential values of democratic citizenship is through teaching the impact of human rights violations. For example, students are taught the issues surrounding and the impact of the persecution of the Armenians in Turkey after the First World War, the slaughter of the Cambodians by the Khmer Rouge at the end of the Vietnam War, and the daily realities of Mao's China or Pinochet's Chile (Shafer, 1992). The intent is to both enhance students' understanding of the importance of respecting rights and their sense of community responsibility in protecting rights (Brabeck & Rogers, 2000).

Second, and arguably the more important difference, is that human rights education is contextualized within human rights instruments (Tibbits, 2002). The benefits of using human rights documents are that they provide an excellent 'means through which the abstract values and utopian ideals of a preferred future can be turned into concrete propos-als and precise images.' (Reardon, 1988, p. 35). Many rights educators and advocates have suggested that the U.N. Universal Declaration of Human Rights should provide the context for human rights education (e.g., Holden & Clough, 1998; Magendzo, 1994; Wronka, 1994).

The creation of the 1948 U.N. Universal Declaration of Human Rights was impelled by the atrocities of the Second World War with the aim of preventing any such recurrence. The rights outlined within the declaration are considered to be basic and universal. Brabeck and Rogers (2000) summarized the four principles of universal basic human rights and how they should be taught as follows. In teaching the overarching principle of the right to human dignity, the focus is on the right of people to not be terrorized, tortured, or assassinated, persecuted by their governments, or deprived of their livelihood or their families. With regard for the principle of civil and political rights, students are taught the legal safeguards that allow the right to human dignity. These include the freedoms of speech, religion, and the press. In teaching the third principle, which is described as economic, social, and cultural rights, the focus is on government provisions for the basic necessities required for human dignity – health care, education and employment. The fourth principle is solidarity rights. These ensure intergovernmental cooperation to decrease the likelihood of war, reduce pollution, and ensure the protection of ethnocultural minorities. Teachings here would include peace education and education for sustainable development.

Human rights education addresses the entire range of democratic citizenship values and knowledge. In addition, because rights education requires a democratic pedagogy, students also should acquire the skills and motivations that provide the foundation for responsible democratic behaviours (Tarrow, 1992). Classroom teachings can be reinforced with rights-respecting school policies and practices such as the inclusion of children with special needs and classroom management styles that respect the dignity of each child.

Of the approaches to developing good citizens summarized above, because it is based on specified values and is the most inclusive, human rights education, has the greatest potential to impact children's citizenship values and behaviours. Nonetheless, human rights education has two important limitations. First, it is focused on the rights that are of greater significance and more salience to the daily lives of adults than of children. Second, and related to the first, human rights education, like all other forms of citizenship education, does not recognize the current citizenship status of the child. Rights education in schools should have as its cornerstone the U.N. Convention on the Rights of the Child.

Limitations of Current Citizenship Education

Each of the approaches to citizenship education described above has had some successes, but none fully realizes the overarching goal of teaching children the values, behaviours, and knowledge that motivate democratic participation. Existing programs have three problems in common (Damon & Gregory, 1997). First, they are fragmented; curricula are typically taught as discrete units. Second, specific skills are emphasized in specific areas. Third, they are negatively oriented.

When citizenship education is presented in discrete learning units, the teachings remain disconnected from each other. During the course of a week or month in school, children may learn about the need for environmental protection, the need to behave in non-discriminatory ways, historic rights violations, and democratic structures. The common concerns or value implications across such issues tend to remain unnoticed because they remain unsaid. Environmental education is taught as a separate subject from civic education, and anti-racist education is most likely taught as a short-term separate unit. A character education lesson may discuss tensions between loyalty and honesty; an environmental education lesson may discuss tensions between the needs of employees or industry and environmental protection. But there will be no extrapolation to the political tensions that these issues have provoked. Cross-referencing the issues, underlying values, associated problems, or behavioural solutions, is rare. Although the varied approaches to citizenship education share a common general goal, they are uncoordinated and unconnected and apparently making generalizations from what is learned in the classroom to students' lives (see, e.g., Torney-Purta et al., 1999; Power, 1997; Schultz et al., 2001). Evaluation findings may reflect, at least in part, the inability of children to link the commonalities underlying various issues without being provided with a coherent framework. What children learn has been described as 'a cacophony of discord and confusion' (p. 122).

The second problem arises from the first and makes generalization among issues even more difficult for children. Specific programs elicit specific learning. Within each unit, the focus is on the learning of issue-related information and, where relevant, problem-solving strategies. Particular skills and solutions are taught. Different types of instruction are used. Some programs, such as character education or anti-racist education, explicitly promote the adoption of particular values or behaviours. Others, such as Kohlbergian moral education programs, attempt to develop reasoning skills. Still others, like civic education programs, emphasize learning factual information. Missing are the underlying common concepts and principles to be abstracted and generalized to the children's experience of daily life. Children need to be provided with a general context in which to coordinate and reconcile the values, behaviours and knowledge they are being taught. Citizenship education must mean 'more than picking up litter and not killing whales' (Alderson, 1999, p. 85). Children need to be taught the overarching decision-making skills that they need to guide their behaviours (Scott & Oulton, 1998). Finally, children need to be motivated to act.

In their negative orientation, many of the programs focus on bad behaviour and how to prevent or control it. Negatively oriented proscriptions for behaviour cannot provide the motivation needed to form the values and goals that promote democratic behaviours (Hauser & Bowlds, 1990). Children are taught that they should not litter, engage in conflict, be discriminatory, be selfish, be unconcerned with the needs of others, and so forth. As any parent knows, such exhortations quickly get tuned out. Such messages are disempowering and demoralizing. Children need to know that it is legitimate for them to be concerned about themselves and protect their self-interest, as well as the interests of others (Haan, Aerts, & Cooper, 1985).

The general implication of these limitations of citizenship education (Damon & Gregory, 1997) is that the current fragmented approaches to citizenship education are unlikely to engage the child or promote the integration of what is being learned into the child's sense of self. It is important that the sense of self be affected by citizenship education. When individuals understand particular values as essential to their core identity, they believe they must act in accordance with those values (Nisan, 1996). The school's task, then, is to bring children to see democratic values to be integral to their personal identity (Nisan, 1996), thereby providing the framework for interpreting experiences and making decisions about behaviour (Colby & Damon, 1992). Australian environmental activist and educator Phillip Payne has written extensively on the need to take into account the child's developing identity in all forms of citizenship education. Payne (2000) has noted that educators tend to focus excessively on the end-state of citizenship education with concomitantly insufficient, if any, attention given to the current condition of their students. In her discussion of human rights education, Tibbitts (2002), too, has pointed to the importance of developmentally appropriate teaching.

There are rudimentary forms of citizenship education at the elementary school level. But for the most part the target age is adolescence, the stage of development in which the child's identity is first being developed. Typically, current approaches to citizenship education either disregard or fail to capitalize on the developmental needs of teenaged

children. It is not our intent here to detail the process of identity formation, but rather to highlight aspects of it that are relevant to the present
discussion. In essence, the development of identity in adolescence is
impelled by maturation of physiological and neurological systems and
the related increases in the capacity for abstract thinking, as well as by
the broadening of one's social world.

How identity develops varies with the child's experiences and the values to which the child has been exposed (Erikson, 1968; Nisan, 1996).
Defining the self as an upholder of democratic ideals requires that adolescents have opportunities to reflect critically on democratic values, participate in democratic decision-making, understand social issues, and feel
empowered to exercise their citizenship responsibilities. The implications for the classroom are as follows. Adolescent students should be
increasingly provided opportunities for cooperative learning in peer
groups, critical thinking, debate, and discussion about social issues and
values of relevance to them, and for meaningful participation. Another
important developmental consideration stems from the heightened
introspection and self-focus that accompanies the definition of a personal identity. Adolescents need very much to believe in and feel good
about the self that is developing (Baumeister & Muraven, 1996). It is particularly important, then, that education for citizenship promote a sense
of efficacy or empowerment, rather than helplessness, and to obviate
feelings of guilt and anxiety there needs to be allowance for self-interest.
So far this has not been the case.

Surveys have found that adolescents are very concerned with such
social issues as environmental degradation, social inequalities, and violence (e.g., Holden, 1938; Holden & Clough, 1998). The same adolescents were also found to be dissatisfied with what they were learning.
They complained that their schools were not teaching them the information they needed to understand their role in shaping the future. One
fourteen-year-old said, 'We learnt the facts about what's happening but
we don't learn what you can do' (Holden, 1998, p. 52). Similar sentiments
were expressed by the students in Payne's study. For example one of
them said, 'Some of my inaction can be attributed to a sense of helplessness ... and the way in which I am made to feel part of the problem but not
part of the solution' (Payne, 2000, p. 69). Students want to translate their
learning into action, but feel disempowered to do so, and then they
become increasingly cynical and disengaged (Holden & Clough, 1998).
Berman (1997) has described how, despite allowing them to select which
current social topics they wished to study, his students always appeared
bored and before long ready to move on to a new issue. Finally, he dis-

covered that their wish to examine a different issue was not a result of boredom, but was in fact elicited by their sense that there was nothing that they could do about the problem under discussion. If education is to increase democratic engagement and participation, students must feel empowered and efficacious.

Engagement and empowerment are more likely if there is allowance for self-interest. Lessons that focus on adult civic rights and responsibilities, or on the plight and needs of others, and ensure that students are admonished to avoid certain behaviours, leave no room for self-interest. Self-interest promotes engagement, and increases the likelihood that what is learned will be integrated into one's developing identity. Self-interest is an especially important component of citizenship education. The reasons have been well put by Diane Goodman (2000), whose essential thesis is that support and action for democratic ideals are motivated jointly by values, empathy, and self-interest. Generally, self-interest has not been included in citizenship education because self-interest tends to be understood as selfishness. As Goodman explained, self-interest is not a zero sum game. Rather, self-interest can be inclusive and involve consideration of others – particularly those with whom one can empathize. There are two key benefits of engaging the interest of the students by linking the issues under discussion to their own rights and their own interests. First, when there is engagement in an issue, exposure to perspectives and information becomes so meaningful that students have the potential to change attitudes and subsequent behaviour. Second, self-interest facilitates understanding and empathy for the situation of others. Empathy is aroused when there is a sense of connectedness with the situation and with the feelings of others. At this time, developments in information technology have increased the potential connectedness of adolescents across cultures. Globally, urban adolescents have similar brand preferences and patterns of consumption with respect to music, videos, T-shirts, and soft drinks (Arnett, 2002; Hornberg, 2002). Communication through e-mail and surfing the Internet are activities that are equally popular among Arab, European, North American, and Latin American adolescents (Booth, 2002; Welti, 2002). Although some may deplore the homogenization of adolescence, there clearly are benefits for the teaching of global citizenship.

A related advantage of acknowledging the importance of self-interest that Goodman (2000) identified is that a focus on benefits for self as well as others should mitigate against attitudes and beliefs that tend to confuse social justice for others with charity. Thus, democratic action is more likely if students' self-focused concerns and interests are legitimized. The successful examples of experiential civic education described above attest to this. To allow for self-interest, and thereby engagement, curriculum content should be relevant to the experiences and interests of the adolescent.

The apparent disregard of citizenship education programs for the developmental needs of the adolescent are reflected throughout the school in pedagogy and governance. Pedagogy is more authoritarian than participatory. Governance structures are rarely democratic. The effect has been to reduce students' engagement in school and their motivations for democratic action and to increase the likelihood of negative self-perceptions. Eccles and her colleagues (1993) developed a theory of stage-environment fit that provides a cogent explanation for these phenomena. Behaviour, motivation, and psychological well-being are influenced by the fit between the characteristics of the individual and those of the individual's social environment. A poor fit predicts decreases in motivation, interest, performance, and behaviour. This theory, applied to the characteristics of adolescence and of typical schools, sheds light on underlying reasons for the evident lack of success of citizenship education programs (see Torney-Purta et al., 2001). The salience of identity issues in adolescence, the self-focus, the desire for increased participation and self-determination, peer orientation, and the capacity for hypothetical and abstract thinking imply a classroom more like that found in a typical kindergarten than a middle or high school. Opportunities for student decision-making, choice, and self-management should increase from childhood to adolescence. But, on the contrary, there is a decrease of such opportunities (e.g., Eccles et al., 1993). Likewise, opportunities for cooperative small group learning and peer interaction should increase. But they, too, decrease as grade level increases, with the emphasis increasingly on individualism and competition. Opportunities for critical thinking, disagreement, and debate should increase; and they, too, decrease, as there is more emphasis on rote learning. The overall result is a poor fit between the developmental needs of the adolescent and the education environment. It is a fit that constrains the provision of effective citizenship education. And it is in sharp contrast to the education goals and promises of the U.N. Convention on the Rights of the Child.

Children's Rights Education as Citizenship Education

Finding that citizenship education has little effect, Torney-Purta and her colleagues (1999) made the following recommendation: for citizenship education to be effective for sustaining and promoting democracy, it should be 'cross-disciplinary, participative, interactive, related to life, conducted in a non-authoritarian environment, and cognizant of the challenges of societal diversity' (p. 30). UNICEF (1992) defined citizenship education as that which promotes understanding of rights and responsibilities with regard to 'the community, nation, and the planet. It promotes the value of active participation ... critical thinking, cooperation and decision-making' (p. 6). These descriptions are similar to and consistent with the rights in and through education as described in the U.N. Convention on the Rights of the Child.

Children's rights education is citizenship education that is contextualized within and informed by the U.N. Convention on the Rights of the Child. It shares the goals of existing approaches to citizenship education, goals that are centred on promoting knowledge, competencies, and values to motivate and enable social harmony and democratic participation (see Print, Ornstrom, & Neilson, 2002). But the content and pedagogy of children's rights education differ from existing approaches in ways that suggest that it may have more potential for success in meeting these goals. Prior to examining these differences, and the advantages of a children's rights approach to citizenship education, it may be helpful to review the most relevant articles of the Convention.

Articles 29 and 42, on the rights through education, provide the foundation for educating children about citizenship knowledge and values. As described in Chapter 2, article 42 obligates teaching children the principles and provisions of the Convention. This, then, recognizes the citizenship status of children and allows for them to learn their contemporaneous, rather than adult, citizenship rights and corresponding responsibilities. Article 29 adresses all other aspects of citizenship education, knowledge, and values. Paragraph 1(d) obligates the provision of education that prepares 'the child for responsible life in a free society, in the spirit of understanding, peace, tolerance, equality of the sexes, and friendship among all peoples, ethnic, national and religious groups and persons of indigenous origins.' In addition, it specifies the the obligations to educate the child in ways that develop respect for human rights, national values, all cultures, and the natural environment. Articles 29 and 42 identify the appropriate content of citizenship education. It is content that subsumes the existing fragmented approaches to citizenship – character education, peace education, environmental education, anti-racist education, civic education, and human rights education. Moreover, article 29, paragaph 1(a), obligates Convention signatories to provide education that is directed to 'The development of the child's personality, talents and mental and physical abilities to their fullest potential.' Thus, children's rights can provide the basis for and the common thread among all school subjects, maths and languages as well as the various strands of citizenship education.

Articles 12 through 15, on the 'freedoms,' identify the appropriate pedagogy and thereby teaching of citizenship behavioural skills. They obligate educators to provide opportunities for the age-appropriate exercise of the rights of freedom of expression; access to information; freedom of thought, conscience, and religion; and freedom of association and peaceful assembly. The rights under the Convention must be respected by teachers and reflected in their teaching and classroom management styles, as well as explicitly taught (Hammarberg, 1997). We note also that limitations on these freedoms are articulated. Pedagogical considerations also require articles 3 and 5 to be taken into account. Article 3, the overarching principle of the Convention, provides that in all decisions concerning the child, the child's best interests shall be a primary consideration. Article 5 obligates teachers, because they are *in loco parentis*, to offer direction and guidance in the exercise of the rights of the child in accordance with the child's evolving capacities. Should these articles be taken seriously in the design and provision of citizenship education, the limitations of the current approaches may well be overcome. Our justification is as follows.

A primary consideration is the nature of the Convention itself. First, the Convention is a legally binding document. What has been suggested for the context of rights education, and what has most often been used, is the 1948 U.N. Declaration of Human Rights (e.g., Pike & Selby, 1997). Declarations do not have the same legal status as conventions. They do not, therefore, have as much legitimacy as a standard or basis for teaching. Rights declarations might be understood as describing rights ideals rather than rights standards. Second, the Convention on the Rights of the Child is the most widely and the most quickly ratified U.N. Convention in world history. As such, it provides a standard that describes a global consensus on societal values for children. Students will learn that the rights of the Convention apply to all children globally. Thus, the Convention can provide a common framework for citizenship education at the national, international, or global level. Third, the comprehensiveness of the education-relevant articles of the Convention allow it to be used as a values base for all school teachings, content, and pedagogy.

A globally agreed upon values base in which to contextualize citizenship education facilitates both learning and teaching. A rights-based approach explicitly provides students with the common principle among the different strands of citizenship education. Recall that the lack of explicit recognition of the commonalities underlying the different components of citizenship education made generalization difficult. Children were not extrapolating general principles or common concepts from their separate lessons. The Convention provides a common principle, the need to promote and protect the rights of all children, which applies equally to issues of racism, sustainable development, interpersonal and world peace, and so forth. When this principle is made explicit, children are provided a general context into which they can link and examine what they are taught.

A related benefit of using a foundation for teaching that reflects the global consensus on values is that it eliminates, or at least limits, concerns that previously have made values-based teaching difficult. On the one hand, the values base avoids the difficulties imposed by values-free styles of teaching. Burwood and Wyeth (1998) have provided an excellent summary of the dangers of value-free teaching that has as its aim children's respect for diversity. The more obvious problem is the promotion of complete cultural relativism. Considerations of what is right or acceptable, of what is needed to sustain human rights and democracy, must be grounded in principles. Burwood and Wyeth also pointed to a related problem of values-free teachings: the danger of inadvertently encouraging judgmental attitudes and behaviours. Instead of children coming to understand that certain lifestyles different from their own are equally valid, for example, they may continue to believe them wrong, but tolerable. Tolerance, rather than acceptance of diversity may be what is learned. On the other hand, potential charges of indoctrination or of teacher bias are precluded. Whereas there may be some parents or teachers who oppose a children's rights value base, they have no legitimate argument. The Convention, once ratified, describes a country's standard for children's rights that is not open for negotiation. The legitimacy of the Convention is unquestionable.

A third consideration is the relevance of the Convention to children. Children learn about their own rights. Consistent with article 42, they must be explicitly taught the details of their rights under the Convention. Children are thereby being provided with the knowledge of rights and responsibilities that enables active contemporaneous citizenship. This will be of much greater interest and relevance to children than is learning about their adult citizenship rights and responsibilities (Barrett, 1999).

The research shows that when concepts such as rights are linked with children's current realities, they are understood better and they are more likely to engage children (Beane, 1990; Griffiths & Davies, 1995; Holden & Clough, 1998). The relevance to self is highlighted by learning that all children have the same rights, not because they have earned them or have otherwise proven themselves worthy, but unconditionally – simply because they are children. Children learn that the purpose of their rights is to maximize their developmental potential, to ensure they are well cared for by their families and by their country. In turn, this teaching allows for self-interest and is expected to evoke in children a sense of interconnectedness with other children and, thereby, empathy for them. The commonality of rights as promised to all children promotes a sense of global interconnectedness among children. Thus, many of the difficulties faced by children, locally or globally, can be understood as systemic violations of rights, rather than as attributable to individual weaknesses or failures. In turn, such empathy-based understanding encourages and empowers social action to counter perceived injustices (Batson et al., 1997).

It may be important to stress at this point that, although the emphasis in children's rights education is on teaching children their own rights (as will be discussed further in Chapter 5), children do learn about their responsibilities as a corollary of their rights. Children's rights education has a unique advantage in being focused on the self, because children are being taught about *their* rights, while being taught that they have a responsibility to respect the rights of others. Children learn, for example, that if each of them has a right to have an opinion heard, then they must respect each other's rights of expression. A related benefit of the focus on rights rather than on responsibilities or on violations of rights is that it enables the maintenance of a positive tone. This should avoid the demoralizing and discouraging messages that children are unable to meaningfully connect with their everyday experiences (Damon & Gregory, 1997). Developing a positive and socially responsible identity is far more likely when adolescents believe in and feel good about themselves (Baumeister & Muraven, 1996). Behaviouristic approaches that reward socially responsible behaviour, and exhortations to avoid engaging in certain behaviours, are equally ineffective in promoting a positive sense of self.

The final consideration, then, concerns the potential for the rights values of the Convention to be incorporated into the child's developing identity. As already noted, for citizenship education to have a lasting impact on the child's democratic values and participation, what is learned must be integrated into personal identity. For children to internalize teachings, the teachings must engage them. It is here that children's rights education may have the greatest potential to be more effective than existing approaches to citizenship education. The participatory pedagogy called for by articles 12 through 15, together with the relevance and self-interest of the content, suggest developmentally appropriate teachings and student engagement. When both curriculum content and pedagogy effectively engage children, they increasingly come to see themselves as being competent to act (Battistich et al., 1999). If the value of rights becomes part of the child's sense of self, we can expect to see that what is learned in the classroom or experienced in the school becomes part of the child's behavioural repertoire. As Scott and Oulton (1998) explained, in their examination of environmental values education, values need to be of such importance to children that they act as 'guides to how they feel they ought to live their lives' (p. 210).

In summary, the U.N. Convention on the Rights of the Child legitimizes a clear and useful values base as the common thread among aspects of citizenship education. It recognizes the citizenship status of the child, and when translated into curricula, it provides the knowledge and values of citizenship as well as practice in the exercise of democratic rights and responsibilities. In so doing, it provides students with a coherent framework that they can internalize and use to identify democratic values and select corresponding democratic behaviours. In essence, understanding and appreciating rights can allow the development of personal values (e.g., respect for the rights of others), provide a context for interpreting experiences (e.g., discrimination is a violation of rights as well as hurtful), and provide a guide for behaviour (e.g., I will not discriminate against others, and I can advocate for anti-discrimination policies and practices in my school). We turn now to an examination of particular children's rights curricula and their impact.

CHAPTER FIVE

Catching Citizenship

The essence of good citizenship may be better caught than taught.
                                    Margaret Sutherland (2002)

Recognizing the difficulties of providing effective education for democratic citizenship, Sutherland (2002) concluded that schools should avoid
teaching democratic values and behaviours. Rather, she says, schools
should limit their citizenship education to the teaching of political
knowledge, languages, and history. We disagree. We do agree, however,
that citizenship can be caught. In this chapter we demonstrate that children's rights education does have a contagion effect. When taught about
their Convention rights in a democratic classroom, children indeed do
'catch' citizenship values. We agree also with Holden and Clough (1998)
that the needs of society can be met if children are taught with a curriculum that develops their competence in critical reflection and provides a
foundation for and practice in values-based participation. Here we
describe such curricula and their impact. We first discuss considerations
in the design of children's rights education.

Curricula Design Considerations

Gaining Teacher Cooperation

Designing curricula such that they evoke a high degree of teacher usage
is not easy. The experiences of those who designed and evaluated the
Resolving Conflict Creatively Program (RCCP), described in the previous chapter, are not unusual. Many teachers did not use the program

activities at all, some used them a little, and few used them as intended (Henrich, Brown, & Aber, 1999). Nonetheless, the research on the effective implementation of new curricula identifies facilitating factors.

Among the most important considerations in the design of new curricula is that there be related professional development opportunities. In the words of Leat and Higgins, 'there is no curriculum development without teacher development' (2000, p. 72). There is considerable evidence that new curricula are implemented more successfully when teachers are given release time for training and workshop attendance, and if they are provided additional supports through the initial phase of implementation (Katz, 1981; Lee, 2000). It appears to be particularly important that training not be focused solely on the content of the new curriculum, but include its objectives and required pedagogy (Ashton & Webb, 1986; Guskey, 1987; Robinson & Gorrel, 1994). However, there is evidence that in-service training is not always helpful. In their study of teachers' responses to a new social studies curriculum, Mabry and Ettinger (1999) found professional development to be ineffective and often disregarded.

Professional development may be the most effective when teachers also have input into the design and implementation of a new curriculum. Many have observed (e.g., Eisner, 2000; Leat & Higgins, 2002; Mabry & Ettinger, 1999) that professional development is more successful when teachers play an active role in shaping the direction and the content of new curricula. Providing such participation opportunities for teachers has two benefits of relevance to compliance and persistence in implementation. One benefit is that it empowers teachers by recognizing the importance of what they believe, how they think, and how they plan for and respond to classroom experiences (Leat & Higgins, 2002). A second and related benefit is that it avoids resentments that tend to accompany teacher perceptions that a new curriculum is being imposed on them and is not sensitive to their conditions or experiences (Mabry & Ettinger, 1999). Earlier studies indicated that teachers who exhibit high levels of self-efficacy and feel that their efforts are appreciated are more likely to persist in the implementation of new curricula (Berman & McLaughlin, 1978; Fuller, Wood, Rapoport, & Dornbusch, 1982). In a more recent study, the extent of usage of a new curriculum was related to class size and years of experience (Covell, O'Leary, & Howe, 2002). Teachers with more experience and small classes were the most likely to use the new curriculum. These factors were believed to reflect the amount of effort involved in implementation.

The less additional work a new curriculum requires, the greater the teacher compliance that can be expected. Since few teachers are trained in children's rights (U.N. Committee, 1996), a rights curriculum must be self-explanatory and inclusive of necessary resources. One of the key criticisms of the Kohlbergian program to teach moral reasoning has been that its use requires highly specialized training for teachers (Noddings, 1997). When teachers perceive a new curriculum to involve significant extra work, its implementation may be undermined (Mabry & Ettinger, 1999). Leat and Higgins (2002) suggested that having flexibility in a curriculum is helpful in this regard. If teachers are provided a range of options from which to select activities whose content and teaching strategy appeals to them, the additional work may well seem less taxing. In an assessment of teachers' responses to a new curriculum in environmental education, Lee (2000) found that a key predictor of teacher compliance was perceived non-monetary cost-benefit, that is, the ratio of workload to perceived benefits of the curriculum. When teachers believe in the goals of a new curriculum, or see the need for it, they are less likely to be concerned about additional workload.

A number of researchers have found that sustained implementation of new curricula is more likely when teachers believe in the curricula's goals (Fullan, 1991; Mabry & Ettinger, 1999; Sarason, 1990). This is a particularly important consideration for implementing a curriculum about which the teacher may have strong beliefs. In evaluating the role of the teacher in the successful delivery of a sexuality curriculum, Goldfarb and McCaffree (2000) found that when the teacher's beliefs were in conflict with the curriculum, the teaching tended to become subversive or ineffective. Some teachers believe that children's rights is a sensitive topic that does not belong in the classroom (Covell & Howe, 2001a). Moreover, there has been a general reluctance among many teachers to educate children about their rights for fear that this will reduce the teachers' authority in the classroom (Franklin, 1996). These teacher beliefs may well stem from a widespread misunderstanding about the nature of children's rights (Howe & Covell, 1998). Regardless of specific concerns about a new curriculum, if teachers do not believe in its goals, a new curriculum is particularly vulnerable to being subverted or defeated (Mabry & Ettinger, 1999). This does not just happen with voluntary use of new curricula as was evidenced with the RCCP (Henrich, Brown, & Aber, 1999). It happened also with the mandated Holocaust education program in England (Brown & Davies, 1998; as described in the previous chapter). Teachers had not used the curriculum because they did not believe that anti-Semitic behaviours or Holocaust denial are problems.

Motivating sustained use by teachers, then, should be facilitated if new curricula are designed with teacher participation and with the provision of supports. In addition, teachers should be persuaded of the need for, or of the benefits of, the learning goals of the curriculum and that the activities are easy for teachers to use.

Identifying Appropriate Student Age

A major consideration for children's rights education is the issue of when it should occur. There is some disagreement in the literature on the appropriate age for introducing children's rights education. UNESCO (1974) recommended including rights education at the preschool level, a recommendation supported by the Fortieth Council of Europe Teachers' Seminar (Abdallah-Pretceille, 1989) and by the Committee of Ministers of the Council of Europe (Starkey, 1991). Many would agree with Humphrey (1987) that it is important to instil the value of human rights in children before they experience prejudice or have time to develop biases. Torney-Purta (1982) suggested that middle childhood is the optimal time to introduce rights education. As she pointed out, the attitudes and values of children between the ages of seven and eleven years are not yet determined. Others similarly have identified this period as the optimum age for developing attitudes towards human rights and global issues (e.g., Schmidt-Sinns, 1980). The cognitive capacities of middle childhood are considerably more advanced than are those of the preschool child, so at least some understanding of rights should be possible.

We believe that the ideal situation may be to introduce the concept of rights at a very basic level in the early grades, but to delay the more comprehensive teaching until early adolescence. There is evidence that even young children have some general understanding of the concepts of rights, fairness, and justice (Helwig, 1997). However, it is only in adolescence that children's cognitive capacity, identity development, and interests in social issues converge to allow both the motivation to learn about and the ability to fully understand the implications of rights education. Prior to early adolescence, no matter how effectively they are taught, there will be some limitations on children's capacity to understand rights. This was well demonstrated in Rahima Wade's dissertation research (1994).

Wade noted that students in social studies often misunderstood important concepts such as the nature of rights. When assessing children's understanding of rights, researchers previously had found that children under age eleven may understand '"free" to mean without payment or the word "equal" to mean numerically balanced' (1994, p. 79). The concepts had been interpreted by the child's existing knowledge and within the child's existing experiences. Interested in examining how children might understand rights when they were specifically taught about rights in a concrete manner, Wade developed and introduced a month long curriculum unit on children's rights to a class comprising seventeen children between the ages of nine and eleven years. She based the content of the curriculum on the 1959 U.N. Declaration of the Rights of the Child. Her curriculum incorporated the elements known to be the most effective in rights education; these include discussion, a democratic pedagogy, cooperative learning, and role-play. To reinforce classroom learning, the children undertook social action projects, and held weekly class meetings to address rights and responsibilities in the classroom. Wade's evaluation data, collected after the completion of the curriculum, indicated that despite this best possible teaching situation, the children had difficulty comprehending rights in ways that were different from their initial conception of rights as freedoms. They had particular difficulty appreciating that there was a link between the rights they were learning about and their own lives. Although by the end of the curriculum, most of the children were able to recognize applications of rights in their daily lives, most could not on their own think of an example of a children's rights issue. Torney-Purta (1984) previously had stressed the importance of integrating the study of human rights with concrete experiences in the children's daily lives. Wade did so, but understanding was not changed. Overall, Wade's data demonstrated that prior to age eleven, children's understanding of rights is likely to be nominal and limited by cognitive capacity.

It is not until around age eleven that children have developed the cognitive skills necessary to understand the nature of rights and the impact of violations of rights. The work of Jean Piaget (1952) suggests that the ability to reason in a hypothetical-deductive way, what Piaget called 'formal-operational thought,' develops between the ages of eleven and fifteen years. Formal-operational thought allows children to consider possibilities as well as reality, to understand abstract concepts such as rights, and to understand relativism. In essence, the child's world expands with the growing ability to consider how the world *could* be, and how the world *should* be. Although others subsequently have found variations in the ages at which children achieve such thought (e.g., Neimark, 1982), there is significant evidence that pre- to mid-adolescence is a period of growth in a number of cognitive skills such as empathic understanding, perspective taking (e.g., Selman, 1980), and rights understanding (e.g., Cherney & Perry, 1996). The improved cognitive skills of late childhood have significant impact on social understanding because they evoke improved perspective taking and empathic understanding. Starting around age ten to eleven years, children become able to consider their own and another's opinion and realize that the other person can do the same. In addition, the child is able to assume the perspective of a third party and to anticipate how each person may react to the other's perspective (Selman, 1980). This improved role-taking ability, together with an understanding of relativism, allows an appreciation that rights can be in conflict, that rights for one person subsume responsibilities towards others, and that it is important to protect the rights of all. As role-taking skills develop, so does sensitivity to the needs and feelings of others. Unlike in earlier childhood, direct experience with another's distress is no longer necessary to arouse empathy. Now empathy can be elicited through information about another's distress (Hoffman, 1984). The empathy elicited by information about the impact of rights violations is expected to have an impact on the child's emerging social and political ideologies and act as a stimulus for the development of rights-respecting self. It is interesting to note also that it is during this same developmental period that children come to understand that conflict in the political or social system is 'as inevitable as it is undesirable' (Berman, 1997, p. 112). Changes in understanding provoke not only questioning about the social and political domain, but also questions about the self.

Changes in identity occur throughout life, but they are of particular salience in early adolescence because it is the first time the child has the cognitive ability to examine and construct a set of personal goals and values. How these values are delineated depends on the child's experiences. Experience with rights – learning you have rights, being treated with respect for your rights, learning how to protect your own and others' rights – can be the catalyst for the development of a rights-based identity. Somewhat reminiscent of earlier concerns with values confusion, Baumeister and Muraven (1996) have noted that there tends to be a broad range of values choices for young people in contemporary society and no clear basis for choice among them. Rights education can fill this void and take advantage of a critical period in development. In turn, the value of rights respect as an integral part of self can provide a framework for interpreting experience and choosing behaviours (as was discussed in the previous chapter).

Teaching Strategies

The Convention must inform the pedagogy as well as the content of any children's rights curricula. This requires that the classroom respect the rights and citizenship status of the child, and that guided by the best interests principle, knowledge from social science research be used to identify developmentally optimal practices. The three essential components of children's rights education are democratic teaching, cooperative learning, and critical thinking – in this case reflecting on rights. Together they teach the behaviours, values, and knowledge that underlie participation in democratic national and global citizenship.

Democratic Teaching

Of fundamental importance is that the teacher practise democratic leadership. The democratic teacher is supportive, recognizes students' accomplishments, and encourages the meaningful participation of students in classroom procedures and practices (Berman, 1997). Classroom management styles respect the rights and dignity of each child. These behaviours model the rights of the Convention. When teachers model and teach about rights in a democratic manner, along with the information they are transmitting attitudes and values about the importance of respecting others' rights. As many have noted, the way the teacher behaves is itself a curriculum (Schubert, 1997), and the teacher's relationship with the children provides the foundation for all learning (Lickona, 1997b). Children with democratic teachers have more positive attitudes towards school, more respect for others, more success, and higher educational and career aspirations (Berman, 1997; Cole & Farris, 1979; Wall, Covell, & MacIntyre, 1999). In addition, children who are allowed meaningful participation in their classrooms develop improved communication and decision-making skills as well as increased social and interpersonal respect and responsibility (Alderson, 2000).

Citizenship is unlikely to be either caught or taught unless lectures about democracy are replaced with the experience of democracy. We stress that a democratic classroom is not one in which children are given decision-making power; that rarely works (Benninga, 1997). It is age-appropriate participation in decision-making that is the core of the democratic classroom. Based on Dewey's theory of democracy, as discussed by Wraga (2001), as well as informed by the U.N. Convention on the Rights of the Child, there are five characteristics of a democratic classroom. (1)

Systematic opportunities are provided for children to participate in decisions that affect them. (2) Children are able to freely think about and express their views on issues of interest and relevance to them. (3) The classroom climate is such that different political and ethical perspectives and opinions can be expressed without threat to personal dignity. (4) Fair and equitable treatment is experienced by each child. (5) Children have opportunities to learn how to be active contributors to their class, their community, and their society, and to discover the social significance of knowledge.

Children's rights education taught in such a classroom would recognize children's rights, their citizenship status and their developmental needs. They would be well positioned to exercise their present and future citizenship rights and responsibilities. In his review of the literature, Berman concluded that 'the more participatory the school, the more the students experience political efficacy, trust, interest and social integration' (1997, p. 127). In essence, children will have caught citizenship. To return again to Dewey, 'the required beliefs cannot be hammered in; the needed attitudes cannot be plastered on' ([1916] 1966, p. 11). A democratic classroom is an essential component of any rights and citizenship education.

Cooperative Learning

A second and related teaching strategy essential for children's rights education is the use of cooperative learning. Advocates and educators of cooperative learning emphasize the utility of cooperative learning for promoting the values of good citizenship (Johnson, Johnson, & Holubec, 2001). Cooperative learning is necessary to the learning and practice of democratic values because it brings into harmony the learning process and the content. Cooperative learning describes situations in which students are placed into small groups to help each other with learning. Group tasks require students to communicate their own ideas, to listen to and respect the opinions of their peers, to learn interpersonal conflict resolution skills, and to share in effort and its outcomes. Students are expected to consider each other's beliefs and knowledge and to work together to ensure the individual success of each member of the group (Veenman, Kenter, & Post, 2000).

One of the seminal developments in cooperative learning was the Jigsaw Classroom; it was designed to reduce prejudice among children of the majority culture and to enhance the self-esteem and academic performance of ethnocultural minority children (Aronson, Blaney, Sikes, Stephan, & Snapp, 1975, 1978). The design was impelled by the ineffectiveness of desegregation policies in the United States in reducing discrimination against minorities. The Jigsaw method involves placing children in six-person heterogeneous learning groups, and providing each child with one-sixth of the material to be learned. Each child must master her own section of the material, then teach it to the others in the group. The total lesson can only be learned through group cooperation and effort. Early assessments of the Jigsaw approach indicated that it was successful in increasing the academic performance of children of ethnic minorities (Lucker, Rosenfield, Sikes, & Aronson, 1977), in increasing children's self-esteem (Geffner, 1978), in reducing negative ethnic stereotypes (Geffner, 1978), and in increasing children's ability to appreciate perspectives other than their own (Bridgeman, 1981). A subsequent assessment of forty-six classrooms in which some version of the Jigsaw approach was being used supported these earlier findings; in particular the cooperative learning style generally increased academic performance and improved relationships among ethnically diverse children (Slavin, 1983). It was especially interesting to note that the benefits of cooperative learning were not reduced when there were also competitive activities in the classroom. The combination of competition and need for cooperation is reflective of contemporary democratic society. As such, these findings clearly are of significant relevance to citizenship education.

Cooperative learning has evolved beyond the initial Jigsaw classroom approach, but has not lost its positive impact on children's attitudes. Subsequent use of cooperative learning strategies, and continuing evaluations of its impact on children provided further evidence of its benefits. When children are afforded the opportunity to work cooperatively with their peers, they are provided the means to develop the interpersonal understanding that is a prerequisite of the development of respect for diverse opinions (Selman, 1980; Youniss, 1980). Group discussion allows for learning about how others feel, think, and are motivated differently from oneself. The peer interaction that occurs in cooperative learning situations also plays a central role in the development of ethical reasoning (Berndt, 1987; Nakkula & Selman, 1991; Selman, 1980). Interestingly, Higgins (1991), in working with the just community schools, found that as children's interpersonal understanding increased, so did their self-image, or identity, as ethical persons.

Cooperative learning is expected to be particularly effective among adolescent students. Peer groups are the prominent context for socialization in adolescence and are potentially powerful models of motivation, achievement and engagement (Ryan, 2000). There are two types of cooperative peer group learning that are particularly effective for the learning and practice of democratic citizenship. One is role-play. The other is discussing controversial issues. These activities are most effective when the role-play or the discussions are related to social or community problems that are of interest to the students (Berman 1997).

The concept of role-play, or role-taking, emphasizes both the cognitive and affective sides of social interaction (Day, 1991). When children adopt the role or character of another person, they must consider what the other person understands, believes, thinks, and feels. Experiences with role-play, therefore, foster both intellectual and ethical development. Role-play in small groups can increase the child's self-esteem. When small groups of children engage in role-play, each member of the group has an opportunity to contribute. Less-able students have an unusual opportunity to experience success (Luff, 2000). And as Luff (2000) also noted, gifted students have an opportunity to express their creativity. These experiences validate the importance of all children, to themselves and to each other, and help each child gain a positive sense of self and personal agency (Higgins, 1991). Numerous benefits have been documented from experience with role-taking. From a pedagogical perspective, role-play is more engaging and memorable to students than are traditional teaching strategies, and it is more effective in developing students' ability to communicate and debate (Luff, 2000). From the perspective of citizenship education, role-play allows the development of a broad conception of the social world and raises social and political consciousness (Berman, 1997). Johnson and his colleagues (Johnson, Johnson, & Holubec, 2001) emphasized the need to use role-play to develop civic values. Overall, the research on the impact of role-play experiences in the classroom shows that role-play is an effective way of exploring differing perspectives and an effective means of promoting empathic understanding and tolerance (Bickmore, 1999). Role-play improves decision-making and conflict resolution skills, reduces the likelihood of interpersonal violence, and increases students' levels of empathy and adherence to democratic principles (Luff, 2000; Sprinthall & Scott, 1989; Sprinthall, Hall, & Gerler, 1992; Thies-Sprinthall & Sprinthall, 1987).

Discussing controversial issues is the second effective means of small group learning. Generally this approach has been found to be very effective in engaging children and in promoting civic values. The rights of the Convention are particularly useful as a context for discussion in that they are both readily applied to the children's experiences, and they are open to some interpretation. For example, children may have differing, albeit equally valid, ideas on how the best interests principle of the Convention might be applied to resolving an issue. Through critical reflection in small groups, they obtain both knowledge of rights and responsibilities and experience with considering and evaluating varying perspectives on issues. Together, this knowledge and experience helps children exercise their rights and fulfil their democratic citizenship responsibilities. As a component of curricula, we use the term *rights reflection* to denote discussion and critical thinking about issues within the context of the U.N. Convention on the Rights of Child.

Rights Reflection

It is obvious that the rights in the Convention are better learned through discussion, debate, and critical thinking, than through instruction. Simply having knowledge of rights is not enough for the practice of citizenship. Citizenship requires both a capacity to participate in public institutions and political life and the ability to contribute to the re-definition of them (Tiana, 2002). Thus, the use of critical reflection to evaluate social issues, ideas, problems, and policies should be a central aspect of citizenship education and democratic teaching (Apple & Beane, 1995; Parker, 1996). In fact, throughout the citizenship education literature, the importance of critical thinking about social issues is emphasized. Cunningham (1991) argued that controversial issues be discussed and debated in classes to help students develop a sense of civic responsibility. The discussion of controversial public issues helps students 'develop an understanding and commitment to democratic values, increase their willingness to engage in political life and positively influence content understanding, critical thinking ability and interpersonal skills' (Parker, 1996, p. 13). More recently, Torney-Purta and her colleagues (2001) observed that promoting the discussion of controversial issues is essential to foster the development of civic commitment. Another important outcome of critical reflection on social issues for citizenship was identified by William Wraga (2001): critical thinking develops the ability to uncover bias and detect propaganda. We believe that for critical reflection on social issues to be effective in promoting democratic citizenship attitudes and behaviours, three conditions must obtain.

First, it is important that students have a context for their discussion. Critical thinking from a democratic values base, such as the Convention, is essential to the realization of citizenship attitudes and behaviours (Reardon, 1988). As discussed in the previous chapter, a value-free discussion of social issues is rarely useful. Citizenship attitudes are unlikely to be developed if controversial issues are analysed in the absence of democratic values or ideals. Moreover, rights knowledge is an important component of the ability to exercise citizenship. Contextualizing social issues discussion within the rights of the Convention more fully enables democratic citizenship, by providing essential knowledge as well as by promoting skills and commitment to the Convention's ideals.

Second, it is essential that critical reflection about issues be itself democratic. In a review of the literature, Doug Harwood (1997) found that students' participation in discussion of social issues is encouraged when teachers adopt the role of facilitator as required by democratic teaching. As facilitators, teachers organize and enable student participation by maintaining rules and limits. Teachers do not express personal views or give feedback to students' expressed opinions. Nonetheless, it is important that the teacher be present and listening to the students. The quality of student discussion is highest when teachers are present and functioning as facilitators (Harwood, 1995). In contrast, with the use of direct instruction, where the teacher explains concepts, asks questions to assess understanding, and provides feedback after student contributions, participation is constrained and decreases over time. Unfortunately, this latter is also found to be the more common scenario.

Third, to maintain engagement and optimize learning, it is important that debate and discussion are centred on issues of interest to the child, particularly issues that spark disagreement (Hahn, 1998). For example, younger adolescents might be given the following scenario. A student is being suspended from school for wearing a T-shirt with a somewhat racist slogan. She complains to her friend that it is her article 12 right to wear what she wants, and wonders why her friend has not been suspended also for his appearance – he is wearing a large safety pin through his eyebrow. Body-piercing, as well as potential weapons, have been disallowed at the school. The task for the group is to consider the thoughts and feelings of the students and whether the suspended student has a legitimate claim. As with Kohlberg's moral dilemma debates, attempts to resolve competing claims to rights promote internal cognitive conflict and thereby improve critical thinking skills (see Leming, 1981). Critical reflection on issues of relevance to children is particularly beneficial because it evokes consideration of why they think, feel, and respond as they do to particular people and situations (Goldfarb & McCaffree, 2000). Since adolescents are in the process of defining their identity, how and where they fit with others and how it feels to be different are highly salient issues to them (Elkind & Hetzel, 1977). In turn, the learning is more memorable and the problem-solving skills learned through critical reflection are more likely to be used by the children in their everyday experiences (Glaser, Ferguson, & Vosniadou, 1996). A rare and excellent example of democratic teaching and the discussion of controversial issues is found in Goldfarb and McCaffree's (2000) assessment of sexuality education. Using a democratic teaching strategy, with critical thinking about sexuality, resulted in students' increased respect for those with different sexual orientations and lifestyles.

Children's Rights Curricula

As noted in Chapter 2, there are a number of children's rights educational materials available. Our discussion here is limited to those whose design includes the three components discussed above and for which there are some evaluation data. These children's rights curricula are quite varied. They have been used with children from ages three to eighteen years in Canada, England, and Belgium. Nonetheless, there are many similarities in their outcome data. Overall, their evaluation findings converge to suggest that citizenship can, indeed, be caught through children's rights education.

In My World is a rights-based citizenship education program developed in Canada for use with children from around five to eight years, Kindergarten through Grade 3 (Murray, 1999). The core focus of the program is participation. The underlying philosophy is essentially that of the Kohlbergian just community school model, in which the encouragement of participation is believed to enable the development of moral reasoning and pro-social responding. The central purpose of the curriculum is to teach children how to become good citizens.

The curriculum is organized around four participatory strategies. First, concept mapping involves students in linking the rights under the Convention to their lives, as they understand their relevance. Second, students work through a decision-making protocol. They identify a problem, consider the response options and possible consequences of each option, and then decide as a group which is the best response. Third, is role-play. Students listen to a story and then respond to questions that require perspective taking through acting out situations and characters. Fourth, is responsive writing. Students listen to, or read, a selection from children's literature and then respond in writing to thematic questions posed about the selection. For example, a story about friendship would have questions such as 'How do you know that a friend understands you?'

Evaluation of the curriculum has centred on its impact on children in Grade 3 (age eight years) and has been limited to qualitative or anecdotal data. Overall, the data and teacher comments have been very positive. Murray (2002) reported the following with regard to the specific strategies. The concept mapping exercises indicated that children were able to organize rights concepts in ways that made them meaningful for them. They were able to discuss rights in relation to their relationships with family, friends, and peers. The decision-making exercises helped the children with their group work skills; they evidenced increased understanding that consensus-based decision-making involves listening to others. The role-play and the responsive writing exercises appeared to promote children's perspective-taking skills, specifically their ability to understand that others have different motivations and intentions. Anecdotal information indicates that the classroom learning had an effect on the children's reasoning and behaviour. As one teacher said, when problems arose on the playground, children tended to deal with them by expressing their rights, for example, 'You are taking away my right to feel safe' (Jeary, 2001, p. 15). Overall, despite limitations imposed by the young ages of the children, the program appears to be an excellent tool for children's early exercise of their citizenship rights and responsibilities.

Similar anecdotal evidence has recently come from England. Impelled by an awareness of how secular schools have been disadvantaged by their lack of universal values or principles, and of the potential of children's rights to provide a coherent values base, existing curricula and approaches to children's rights education (Covell & Howe, 1999, 2001a) were being adapted for use among schools in Hampshire, England. Under the leadership of County Education Officer Andrew Seber and County Inspector for Intercultural Education Ian Massey, a county-wide initiative for the inclusion of children's rights education has been implemented. One of the first schools to become involved in the initiative is Knights Enham Junior School in Andover. Head teacher Anne Hughes and classroom teacher Helen Filer have provided anecdotal evaluation data on their experiences with teaching children's rights to a class of ten- and eleven-year-olds over a six-month period (Hughes & Filer, 2003). Children's rights was taught as a separate subject and also was integrated into the students' literacy classes. The data from England are consistent with data obtained from other children's rights education as described.

Overall, the children and their teacher commented on the improved classroom atmosphere and the greater opportunity for focusing on learning. Children were reportedly calmer, more caring, more tolerant, and more respectful of each other. Hughes and Filer observed that students had started to appeal to rights to solve their interpersonal problems. For example, one child asked another to take 'time-out' because her disruptive behaviour was interfering with other students' right to an education. The child in question complied. Another example was provided by a parent who said that her child had stopped arguing about bedtime, understanding it as the mother protecting the child's right to a healthy good night's sleep. Students have been more careful with their classroom materials and equipment than they were previously and more so than children in a comparable class which was not yet receiving children's rights education. Among the more notable findings was the concern that the children expressed about the rights of Iraqi children when Britain joined the United States in the war on Iraq; in contrast, children in other classes were focused on bombs. Perhaps the most significant finding of this initiative is seen in the summary comment given by Helen Filer: 'I have been teaching for seven years, using the same ways of teaching, but I have never had them [the children] so cooperative and so understanding.'

A positive impact of teaching children's rights was also reported from an earlier program in Belgium. The children's rights education project in Bruges (Decoene & De Cock, 1996) was a comprehensive children's rights education initiative with younger children. All children, ages three to twelve years, attending the De Vrijdagmarkt primary school, their teachers, and their parents were involved in the project throughout the school year 1993/4. It is noteworthy that not only were parents involved with this project, it was the school's parents' association that had initiated it as a means to greater child involvement in the learning process. The goal of the project was to teach the contents of the U.N. Convention on the Rights of the Child, using a democratic pedagogy with emphasis on child participation. Similar to the Murray curriculum (described in the previous chapter), in the Bruges project, children were taught about their rights through a variety of media including art and poetry, and there was considerable provision for child-initiated and small group activities. Also like with the Murray curriculum, there was extensive use of role-play and group discussion. In addition, the curriculum activities described reflect a keen awareness of the importance of engaging the student through age-appropriate salient issues. For example, with the younger children, learning about the Convention started with a focus on the right to food. The children created a very large doll with illustrations of food. This project then led to activities surrounding the right to play. Older children engaged in discussions and role-play regarding rights to adoption, privacy, education, and family. Art activities included newspaper collages representing examples of rights violations.

To facilitate sustaining the rights education across the school year, a workgroup was established comprising one teacher and four parents. The purpose of the workgroup was to agree on the parameters of the project and to set up a structure for continuous dialogue between parents and teachers to monitor the progress of the project throughout the school year. In addition, there was cooperative planning of supportive activities such as visiting speakers and a UNICEF exhibition at the school.

The evaluation of the project involved interviews with children and teachers (Decoene & De Cock, 1996). Some concerns were expressed about allowing children participation rights, and about an emphasis on rights rather than responsibilities, but the teachers were generally very enthusiastic. They reported that although they had had some previous knowledge of children's rights, it was the first time that they had worked with them. The enthusiasm with which they had initiated the project was still with them at the end of the year. Teachers were very positive about the parent involvement. The teachers had monitored the impact of the children's rights curriculum by observing the students' social behaviours. They reported that their students had made obvious gains in interpersonal understanding and respect as a result of the project. Their observations were consistent with comments from the students.

Learning about rights had evoked concerns among the older children about issues such as peace, injustice, war, and hunger. The children spontaneously discussed the rights of minorities, of children who were adopted, and of children with disabilities. They expressed concern about the rights of children living in institutions, rather than with their family, especially children in juvenile facilities. And these children took action. They requested visits to peers living in different situations such as in medical or juvenile justice institutions. One class, after learning about their right to freedom of speech made an appointment with the local mayor and read a letter to him that they had written to express their concerns. After learning about how rights are respected or violated in other areas, a class wrote letters to a U.N. soldier in the former Yugoslavia and to a school in Zimbabwe. In their own school, the students displayed behaviours that reflected an increase in appreciation for diversity. The researchers concluded that children's rights education can be an effective tool for increasing socially responsible behaviours and tolerance for differences in preventing the common school problems of truancy and disinterest in school. Clearly, children's rights education is of relevance to democratic citizenship.

Building on the success of the Bruges project, we at the Children's Rights Centre of the University College of Cape Breton developed children's rights education curricula in Canada for use with students in Grade 6 (ages eleven to thirteen), Grade 8 (ages thirteen to fifteen), and Grade 12 (ages seventeen to nineteen).[1] Grade 6 was selected for the introduction of children's rights education because cognitive development at that age allows for understanding abstract concepts such as rights and justice and for greater interpersonal understanding (Selman, 1980). Of particular relevance to the selection of curriculum content, is the growth of a sense of community and political understanding that develops through adolescence. Initially, the benefits of policy are seen primarily as they relate to the self. By the end of adolescence, the ability to judge public policy from the standpoint of the broader community and the common good has developed (Gallatin & Adelson, 1970). We attempted to reflect this growth by focusing the content of the Grade 6 curriculum primarily on the relevance of the U.N. Convention to the individual child, the Grade 8 curriculum to relationships the child is likely to be engaged in, and the Grade 12 curriculum to issues of global citizenship. The other age-related consideration was that the issues, as well as the pedagogy, be salient to the developmental interests of the students. It is important to state here also that children themselves were involved in the design of the activities in the curricula. For each level we first used the social science literature to identify developmentally appropriate issues. We then sought students' opinions on the content and nature of activities and altered the activities to be consistent with what the students themselves found the most interesting and relevant. It is rare for students to be involved in curriculum design, but when they are, they request that there be more opportunities to do

1 We acknowledge funding from Canadian Heritage for the funding of the Grade 6 curriculum, Canadian Race Relations Foundation for the development of the Grade 8 curriculum, and Canadian International Development Agency (CIDA) for funding the development of the Grade 12 curriculum. Evaluation research was supported by a standard research grant to the authors from the Social Sciences and Humanities Research Council of Canada. The curricula are available in PDF format in English and in French on our website, http://discovery.uccb.ns.ca/children/.

research and projects than they usually are allowed, and they ask that there be fewer note-taking and rote-learning tasks (Keighley-James, 2002). Our student consultants were delighted with the small group tasks and provisions for student participation.

Each curriculum is designed to maximize students' participation in learning. The types of activities used, the role-playing, discussions of case studies, analyses of popular song lyrics, story-writing, self-directed community projects, and cartooning, are centred on the issues salient to the target age groups and provide for meaningful participation. To ensure that the rights being taught are being respected and modelled, the curricula are designed to provide opportunity to express opinions (consistent with articles 13 and 14 of the Convention) and to have views heard and taken into account (article 12). In essence, the activities are designed for an egalitarian approach to classroom interaction in which teachers' and students' opinions are listened to with equal consideration. Each unit of each curriculum comprises a variety of activities, most of which are designed for small group cooperative learning and to promote critical thinking.

The Grade 6 curriculum includes units on healthy living, personal safety, drug use, families and family life, discrimination and freedom of speech, and problem-solving and decision-making. For example, to learn about their article 33 right to protection from narcotics, students role-play children and drug dealers to examine ways of dealing with pressure to try drugs or sell drugs. There is also a discussion on how parental alcoholism might violate a child's rights, and a case study in which children are asked, among other questions, how they might prevent future occurrence of a situation in which a child is taken to hospital with an asthma attack after being exposed to second-hand smoke. Freedom of expression rights are taught through acting out a trial, which teaches the importance of listening to different views and reconciling them, and through participating in the development of a 'Graffiti Wall' in which limits on expression in order to respect others' rights are taught. These types of activities allow the students to develop understanding that rights can be in conflict and that they can identify circumstances under which reasonable limits should be placed on rights.

The Grade 8 curriculum includes units on equality, alcohol and drug use, the environment and health, youth justice, abuse and exploitation, rights and sexuality, and employment and education. Sample activities include an analysis of popular songs to identify how rights and responsibilities in sexual activity are represented in contemporary music (discussed in the context of Convention articles 13, 16, 19, and 34), the design of alternative advertising for tobacco and alcohol that includes messages about rights violations (articles 3, 24, 27, and 33), and the completion of a cartoon in which freedom of expression rights come into conflict.

The Grade 12 curriculum is designed to build on previous learning and to expand the sphere of application of children's rights to the consideration of global issues, children in especially difficult circumstances, and issues of particular relevance to developing countries. The units of the Grade 12 curriculum include war-affected children, sexual exploitation, child labour, education, discrimination, health, the environment, family, and participation. Activities include analysing law on child sex tourism, researching and debating the situation for child soldiers, role-playing racial discrimination, keeping a diary to describe the life of a child labourer, comparative analysis of educational situations, and writing marriage announcements that reflect a variety of cultural traditions on dating and marriage. Again, many of the activities require that the students work together in small groups to reach consensus about social issues, to solve problems, and to achieve common goals. Some activities also are designed to bring the small groups together for a whole class project. For example, there is a sweatshop talk show, in which different groups role-play the varying actors in a typical talk show, and there is a mock U.N. conference on war-affected children in which each of the small groups have responsibility for representing the players at the conference.

A number of measures were taken in the hope of gaining teachers' cooperation in using the curricula and enabling their evaluation. Teachers in the school district in which the curricula were developed had expressed three concerns. First, they were reluctant to accept any new responsibilities, and but few were interested in adding a new area to their teaching. Second, some teachers believed that children's rights was too sensitive an issue and would better be taught in the home. Third, and of greatest concern to us, was that many of the teachers, being themselves unfamiliar with the Convention, expressed concerns about the loss of authority that they anticipated experiencing in the classroom if they let their students know they had rights. In response to these concerns, we took the following measures. To ease the implementation of the children's rights education and allay concerns about additional responsibilities, we designed the curricula to fit into and complement existing school curricula: at the Grade 6 level this was health and social studies, at the Grade 8 it was personal development and relationships, and at the

Grade 12 level, global studies. For example, the article 33 right to protection from narcotics was linked with the existing health curriculum section on drug prevention. Each section included an overview of the relevant articles of the Convention and a choice of corresponding activities. For additional support, we developed an Internet site with further information and resources for teachers and parents. We also held workshops with teachers and administrators at which they were informed about the Convention as well as the pedagogy required by the curricula.

The Grade 6 curriculum was the first to be developed and evaluated (Covell & Howe, 1999). It was used by seven teachers who had a total of 175 students. The students who received the children's rights curriculum described above, when compared with those who did not, showed a more adultlike understanding of rights, perceived their classmates to be more accepting of ethnic minority children, and perceived greater levels of peer and teacher support. Children who did not receive the rights curriculum understood rights to be freedoms and wants - the right to stay up late, for example – and did not believe that all children should have rights, only those who 'deserved' them or were old enough to know 'how to use them.' In contrast, the children who received the children's rights education understood rights to be entitlements that are qualitatively different from wants and freedoms. They understood rights to mean that they should be protected from abuse and exploitation and that they should be provided with their basic material needs. In turn, this understanding was reflected in their assertions about the importance of rights being met for all children and their expressed concerns with rights violations. The children's perceptions that their peers were more accepting of ethnic minority children were reinforced by comments from their teachers, who reported to us a notable behavioural change and a change in classroom atmosphere. Interestingly, some of the children also commented to us that knowing they had rights made them feel good about themselves and made them feel wanted. We examined these findings further in the evaluation of the Grade 8 curriculum (Covell & Howe, 2001b).

At the end of the school year in which the Grade 8 curriculum was implemented, comparisons between the eighty-nine students who received it and the ninety-one who did not indicated that the rights education again had led to an adultlike understanding of rights. In addition, the curriculum had a significant impact on self-esteem, perceived peer and teacher support, and on support for the rights of all other persons – children, and adults including ethnic minorities, native peoples, people with disabilities, and homosexuals. Again, anecdotal data from the teachers who used the curriculum indicated that behavioural changes accompanied the attitudinal changes. For example, one teacher commented that his class used to complain about their Personal Development and Relationships class in which the rights education was being used, but now they asked for more time in it. Another teacher anecdote was that he had met a parent at a sports event who commented, 'whatever you are now teaching my son, please keep it up – he's never been so cooperative.' Beyond individual examples were pro-social initiatives directed by groups of children and undertaken in the context of rights education. One class established a breakfast program for their school, another worked towards helping Kosovar refugees who were coming to Canada at that time, and a third worked for a local food bank. Rights respecting attitudes and rights promoting behaviours resulted from the rights education. These outcomes were similar to those reported in the Belgian study.

Our evaluation of the Grade 12 curriculum was less successful. Twelve teachers of Grade 12 global geography or global history attended a one-day workshop where they were introduced to the Children's Rights Global Studies curriculum. Each agreed to use the curriculum over the next four months and to allow for its assessment. Pre-test data on knowledge of rights and international responsibilities as well as attitudes towards the provision of humanitarian assistance were collected from the students in the twelve classes and from those in four comparable classes which were not using the curriculum.

Unfortunately, the actual use of the curriculum fell short of promises. Five teachers did not use the curriculum at all, two for reasons unknown, one because of illness, one received a change in classroom assignment, and there was the physical collapse and ensuing closure of one school (apparently the school had been constructed on an old mine shaft). Among the remaining seven teachers, use of the curriculum was sporadic and infrequent. The overall lack of cooperation in using the curriculum may well have resulted from the unforeseen confluence of curriculum test time with teachers union negotiations. Citing the possibility of strike action, or lack of time, no teacher reported using more than half the curriculum. Similarly, shortage of time was cited for non-compliance with post-test survey completion, among both the rights education and control classes.

Despite this, teachers who did use the curriculum were enthusiastic about the level of student interest and the positive student response. They noted an obvious improvement in their students' appreciation of global problems and the complexity and importance of human rights.

These observations were supported by students' post-test survey data. Students who had experienced some of the curriculum activities were three times more likely than were those in the control group to understand humanitarian assistance and assistance for children in difficult circumstances as a fundamental human right. However, the usage patterns and poor return rate of evaluation surveys precluded statistical analyses.

We were interested in teachers' responses to using the children's rights curriculum (Covell, O'Leary, & Howe, 2002). To examine the impact of teaching children's rights on teacher attitudes, we held a one-day workshop with the thirty-five Grade 8 teachers in the school district. At the workshop, we first assessed the teachers' existing attitudes towards human rights and the idea of teaching children's rights. We then introduced them to the U.N. Convention on the Rights of the Child and to the Children's Rights Global Studies curriculum. During the school year, contact was maintained with the teachers and supports provided as desired. At the end of the school year, the 906 students from the classes surveyed completed a rights values survey. A subset of eighty-three students, half from classes where the curriculum had been most used and half from where the curriculum had been least used, were interviewed. Teachers were again asked to complete surveys as they had prior to experience using the curriculum. The following findings were of particular interest. There was no relation between the teachers' pre-test attitudes towards rights or teaching children's rights and their subsequent use of the curriculum. However, the more the teachers used the curriculum, the more supportive they became of children's rights and the more enthusiastic about the curriculum. Comments at the end of the year included the following: 'The understanding [of rights] was accompanied by a reduction in behaviours that infringe upon the rights of others.' And, 'as they [the children] began to understand diversity and realize that everyone is equal, students became more accepting of others. This led to a decrease in teasing and bullying.' Did teaching children's rights affect teacher behaviour as well as attitudes? We were unable to address that question in this study. However, during a recent visit to the Hampshire project in England, we asked the Year 6 students if Ms Filer had changed in any way as she taught them about their Convention rights. After a brief discussion, the children agreed that she had. She had, they explained, become 'more normal.' First, they said, she was too strict, then not strict enough, but now, she was 'just right.'

Overall, the evidence supports the assertion that appropriately designed children's rights education has the potential to affect children's behaviours, values, and sense of self in ways that are consistent with the goals of citizenship education. Indeed, we believe that rights education has a contagion effect.

The Contagion Model

The contagion effect is in part a result of the democratic teaching and participatory learning and in part a result of children learning about their rights. As children learn that they have rights, and are persons worthy of rights the value of rights spreads to a support for the rights of others. The curricula described above differed from each other, were taught to different age levels, and in different countries. But each had similarly positive outcomes on the children. In terms of content, each was centred on teaching children about their rights under the Convention using age-appropriate activities about issues salient to the age group. In terms of process, each curriculum incorporated the three components: democratic teaching, cooperative learning, and rights reflection. How these affect the learner is shown in the contagion model (Figure 5.1).

In the contagion model, the first row represents the three essential components of a rights-based citizenship education curriculum. The middle row describes the factors that mediate between the curriculum and its outcomes: rights understanding, positive classroom climate, and self-esteem. The outcome variables are the rights-respecting values and their consequence: socially responsible behaviours. Each of these will be discussed in turn.

Rights Understanding

The evaluation data from the Cape Breton studies demonstrate quite clearly that it is not simply age or the development of reasoning capacity that allows an understanding of the concept of rights. When compared with those who had not received the children's rights education, children who had received the education showed a significantly different understanding of rights. At both the Grade 6 and Grade 8 levels, when asked what they had learned about rights and what it means to have rights, children who had not been educated about the Convention were likely to either be unable to answer the question or understand rights to be freedoms. In contrast, children who had received the rights education focused on themes of rights of protection, the provision of basic needs, and the right to be treated with fairness. These differences are especially noteworthy because the concept of rights was introduced

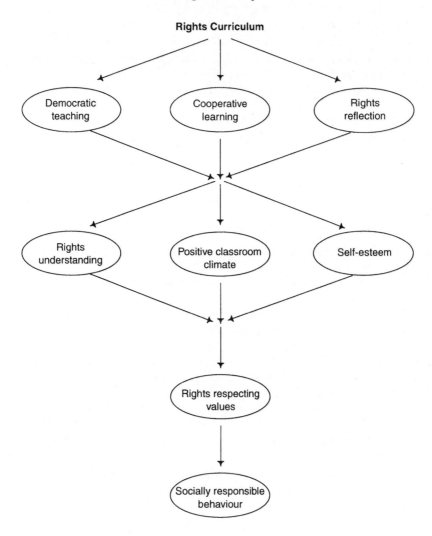

Figure 5.1 The contagion model

explicitly only at the beginning of the year and only with reference to the difference between rights and needs. Subsequently, the rights of the Convention were taught (as described above) through applied activities. These data underscore the importance of the democratic classroom and the opportunities for critical thinking in small groups.

One of the most important aspects of the adultlike understanding of rights that was gained by those who experienced the curricula is that responsibilities are inevitable corollaries of rights. Although the emphasis throughout the teaching was on rights, the students learned that rights cannot exist without responsibilities. They learned that part of having rights is respecting and promoting the rights of others. Thus, their understanding of rights included a consideration of others. In contrast, those who were not taught children's rights, and who understood rights to be freedoms, understood rights only in relation to the self. It is only through experience with rights, it would seem, that children can fully understand the nature and importance of rights.

Positive Classroom Climate

As children are learning about and reflecting on their rights in cooperative learning situations guided by democratic teachers, they are developing a positive classroom climate. The positive classroom climate is one characterized by a sense of group membership; shared values, goals, and successes; and mutual respect. The importance of such a classroom to both teachers and students was highlighted in an extensive cross-national study of affective education (Puurula et al., 2001).

Affective education is defined as the non-cognitive dimension of education that deals with students' moral, spiritual, and values development. It involves teachers being supportive and concerned with students' feelings, interpersonal relationships, and social skills. Affective education can be, and often is, a by-product of classroom practices – the hidden rather than the formal curriculum. Beliefs about affective education were assessed in a comparative study of a total of 2,230 students and 1,507 teachers in England, Finland, Germany, Greece, Hungary, Ireland, Israel, Italy, the Netherlands, Northern Ireland, Portugal, and Spain. An interesting pattern of data emerged that was consistent across countries. Both students and teachers identified a positive classroom climate as the most important aspect of affective education. The specific characteristics of the positive classroom included the promotion of a caring atmosphere, respect for self and others, the fostering of the talents of each student and allowing each student to experience success, and providing opportunities for the practice of responsible democratic citizenship. The second most important aspect of affective education, again identified by both teachers and students, was that teachers be supportive of students, recognize their difficulties, and allow them to express their feelings.

It is not surprising that other researchers have observed relations between students' perceptions of a positive classroom climate and positive outcomes. The classroom climate is a key predictor of student behaviours and values (Nucci, 2001). Ryan (2001), for example, in a study of Grade 8 students, found that students' perceptions of teacher support and respect were related to students' increased motivation and engagement in school. Adolescents who perceive themselves to have teacher support have more positive attitudes towards school, more success, and higher educational and career aspirations (Wall, Covell, & MacIntyre, 1999). Others have demonstrated a link between a positive classroom climate and the development of students' self-confidence, increased levels of self-esteem, more positive peer relationships, and a decrease in problem behaviours (Demaray & Malecki, 2002; Stuhlman, Hamre & Planta, 2002). In particular, perceived peer support has been correlated with psychological well-being (see Dunn, Putallaz, Sheppard, & Lindstrom, 1987) and with heightened self-worth (East & Rook, 1992).

One of the most consistent findings in the political socialization research is that a positive classroom climate is a major contributor to the development of positive civic attitudes, civic values, and civic participation (Hahn, 2002; Torney-Purta, 2002). Students who perceive their classrooms to be respectful and supportive report higher levels of civic tolerance and political interest than do other students. Constance Flanagan and her colleagues (1998) examined potential predictors of civic commitment of adolescent students from Australia, Bulgaria, the Czech Republic, Hungary, Russia, Sweden, and the United States. Their data demonstrate the importance of students' perceptions of their classrooms. A sense of community among classmates – of membership, belonging, and solidarity – was a key predictor of identification with the common good. When students perceived their peers to be supportive, the group took precedence over the self. A sense of being a valued member of a community is a powerful force in promoting commitment to shared values and shared needs (Battistich et al., 1999).

Self-esteem

The observed increases in self-esteem result from both the content and process of the rights education. In terms of the process, the democratic teaching, small group cooperative learning, and discussion of social issues all contribute to increasing students' self-esteem. The participatory and democratic nature of teaching means that students have their thoughts solicited and listened to by their peers and their teachers. Within this democratic teaching context, through cooperative learning, each student also has opportunities to contribute to group problem-solving and decision-making. Such experiences allow students to feel a sense of being a valued member of a group and, in turn, a sense of belonging. Adolescents who experience a sense of belonging at school report higher levels of emotional well-being (McNeeley, Nonnemaker, & Blum, 2002). Cooperative group learning provides opportunities for every student to experience some success, a commonly believed antecedent to self-esteem (see Harter, 1988). The discussion of social issues in cooperative learning structures promotes supportive relationships among students which, in turn, increases their self-esteem (Berman, 1997). The support and encouragement experienced may be particularly effective in raising the self-esteem of children who do not receive support and encouragement at home (Battistich et al., 1999). It is these children who typically are less likely to experience success or a sense of belonging at school.

To explain the link between the content of the curriculum, children's rights, and the increases in self-esteem seen in its impact, we draw on the work of F. Clark Power (1997). Power rightly pointed out that much of the self-esteem literature is concerned with the child's level of self-esteem to the neglect of the very important aspect of its source. The source, he believes, is a match between the child's real and ideal moral selves. Building self-esteem involves the construction of moral standards of self-evaluation. Power proposes the following levels of development. At the earliest level, the child's ideal and real moral attributes are described in very general terms such as 'nice.' Descriptions of self reflect parental expectations and exhortations. Because this stage comes before the acquisition of cognitive capacities that allow abstract thought, the ideal self and the real self are consistent, and conscience and guilt are expressed as trepidation about punishment in response to misdeeds. At Stage 2, the ideal and real selves are described in terms of dispositions for action. The child sees the self as kind and helpful towards others and tries to avoid behaviours that would be inconsistent with this self-concept. By Stage 3, the self is described in terms of traits and attitudes that typically reflect a concern for being caring and unselfish, and fear is expressed about being self-centred. The children in the Murray (2002) and the Decoene and De Cock (1996) studies would likely be at Stage 2 or 3. Stage 4 would describe the level reached in adolescence – the age of the students in the children's rights education studies upon which the contagion model is based.

By Stage 4, the ideal self reflects the identity that the adolescent is developing, and there is some construction of standards for self-evaluation. As identity develops, there is a dread of failure to live up to ideals or role expectations. There is a strong need to behave in ways that are consistent with the ideal self, to bring into harmony the real and the ideal selves. Power, as did many earlier theorists, noted that many adolescents at this time express a desire to make a difference to society or to the world. Thus, Power understands self-esteem to be intrinsic to the development of self and identity. The adolescent's ideal self is of intrinsic value; to achieve self-esteem requires that the adolescent believe the real self to be of value. The more valued the adolescent feels, the greater the match between the ideal and the real self and the higher the self-esteem.

The source of self-esteem, the sense of personal worth, Power suggested, is not dependent on natural or achieved characteristics, but on personhood. Self-esteem may be bolstered by achieving high grades or by athletic awards. But the essential source of self-esteem is knowing one has value simply because one exists. The intrinsic value of a person regardless of achievement or characteristics is emphasized in many theories of justice. For example, Power notes that in John Rawls's theory of justice (1971), the emphasis is on the value of every individual regardless of the individual's age, sex, ethnocultural, health, or socioeconomic status. The message of the U.N. Convention on the Rights of the Child is the same. Children learn that each of them, and all children everywhere and in all circumstances are equally worthy of rights. All children possess fundamental rights simply because they are children. They do not need to earn these rights or achieve any societal or parental standards. It is their status as child citizens of the globe that makes children valuable, rights-worthy, and rights-bearing citizens. Learning about rights provides a standard for self-evaluation and a sense of being valued. As such, it facilitates a match between the ideal self (rights-worthy) and the real self (rights-owning).

Power argued that the value on personal worth leads to respect for others, and a concern for the dignity and the rights of others, because a concern for the other based on the other's personhood is a concern for the self. In essence, Power is reflecting the argument described in the previous chapter for the benefits of self-interest. It is only through promoting and protecting the rights of all that one's own rights are respected. Our data are consistent with Power's assertions. A sense of intrinsic self-worth empowers and challenges the child to think and act in ways that are consistent with it. Thus, Power concluded that an appreciation of self-worth is both a source of self-esteem and a goad to action. We agree.

Rights-Respecting Values

One's self-concept is a powerful force in delineating values, and goals and in motivating behaviours. The effects of increased self-esteem, a positive classroom climate, and an understanding of rights interact to produce a rights-respecting self-concept. We note that increased rights-respecting attitudes were reported in all the children's rights education described above. Decreases in anti-social behaviours and concerns for the rights of others were observed in both the Canadian and Belgian studies. However, it is only from the Grade 8 level curriculum evaluation that we have more than anecdotal data.

For the evaluation of the Grade 8 curriculum, a rather stringent measure of rights-respecting values was used (Covell & Howe, 2001b). It comprises two subscales; one assesses rights-supportive values for the rights of adults and the other for the rights of children. The adult rights described in the measure are rights given to adults in Canada under the Canadian Charter of Rights and Freedoms; these include rights of ethnocultural and sexual minorities, native peoples, and people with disabilities. The items describing children's rights are taken from the U.N. Convention. Respondents rate their beliefs about the importance of each right. To avoid socially desirable responses, each right is presented with a competing consideration: for example, 'the right of children in trouble with the law to be sentenced differently from adults even if they commit serious crimes.' Grade 8 students who participated in the children's rights education showed significantly higher ratings on both the child and adult subscales of the measure than did their non-participating peers. Learning about their own rights had made these students more supportive of the rights of all others. In their own words, 'We learned that we need to respect other people's rights.' In the words of one of their teachers 'They realized that since all children are the bearers of rights, it is important to ensure that they respect the rights of others.' (Covell & Howe, 2001b, p. 310). That this sense of respect was connected to the possibility of self-interest and a growing sense of socially inclusive identity was reflected in student comments such as the following: 'I learned to know when I am being disrespected and disrespectful,' and 'learning about my rights, helped me learn about myself and how to respect myself.'

The indications are that the rights education affected the children's evolving sense of identity and emerging understanding of social concepts. The empathy elicited by discussion and by identification with all children would be expected to have an effect on the child's understanding of social concepts such as justice and rights and to act as a stimulus for the development of rights-respecting attitudes. Wringe (1999) explained how education about social problems impels reflection beyond personal concerns and forces examination of values. Such examination is particularly likely during early to mid-adolescence when one's personal identity is being defined. The comments from the students who participated in the rights education suggest that what was salient to them were general concepts and value orientations. What they learned, then, was more likely incorporated into the self and less readily forgotten than are memorized facts. Berman (1997) summarized the four aspects of principles thinking that emerge in early adolescence and influence the development of identity. First, there is reflection upon abstract concepts such as social justice. Second, democratic tolerance and dialectical thinking are likely to replace the authoritarian attitudes of earlier childhood. Third, a sense of principle develops and allows for the formation of an ideological position. Fourth, there is an ability to move beyond an individualistic orientation and to understand the needs of various other members of the community.

That this process occurred through implementation of the Children's Rights and Global Studies Curriculum is reflected in the students' comments. When asked to describe what they had learned about children's rights, typical answers included the following: 'that I should learn what's going on around me'; 'the hard truth about poverty'; 'that everyone deserves a future'; 'how traumatic it is for kids whose rights are violated'; 'respect and equality are important for everyone'; and 'how to become better citizens and understand each other.' The students, it would seem, had become confident to assert their own rights and to support the rights of others. The relevance to democratic participation is self-evident.

Socially Responsible Behaviours

Consistently noted by teachers in each of the children's rights education assessments were two behavioural outcomes: an increase in cooperative and pro-social behaviours, and a decrease in teasing and bullying. We believe these to be behavioural manifestations of rights-respecting values.

There is significant evidence in the literature that values affect behaviours. As Berman noted 'a sense of self that is defined by values and a sense of connectedness with less fortunate others' (1997, p. 56) is the root of rights-respecting behaviours. The incorporation into the child's evolving sense of identity of self as bearer-of-rights and, therefore, worthy, and of self as sharing rights with peers is likely to impel behaviours that are consistent with that self-schema (Damon & Gregory, 1997). In particular, values that are seen to be essential to the sense of self motivate consistent behaviours because of importance of not violating one's sense of self. Nisan (1996) provided an interesting and cogent explanation of why rights-respecting attitudes about others emerge from rights being part of the child's definition of self. Nisan suggested that identity-based values make individuals more tolerant of diversity because they can understand values as being part of essential identity. When a child discovers that another person has different opinions, experiences, or beliefs, that child is unlikely to reject these without exploring their possible legitimacy. Such a child is willing to consider and accept differences as part of the other person's self. The reportedly more harmonious peer relations and acceptance of those with differences are clearly consistent with Nisan's suggestion. And as demonstrated in the self-initiated projects such as the breakfast program, identity-based motivation is not directed only at avoiding inconsistent behaviours, but also at actively affirming the self through consistent behaviours. Thus, self as bearer and respecter of rights is expressed in attempts both to actively promote the rights of others and to avoid the violation of others' rights.

One of the most pleasing outcomes of the rights education noted by teachers in Belgium and in Canada was the decreased incidence of behaviours that infringe on the rights of others. There have been many concerns about bullying behaviours over the past decade and many attempts to reduce tensions at school through the reduction of teasing and bullying. To consider why children's rights education can reduce interpersonal violence at school, we can consider its nature and causes.

Bullying behaviours comprise verbal aggression such as name-calling, social aggression such as exclusion or shunning, and physical aggression such as hitting (Crick & Grotpeter, 1995; Lagerpetz et al., 1988). The frequency and severity of bullying tends to be high in late childhood and early adolescence, where it is focused on competence, dress, appearance, sexual orientation, and ethnic identity (Lickona, 1991b; Pellegrini, 1998). Bullies and their victims tend to have poor social skills and low self-esteem (O'Moore & Hillery, 1991; Pellegrini, 1998). The bully-victim relationship is maintained because (1) the victim lacks the competence for self-defence, (2) other children typically do not become involved, and (3) the bully finds her or his behaviour reinforcing (Pellegrini, 1998). Rights education can affect bullying in the following ways.

When children value themselves they are more able to command respect and assert their rights (Lickona, 1991b), and the victim's vulnerability should be diminished. When children work together in cooperative learning situations they feel both a sense of belonging to a group and a sense of accountability to the group (Lickona, 1991a). The communication and interdependence that are the essence of cooperative learning provide opportunities for the promotion of self-worth and group membership through a sense of collective responsibility. Such feelings should challenge the bully's characteristic belief that others have hostile intent, and they should counter the apathy of the group to the plight of the victim.

In summary, the data suggest that children's rights education has the potential to impart the knowledge and impel the growth of values and behaviours that are consistent with the principles of democratic citizenship. Rawls (1993) identified the 'political virtues' essential to promote and sustain democracy: a sense of justice or fairness, civility, tolerance, and mutual respect. Children's rights education facilitates the development of these virtues, as well as the sense of empowerment to act on them. As such, we believe children's rights education to be an effective means to citizenship. Children's rights education, as described above, is based on previously identified best practices in education. As Victor Battistich and his colleagues (1999) described in their call for school reform, we have known since Dewey's writings in the early part of the twentieth century that students can acquire the dispositions and skills necessary for participation in democratic societies – if they have experience in collaborative deliberation in democratic classrooms. The need for supportive relationships among students and teachers, students' active participation in the classroom, and discussion of social issues have all been identified as essential components in effective teaching. What makes children's rights education different is that it engages and empowers the child by acknowledging the child's contemporaneous rights and citizenship status. It is this difference that accounts for the contagion effect. Children's rights education influences the child's sense of self.

The importance of children's rights education being included at school is highlighted by findings that its impact is less when experienced later. At the university level, children's rights education increases students' rights-respecting attitudes towards children, but it has no impact on their respect for the rights of ethnic or sexual minorities (Campbell & Covell, 2001). Thus, children's rights education is unlikely to alter the democratic attitudes or citizenship behaviours of young adults. Many years ago Mohandas Ghandi said, 'If we are to have real peace in this world, we shall have to begin with the children.' If we are to promote and sustain democracy, likewise, we shall have to begin by empowering child citizens.

CHAPTER SIX

Confronting the Challenges

It is easier to change the location of a cemetery than to change the school curriculum.

Woodrow Wilson (1856–1924)

Woodrow Wilson's comment certainly reflects the challenges faced in attempting to implement a new curriculum. It also provides an explanation for the lack of real curriculum reform since compulsory education was introduced in the 1800s. Despite all the expressed concerns about educating for citizenship, and despite almost a century of literature in which consensus on best practices is evident, there has been relatively little change in schools. We agree strongly with Allan Collins (1996), who urged that educators address the issue of the potential use for what is taught. Does the material have relevance? Does it empower students for their role as national and global citizens? Does it facilitate the sustaining of democracy? These are some of the key questions that need to be considered. With the exception of the recent inclusion of information technology, schools have tended to teach and test the same subjects. But consider the relative benefits to society of citizens who have memorized formulas or trigonometric functions compared with citizens who understand and value their rights and responsibilities.

In this chapter we identify the major challenges to implementing children's rights-based citizenship education and suggest some means of overcoming them. The challenges that we confront are the persistence of traditional attitudes towards children, teaching difficulties, and the persistence of traditional school practices that together make for an educational environment inhospitable to children's rights and offer symbolic support for – rather than commitment to – the implementation of the U.N. Convention on the Rights of the Child. We conclude by examining the prospects for political will in empowering children with the knowledge that they are rights-bearing and worthy citizens.

Traditional Views of Children

A first challenge for education on children's rights and citizenship is traditional views and beliefs about children. Officially, through signing and ratifying the U.N. Convention on the Rights of the Child, virtually every country in the world recognizes children as bearers of rights and valued citizens. Virtually every country also recognizes the principle that children should be educated in their basic rights and not left in the dark about them. However, unofficially and informally, children's rights education is resisted because of the persistence of traditional attitudes and beliefs about children, which are at odds with the principle of children's rights and children as citizens. As already discussed, the persistence and strength of these views is reflected in many areas including the opposition to the UNICEF student elections on children's rights (discussed in Chapter 1), resistance to the inclusion of children's rights in Britain's new citizenship education program, American resistance to the ratification of the Convention, and general debate over policies and laws involving children. Most noteworthy here is the obstacle that traditional views place on the systematic provision of children's rights education.

A number of traditional views about children share responsibility for holding up children's rights education. We identify and respond to five major ones: children as parental property, children as incapable not-yets, children as innocent creatures in need of protection against politicization, children as unruly creatures unfit for the rights and responsibilities of citizenship, and children's rights as an individualistic and anti-social concept.

First, among some adults and parents is the lingering traditional view of children, which usually is unstated and perhaps unconsciously held, as essentially the property and responsibility of their parents (Archard, 1993; Onheiber, 1997). This view periodically comes to the surface in debates over issues such as the physical punishment of children. This view can be summarized as follows. Although parents do not have absolute authority over their children (as Roman fathers did), they do have a wide and substantial degree of authority. On the one hand, they acknowledge, parents have minimal obligations such as providing their children with the basic necessities of life, sending their children to school, and not abusing or neglecting their children. But on the other hand, beyond these minimal obligations, parents have the basic right to determine how their children will be raised. This includes the right to discipline their children as they see fit and, as part of this, to use physical punishment if they choose to do so. Parents have the fundamental right to a 'protected sphere' in which to raise children and to use discipline, free from regulation by the state in the interests of society or the rights of the child (Howe, 2001). Children are not independent bearers of rights but the dependent offspring, possessions, and responsibilities of their parents. Parents have a natural bond with their offspring and act in their best interests. Children acquire independent rights and the status of citizenship only when they become adults. Thus, citizenship education based on children's rights is to be opposed because children do not have rights independent from their parents and because such education would be an improper intrusion into family life and parent-child relations.

This view deserves sharp criticism and to be exposed for its highly authoritarian and outdated view of parent-child relations. What it tries to do is legitimize the disempowerment and oppression of children, just as the patriarchal view of husband-wife relations tried to legitimize the traditional oppression and exclusion of women from citizenship (Kulynych, 2001). Just as it was wrong to consider wives as the appendages and possessions of their husbands, without rights independent from their husbands and without citizenship, it is wrong to consider children as the appendages and possessions of their parents, without individual rights and without value as independent persons and citizens. And just as it was appropriate to bring women a sense of dignity and social belonging through recognizing them as independent bearers of rights and as valued citizens, it is appropriate to provide children with a sense of value and belonging through recognizing them, too, as rights-bearing citizens. It is no longer acceptable for one person to treat another person as property, whether that person is a husband or slave-owner or parent.

To oppose children's rights in the name of traditional parental rights and authority is no longer a tenable principle, whether the issue is children's rights education or physical punishment. As stated by the U.N. Committee on the Rights of the Child, in reviewing the United Kingdom's first report and its allowance of physical punishment by parents, the view that parents have a fundamental right to use physical punishment on their children or to raise their children as they see fit, is a vestige of the outdated and illegitimate position that children are their parents' chattel or property (U.N. Committee, 1995). Parental authority and parental practices may be justified through reasoned arguments, but not simply on the basis of parenting as a fundamental or natural right and children as possessions of their parents.

Furthermore, whether citizens approve of it or not, the principle of children's rights and children's rights education has been officially embraced by virtually all states of the world and by the international community. In signing and ratifying the U.N. Convention on the Rights of the Child, there is now international consensus that children have fundamental rights and that parents and the state have responsibilities to provide for the rights of the child. To the extent that parents have rights under the Convention, these are not fundamental rights but rights conditional on the fulfilment of their duties to children (Howe, 2001). The countries did not ratify a U.N. Convention on the Rights of Parents. Rather, in recognition of children as a special vulnerable group in society, they ratified a children's rights convention in which parents have a primary responsibility – not a right – to provide for the best interests of the child (article 18). Contrary to the statements of family values critics, the Convention is a document that is highly supportive of strong families and family values (Melton, 1996). In the preamble of the Convention, the family is referred to as a 'fundamental group of society and the natural environment for the growth and well-being of all its members and particularly children.' Parents are assigned the duty of guiding children in the exercise of their rights (article 5) and providing for their best interests (article 18). The state is given the responsibility of supporting families and of assisting parents or guardians in such areas as child care or day care (article 18), care for children with disabilities (article 23), child health care (article 24), and nutrition, clothing, and shelter (article 27). The Convention assumes that parents and a family environment are so important to the child that the state has the obligation to provide the family with support when this is necessary. Thus, far from being an anti-family document, the Convention is very much pro-family.

A second traditional view of children is that, although not the property of their parents, children are immature and vulnerable not-yets – people not yet in a position to exercise rights and responsibilities and to participate as citizens in the decision-making of their political community (Verhellen, 1999). This view can be summarized as follows: Children are not yet in a position to exercise rights or to be responsible citizens because they do not have the capacities and competence to make informed and rational decisions, they lack the necessary experience to make reasoned and mature judgments, and they have insufficient control over themselves and their emotions but look to their immediate and not their longer-term interests (Purdy, 1992). Short on maturity, cognitive development, and the capacity for self-control, not-yets need to be protected and nurtured, and they should not be given the rights and responsibilities of citizenship. It is in the best interests of children to have their needs and their interests taken care of by adults and to be protected from harm. It is not in their best interests and not in the best interests of society that they be given rights, particularly the participation rights of citizenship. Without experience and capability, not-yets would exercise their rights unwisely and irresponsibly to the detriment of themselves and society. Children, being not-yets, need to have their rights and freedoms limited, and they need to be under the control of their parents and adult authorities so that they have the time and opportunities to develop their capacities, gain experience, and acquire self-control so that they are prepared for the rights and responsibilities of citizenship. Thus, because children's rights is a faulty concept, children's rights-based citizenship education is a faulty concept.

This view needs to be challenged and exposed for its undue paternalism. It is essentially a protectionist view of children in which children are to be excluded from citizenship in a manner similar to the old patriarchal view of society in which women were paternalistically excluded from citizenship (Kulynych, 2001). Just as it was historically argued that women should be denied citizenship rights for their own good – that they would not have the additional burdens of citizenship placed on them – it is argued that it is beneficial for not-yets to not have to assume the rights and responsibilities of citizenship. And just as it was argued that the interests of women would be well provided for by their husbands, it is argued that the interests of children are best protected by parents and adult authorities. As was the case with women, rights are both unnecessary and contrary to the best interests of children. Certainly, the situations of women and of children are quite different. Nevertheless, the paternalistic assumptions are faulty in both cases. Just as husband-wife relations were idealized, so too are child-parent relations. The caseloads of child protection agencies are just one reflection of this reality. While parents generally do work to protect the interests of their children, this cannot always be assumed. Children cannot depend alone on the paternalism of their parents to protect their interests. They require protection in the form of having rights. Rights do not have as a pre-condition the elements of self-control and the capacity for rational decision-making. Rather, like adults, children have basic human rights because they are human beings, and they have the rights of citizenship because they are valued members of a political community.

Furthermore, whether citizens approve of it or not, the participation rights of the child citizen have been widely endorsed by the international community. The U.N. Convention on the Rights of the Child does not see citizenship as an all-or-nothing concept, and it does not rule out children as participating citizens simply because they do not have a full capability for exercising rights and responsibilities in a rational and mature manner. Rather, in reference to the principle of 'evolving capacities,' the Convention recognizes that children are worthy citizens who have a right to be heard and to be listened to, in relation to their age and level of maturity (Flekkoy & Kaufman, 1997). On the one hand, the child citizen does not have a right to complete autonomy or self-determination. There is room for guidance by parents and adult authorities and, indeed, such guidance is a responsibility. But, on the other hand, the child's participation cannot be blocked in the name of paternalism. Child citizens do have the right to age-appropriate participation in matters that affect them. This is consistent with good child-rearing practices and with the learning and experience required for democracy (Flekkoy & Kaufman, 1997). People do not become autonomous and capable persons overnight, and they do not become responsible democratic citizens overnight. The exercise of rights and responsibilities and the practice of democratic citizenship are learned in steps from childhood to adulthood. In the earlier stages of development, there is a great deal of adult protection and guidance, but this guidance gradually gives way to increasing participation and independence in the later stages. In short, as officially recognized through worldwide ratification of the Convention, children have basic rights, including the basic rights of citizenship. And by ratifying the Convention, a country has the obligation to implement not only children's rights but also children's rights education.

A third traditional view, associated with the second, is that children should be protected from politicization (Kulynych, 2001). This view can be summarized as follows: Granting rights to children, recognizing children as citizens, and implementing programs of children's rights education should be avoided because these would bring children prematurely and unwisely into the realm of politics and partisan political activity. According to Hannah Arendt (1961), for example, the politicization of children should be avoided because children should remain part of the private realm of society, both for their own good and the good of soci-

ety. Childhood, argued Arendt, is a time of preparation and conceal-
ment, where children should be able to develop free from the stresses
and burdens of adult life. Children are vulnerable and fragile beings
who must be hidden from the public realm and protected from the
world of politics in order to develop and mature, undisturbed, into
adults capable of genuine and responsible political action. Exposing
children to the realm of politics and indoctrinating them with political
ideas and ideologies disturbs and impairs their development, making
them less capable of being independent, thoughtful, and responsible
adult citizens. Such exposure, Arendt contended, is also harmful to society. It undermines the influence of parents and adult authorities in the
private realm and increases the influence of political educators and
childhood peers. If children are recognized as citizens with rights of participation, they will have no clear authority figures and thus will be more
heavily influenced by their peers. Pressured by peers and political cor-
rectness, children will conform to accepted standards and beliefs,
becoming incapable of independent judgment and responsible action.
The development of a free and democratic society is sure to suffer.

A serious problem with this view is that it ignores the political character
of child development, regardless of whether children are recognized as
citizens and bearers of rights. In the so-called private realm of the family,
some children learn democracy and others learn authoritarianism. Families are not politically neutral. Through authoritative or democratic
parenting styles, parents teach democratic values and practices consistent
with democratic citizenship; through authoritarian styles, they teach
authoritarian values and practices less consistent with such citizenship
(Covell & Howe, 2001a). Similarly, schools are not politically neutral
institutions. Through school practices and structures, through both formal and hidden curricula, schools teach political attitudes and values,
with a greater or lesser degree of effectiveness. And through democratic
teaching styles, some teachers educate children in self-direction, critical
thinking, and independent judgment, supportive of participatory democracy and democratic citizenship, while through authoritarian styles,
other teachers educate children in discipline, obedience, and rote learning, less consistent with the practice of democratic citizenship (Covell &
Howe, 2001a). The point is that in families and schools, as well as through
the media and peer groups, children are exposed to the political realm.
The task is not to direct them away from such exposure – which is not possible anyway – but to expose them in a way that is consistent with the
development of a democratic and human rights-respecting society. Chil-

dren's rights-based citizenship education is an important means of doing this.

Moreover, it must be kept in mind that the U.N. Convention on the Rights of the Child was brought forward and ratified by governments, governing parties, and politicians representing a wide diversity of political views across the political spectrum. It was not and is not a partisan document. Rather, it is an expression of worldwide and official agreement on the fundamental importance of the rights of the child, which cuts across differing political perspectives. Thus, it is inaccurate to say that a program of children's rights education in schools is driven by a partisan political agenda and that such a program involves children in improper partisan political learning and activity. It is more accurate to characterize children's rights education as based on widely endorsed political values that place human rights and democracy above partisan politics and to describe the involvement of children as learning and activity in pursuit of these important values.

A fourth traditional view of children is their general tendency to be unruly, disruptive, and disorderly (Kulynych, 2001). This view can be summarized as follows: Granting children the rights of citizenship and making them aware of their rights would serve only to encourage or reinforce this tendency. Historically, children's unruly characteristics were held in check through social norms in which parents and teachers were expected to discipline and control children and through laws and practices in which police and adult authorities were directed to ensure youth compliance with the law and to keep public order. However, in recent decades, with such factors as the decline of the traditional family unit, the liberalization of society, and the influence of the mass media, the unruly impulses of children and youth have been less held in check, with a resulting increase in disorderly behaviour, youth rebelliousness, youth gangs, and youth crime. Given these trends, an emphasis on children's rights is ill-advised. Programs of children's rights education and a resulting culture of rights would only lead to further youth defiance, disorder, and social unrest (Lansdown, 1995a; Lawson, 2001). Children and youth would be encouraged to become even more unruly, demanding, and self-centred, leading to the further growth of a culture of entitlement in which citizens focus more on their personal rights than on their social obligations. In the interests of a more orderly society and more responsible social behaviour, what should be emphasized in schools and in programs of citizenship education are not the rights of children but their duties and social responsibilities.

There are several problems with this view. First, it is not clear that the apparent unruliness of children, youth rebelliousness, and youth crime are any more serious now than in the past or any more serious than adult disorderly behaviour and adult crime (Kulynych, 2001). The recent media focus on school shootings and other incidents of youth violence in North America and Europe suggests that there has been a rising tide of youth crime and disorderliness. However, such a tide is not evident in youth crime statistics. Indeed, what the evidence indicates is that youth crime has been decreasing in recent years (Bala, Hornick, Snyder, & Paetsch, 2002). The belief in rising unruliness is based on unreliable information about trends in youth behaviour and on unhelpful stereotypes of youth. Like adults, some youth do have problems from time to time, which may lead to disorderly behaviour. And like members of previous generations, some youth experiment with non-conformist lifestyles, which may appear as 'unruly.' But most of the time, like adults, the majority of youth are law-abiding citizens who do not like to be negatively stereotyped.

Second, it does not follow that the apparently unruly impulses of youth would be increased through education on rights. It obviously is true that some children and youth do become distressed and angry and do engage in varying degrees of disorderly or rebellious behaviour for a variety of reasons, including the effects of divorce or maltreatment by parents. It does not follow that knowledge of rights would reinforce or encourage such behaviour. For seriously troubled young people with psychological and social problems, information about the rights of the child may be beside the point. What they require are measures to deal with their problems such as counselling or therapy. But for youth in general, knowledge about rights is a recipe not for demanding and irresponsible behaviour but for social responsibility. As discussed in Chapter 5, children and youth who learn about their own rights – in a systematic and comprehensive way based on the U.N. Convention on the Rights of the Child – are learning about the rights of others, about limitations on freedom, and about corresponding responsibilities that go along with rights. In learning about the rights of the child, children are developing a sense of value about themselves and about others. They are learning to respect themselves and others and to respect the rights of others. Respecting the rights of others and having empathy for others is a basis for the development of a sense of social responsibility. Thus, contrary to the view of rights bringing forth unruly and irresponsible behaviour that is at odds with good citizenship, there is good reason to believe that children's rights education is a positive vehicle for democratic citizenship.

Finally, a fifth traditional view of children, most often held in societies and communities with collectivist traditions and values, is that the principle of children's rights is to be opposed because of its basis in Western values and its individualistic anti-social conception. For example, in non-Western countries such as Vietnam, although government authorities did sign and ratify the Convention, there is opposition to children's rights on the grounds of the traditional view of children as members of families rather than as individuals (Burr, 2002). According to this view, the Convention is largely a Western-inspired document, centring on the individual rights of the child that does not fit with Vietnamese values, which prize the well-being of the collectivity and traditional institutions such as the family. It is contrary to Vietnamese tradition to see children as separate from families and to see children's rights as separate from parental rights. Similarly, in communities within Western societies that have long-standing collectivist traditions, there is resistance to the Convention and to the concept of children's rights. For example, among aboriginal communities in Canada and New Zealand, there is the view that the concept of children's rights is alien to collectivist aboriginal traditions, and its acceptance is undesirable because it would pit children against their parents and their elders. Thus, children's rights education is to be opposed because the principle of children's rights is inappropriate to communities and societies with collectivist traditions.

In response to this view, it is important to emphasize that the Convention is a piece of international law that values children *both* as individuals and as members of groups and that values families and different cultural traditions. It is true that the Convention does value children as individuals with rights separate from their parents and their society. This is in keeping with experience that shows that not all parents and not all societies act in the best interests of children. Law is a necessary and positive means of protecting individual children against adults who may do them harm. But it is true also, as previously discussed, that the Convention values children as members of groups, including aboriginal communities and communities with collectivist traditions. Under the Convention, children have the group-differentiated right to enjoy their own culture, religion, and language. And it is also true that the Convention not only recognizes the importance of the family as a natural and primary institution to care for the child, but also promotes the family through the requirement of state support for the family. The Convention is neither Western nor non-Western and neither individualistic nor communitarian. The U.N. Convention on the Rights of the Child is based on a worldwide official consensus that children have protection, provision, and participation rights, and individual and group rights, that warrant recognition and implementation. It also is based on an official consensus that children are to understand that they have basic rights.

Teaching Difficulties

A second major challenge for children's rights education is seen in three areas of teaching-related difficulties: teacher attitudes, teacher stress, and teacher training. There are, of course, many outstanding teachers who themselves have argued for the inclusion of children's rights education and who make every effort to respect children's rights in their teaching. Some of these teachers have helped with the development and testing of children's rights-based citizenship curricula. Nonetheless, the data indicate that many teachers oppose the inclusion of children's rights, have rather negative conceptions of children, experience stress, and lack adequate training in the essential content and pedagogy for citizenship education.

The attitudes of teachers towards their students may present an obstacle to the implementation of children's rights education. Like adults in the general population, many teachers believe that children are unable to competently exercise rights. The resistance or ambivalence about teaching children's rights, or allowing their practise in the classroom, most often comes from fears concerning loss of authority (e.g., Alderson, 1999; Torney-Purta, Schwille, & Amadeo, 1999). Some teachers are concerned that if children are made aware that they have rights, there will be rebellion and chaos in the classroom. In Australia, when a rights information kit was distributed to students, it was met with derision, resistance, and teachers' comments such as, 'the Kit could lead to United States–style schools where weapons and drugs are common and the enforcing of school rules may turn into a lawyer's picnic' (Ludbrook, 1996, p. 93). Other teachers are less concerned with potential anarchy, but want to maintain their dominance in the classroom. As Kathy Bickmore of the Ontario Institute for Studies in Education has noted, educators, like other adults, are not often disposed to sharing their power with children (1999). Misunderstanding the nature of children's rights, or perhaps the nature of childhood, many teachers have expressed a strong belief that their students need to be taught about responsibilities and that the teaching of rights is antithetical to what is needed (e.g., Covell & Howe, 2000).

Negative conceptions of children may be at the root of many of the expressed concerns about informing children that they have rights.

Many child psychologists, educators, and child advocates have written on the difficulties of raising children in contemporary society and the particular difficulties faced by children at this time. Sheldon Berman, superintendent of schools in Hudson, Massachusetts, is one such example. He has written extensively on the need to focus education on raising social consciousness and social responsibility (Berman, 1997) and has highlighted the challenging social environment for children. Children experience poverty, the increasing acceptance of violence, a societal emphasis on the self, a sense of disenchantment with government, growing alienation, and so forth (Berreth & Berman, 1997). James Garbarino, child psychologist, also has written extensively about what he calls the 'socially toxic' environment in which children develop – an environment characterized by violence, inadequate parenting, and inadequate social policies and supports for families and children (Garbarino, 1995). Do teachers share these beliefs and how might they be influencing teachers' perceptions of children?

It can be very difficult to obtain accurate information on teacher perceptions of children. As with any target group, concerns with social desirability can influence teachers' responses to opinion-based questions. One rather cleverly designed study overcame this difficulty by interviewing teachers in small groups over dinner in restaurants and with wine available (Hartsell & Ricker, 2002). Forty-six teachers of Kindergarten through Grade 12 from six different American states representing private, religious, and public schools took part. Dinner discussions were teachers' responses to the question of what changes they had seen in their students over the past decade. They were asked to comment on four aspects of children: their intellectual, physical, academic, and social characteristics. The discussions indicated consensus among teachers of all age groups of students and from the whole variety of school contexts that children had deteriorated in all aspects over the past few years. With regard to the intellectual domain, children were perceived as having shorter attention spans, a greater inability or unwillingness to do research projects, and a preoccupation with video games. Overall, children were described as easily bored and not motivated to learn. The academic domain was described similarly. Children now, these teachers said, had a greater tendency to plagiarize, lack effort, have a less mature vocabulary, and are more unwilling to do homework; again, teachers commented on children's short attention spans. The comments concerning the social domain were clearly consistent with the writings of James Garbarino and Sheldon Berman (as described above). The children were perceived as showing less empathy, more anger, and more stress than their earlier cohorts. The children's physical status also had deteriorated, according to these teachers. Children were more tired and less healthy and made poor food choices; again, it was emphasized that children were addicted to video games. The authors of the study reported that in the physical health category there was one positive change noted. Unfortunately, it was the only one, and it was from one educator at one school, in an upper-income suburb. At this school, students were perceived to show a preference for healthy foods and to have increased athletic participation. With that one exception, all else was negative. In fact, the teachers added two categories of new problems to the four areas the researchers had asked them to discuss. First, parents were generally portrayed as on a continuum with incompetence at one end and dysfunctionality at the other. Second, school administrators were described as unsupportive with a tendency to engage in harassment. Whereas we must be cautious generalizing from one study, the design suggests its validity, and the data are consistent with considerable anecdotal information, with our own experiences in Canada, and with a recent analysis from Russia of children's rights to education.

Throughout the 1990s Russian schools were in a state of transition from an ideology of duty to an ideology of rights (Lebedev, Maiorov, & Zolotukhina, 2002). Now, in Russia, schooling is no longer seen as a state-conferred privilege but as the child's right. With that in mind, Oleg Lebedev and his colleagues undertook an analysis of the extent to which the change in ideology has affected practice. Included in their findings was that teachers frequently infringed on the rights of children. Students said that it was rare to have a teacher who is fair and respectful. More than two-thirds of administrators reported that they had received complaints from parents about teachers' belittling students and or unfairly assessing students' work. A surprising 13 per cent also reported that administrative measures had been taken against teachers for committing physical violence against their students. Although few data were collected about teachers' beliefs about students, we might assume that some negative attitudes underlie the teachers' negative behaviours to children. Moreover, when the researchers asked the teachers why they thought students fail, around half replied that students simply are not interested in learning. It may be that Russian teachers have not yet adapted to the new ideology. Or perhaps like their North American counterparts, they tend to have negative conceptions of children.

It may be that the current cohort of school students is unprepared for school and difficult. We have no systematic data that make the necessary comparisons. We do know that the impact of teachers' negative perceptions likely will be reflected in behaviours such as those reported in the Russian study. Teachers respond to their students in ways that are consistent with their perceptions of their students (McLoyd, 1998). Resistance to the appreciation of children as rights-bearing citizens and the teaching of children's rights may at least, in part, be a function of the negative attitudes teachers appear to hold about their students. It may also be related to teachers' frequently reported sense of role-overload and related stress. In fact, both negative attitudes towards students and resistance to implementing new curricula may be related to stress (Evers, Brouwers, & Tomic, 2002).

Significant evidence has been obtained over the past decade to suggest that teaching is one of the most stressful of professions. Not only are teachers generally more stressed than is the general population, their levels of stress are higher than are those of people who work in other client-related professions including nurses and doctors (Travers & Cooper, 1993). Workload appears to be a major factor. In a comparative study of workers in the Netherlands, teachers reported higher levels of workload-related stress than did civil servants, commercial workers, caregivers, or industrial workers. In Canada, teachers have expressed many concerns about increasing workload because of new responsibilities, larger classes, fewer resources, and loss of support personnel (Covell & Howe, 1999). Canadian teachers are left exhausted by cutbacks to funding, new curricula, new assessment protocols, and many policy changes (Majhanovich, 2002). Feelings of exhaustion also are commonly reported among teachers in the United States (e.g., Friedman, 1996). Statistics from the Netherlands indicate that almost half of the total number of persons considered disabled for work are teachers, many of whom are suffering burnout (Evers et al., 2002). And in the survey of teachers in Russia, 13 to 20 per cent (varying by region) reported wishing to leave the profession, complaining of excessive general paper work, documentation, and record-keeping (Lebedev et al., 2002).

A number of global trends in education have been identified that are likely to increase teacher stress regardless of actual workload. Mark Priestly (2002) summarized them as follows: (1) Education has become framed in economic terms and marketized. (2) Education increasingly is criticized. (3) There are many demands for improvement in education without the needed resources. (4) Promotion of educational change has been through changed governance. (5) There is an ever-increasing emphasis on standards, accountability, and testing. What is missing in these global trends is teacher involvement, teacher supports, and fundamental respect for the role of the teacher. The changes are understood by teachers to indicate the inadequacy of the existing system and their failure in the classroom (Majhanovich, 2002). The rigidity of new programs, the lack of teacher involvement in their development, and the increased emphasis on testing rather than educating the child, leave teachers feeling that their expertise and professionalism has been questioned and found wanting (Hancock & Mansfield, 2002; Majhanovich, 2002). Teachers need to be involved in the development of educational changes, and teachers need to feel respected (Leat & Higgins, 2002; Richardson, 1988). The general failure to recognize the teacher must be considered a significant source of stress.

The changes in education themselves have also tended to increase the daily stress on teachers. One difficulty is that many new curricula encourage highly ritualized and hierarchical teacher-student relationships (Hancock & Mansfield, 2002). Another is the constant tension from attempting to use rigid curricula and ensure that standards are met, while also attending to the increasingly wide variety of needs and learning styles of the individual children in the class (Katz, Earl, & Olson, 2001). In essence, teachers are feeling under siege. Teachers are overwhelmed with demands and believe that their professionalism has been under attack and their ability questioned. The resultant level of stress increases the likelihood that they will perceive their students negatively and increases the likelihood that they will experience failure in the classroom (Evers et al., 2002).

What often happens in such circumstances is the questioning of one's ability to continue to function effectively, one's sense of self-efficacy. Will Evers and his colleagues assessed the relation among burnout, sense of self-efficacy, and willingness to try new classroom practices with 490 teachers in the Netherlands. Their data underscore the importance of beliefs about self-efficacy. Teachers' sense of self-efficacy was related to their burnout level as well as their willingness to work with new educational practices. It may well be that difficulties in feeling efficacious with their students are the root cause of much teacher stress. If we are to expect teachers to shoulder the responsibility of promoting citizenship values and behaviours in children, steps need to be taken to increase teachers' sense of self-efficacy and professionalism. One obvious means to this end is to ensure the involvement of teachers in any changes to educational programming and policy, to explicitly recognize the importance of what teachers believe, and how they think, plan, and respond to classroom experiences (Leat & Higgins, 2002). It is arguably even more important to maximize the likelihood of teachers experiencing success in the classroom by ensuring that practices are consistent with those known to be effective for improving classroom climate and student success and by ensuring appropriate and adequate training for teachers. As described in the previous chapter, the essential characteristics of the ideal classroom, and the classroom required for rights-based citizenship education, have been identified as democratic leadership, cooperative learning, and discussion of controversial social issues. Does teacher training prepare teachers for this?

The overwhelming evidence throughout the education literature is that teachers are poorly prepared to teach in other than traditional ways. Changes in the goals of education, in curricula, and in education policy have not been accompanied by changes in training of new teachers nor in professional development of experienced teachers (e.g., Torney-Purta, Schwille, & Amadeo, 1999). Nowhere is this more apparent than in rights-based citizenship education. Teachers lack the knowledge of children's rights and citizenship status, and they lack training in the pedagogy required. Teachers need training that provides the basic knowledge of children's rights and that also convinces them of the importance of rights education (Best, 1991). Essentially, teachers need to be trained in the value and methods of democratic leadership, cooperative learning, and discussion of controversial issues.

Fundamental to democratic teaching is the ability of teachers to listen to their students. Building on Dewey's (1933) concept of reflection, Carol Rodgers (2002) emphasized the importance of teachers developing their capacity to think critically about what and how their students are learning. Part of this requires that teachers respect the participation rights of their students. Teachers should solicit, take into account, and value student feedback as critical to their understanding of students' learning. Teachers must create conditions that 'reveal learning rather than just answers' (2002, p. 233). This is an evaluation practice that is quite different from the usual testing procedures. It involves engaging students in dialogue and requires using students' comments to guide future teaching and students' further learning. Rudduck and Flutter (2000) highlighted the need for teachers to be trained to listen to their students, help students express their learning needs, and respect the participation rights of the child. Fullan asked, 'What would happen if we treated the student as someone whose opinion mattered?' (1991, p. 70).

We would have a democratic classroom that modelled and respected children's citizenship rights.

Not having been taught the importance of children's voices and agency in their own learning is reflected also in the difficulty many teachers have expressed in allowing their students to engage in non-traditional learning activities such as role-play or drama. Innovative history teacher Ian Luff (2000), for example, found that many teachers are sceptical about the value of role-play or drama and dismissive of such activities which they see as a waste of time, fun, or a break from real teaching. We experienced similar reactions from teachers when pilot-testing our children's rights education activities. While teachers readily acknowledged that their students enjoyed the role-play activities, they also expressed reservations about their use and commented that students enjoyed 'the greater opportunity to socialize.' It would appear important for teachers to be taught not only the benefits of role-taking, but also of student engagement in and enjoyment of classroom activities. Effective teaching strategies such as role-play should not be dismissed because the students have fun with them. It is time for teachers to be taught how to guide student learning and to move away from factory models of teaching with their emphasis on information in, testing and grades out (Rudduck & Flutter, 2000).

Teachers lack training in cooperative learning. The effectiveness of cooperative learning has been well established (e.g., Slavin, 1995), yet its techniques are not often part of teacher training. In the absence of adequate training, cooperative learning often fails and, like role-play, becomes dismissed as a waste of time. In their study of teachers' use and evaluation of cooperative learning in Dutch classrooms, Simon Veenman and his colleagues (2000) identified the issues. Cooperative learning involves a lot more than simply placing students in small groups. For cooperative learning to be effective, it is imperative that teachers understand the nature of cooperation and the essential components of a cooperative activity. Five essential components of cooperative learning can be summarized as follows. (1) The success of the group should be dependent on the contribution and success of each member thereof. (2) Individual group members should be accountable to the group. (3) The size of the group should be small enough to allow meaningful face-to-face interaction. (4) As necessary, social skills training should be provided to facilitate group collaboration. (5) Time should be allowed for group members to discuss their progress and working relationships. When teachers have not been trained in how to organize and facilitate effective groups, there can be individualistic learning or competition within a group, or there can be some students who do the work for the entire group. Teachers need to be taught how to design and supervise cooperative learning so that these problems do not occur, and teachers need to be taught the benefits of cooperative learning over whole-class competitive approaches. An excellent short summary of the benefits and best practices in cooperative learning is provided by Mary Hamm and Dennis Adams (2002). This summary could readily be used as the core for teaching.

The discussion of controversial social issues is an essential component of rights-based citizenship education. It is also an area in which teachers lack pedagogical confidence (Hess, 2002). The discussion of controversial social issues promotes democratic understanding and values, critical thinking skills, acceptance of diversity, and support for equality. Recognizing the importance of social issues discussion in citizenship education, French educators have suggested that teacher training should include the development of skills to facilitate such discussion (Sutherland, 2002). Studies of teacher responses to the concept of discussing controversial issues suggest that training should include dealing with affect-laden issues and increasing tolerance for ambiguity as well as basic facilitator skills. Teachers, generally, have difficulty with classroom discussion of sensitive or affect-laden issues. This was particularly evident in the examination of Holocaust education by Brown and Davies (1998). Teachers reported significant discomfort discussing the issues and worrying about the possibility of students becoming emotional. In Hungary, one difficulty faced in citizenship education has been teachers' avoidance of sensitive or problem-oriented issues such as diversity, ethnicity, poverty, and prejudice (Zsuzsa, 1999). Similarly, in Canada there is a gap between official policy, which advocates citizenship education that promotes active involvement in classroom discussion, and public action and actual practice, in which teachers' reluctance to allow student discussion of controversial issues is seen in their avoidance of classroom debate and dependence on rote-learning (Sears & Hughes, 1996). And in Britain, a surprising 96 per cent of teachers report being uncomfortable with teaching some aspects of citizenship education (Arnot et al., 1996). The observed discomfort of teachers may, in part, be attributed to the inherent nature of discussing controversial issues. Unlike with the majority of their teaching, controversial issues discussion has no 'right answer.' That is, of course, its value. But it requires a tolerance of ambiguity that is antithetical to the norm of teaching facts.

Observing how rarely controversial issues discussion is implemented in practice, Diana Hess (2002) identified the common behaviours of those few teachers who successfully used it. First, they teach *for* rather than *with* discussion. The emphasis is on how to participate in discussion, rather than on the topic under discussion. Second, the discussions are the students' fora. Teachers avoid expressing their opinions, and they do not decide the discussion guidelines. Teachers facilitate. Third, students' participation in discussion is formally assessed. The assessment reinforces the message that it is the participation that is important. Finally, successful teachers have administrative support. These characteristics of successful controversial issues discussion can inform the design of teacher training. It is important also that teachers are provided ongoing support when they implement newly learned practices; this may be especially important after professional development training, when teachers must learn to change their existing practices and sometimes beliefs about teaching (Veenman, Kenter, & Post, 2000). Four approaches to skill development are relevant here: peer coaching, collaborative teaching, feedback from students and parents, and videotaping self in the classroom (McQueen, 2001).

It seems obvious that successful use of social issues discussion and cooperative learning would do much to increase teachers' sense of self-efficacy and, thereby, reduce their stress levels. Once implemented, these teaching techniques are likely to become self-reinforcing. Students are more engaged, and learning outcomes are more readily met. As in the contagion model (described in the previous chapter), a more positive classroom environment would be expected to develop with all its attendant benefits to teachers and students. Adequate teacher training is one precondition for this; the other is the support of school administrators.

Traditional Schooling

A third challenge for education on children's rights and citizenship is the problem of traditional school practices. We must be clear at the outset that this problem is not reducible to one of inadequate funding for education. There is no question that inadequate funding often is a problem. In the developing world, for example, it is commonly noted that inadequate portions of government expenditures are allocated to education (LeBlanc, 1995). In the developed world, although to a much lesser extent, there are problems of funding cuts and financial restraint on education budgets. However, funding cuts also have been wrongly used to explain – if not excuse – the shortcomings of schools in the wealthier nations (see Majhanovich, 2002; Ruxton, 1996). Clearly, if funding cuts mean a lack of resources for students or a lack of assistance for children with special needs then there are serious funding shortages that must be overcome. However, it is important to not assume that the injection of money into any education system will in itself overcome shortcomings. A case in point is the experience of the state of Georgia in the United States, where between 1993 and 2003 spending on education increased by 116 per cent. There has been no measurable impact on student outcomes. Rather, issues of policy and accountability have been identified as underlying the difficulties experienced by students.

Some concerns have been expressed about the expectation that schools should solve social problems or promote democratic citizenship (Torney-Purta et al., 1999). Nonetheless, the efforts of education officials to include citizenship education in its variety of manifestations suggest that, for the most part, schools have accepted this responsibility. To date, however, the fundamental changes needed for effective citizenship education have not been made. Rather, we witness a 'flavour-of-the-month' approach. As social problems become more or less salient, programs to cope with them appear and disappear. For example, there are anti-bullying, anti-racist, anti-gambling, drug prevention weeks, and so forth. As concerns with school violence have risen so have zero-tolerance responses. But these are little more than attempts at quick fixes. There has been no serious restructuring of school programs, policies, procedures, or pedagogy. A gap remains between educational knowledge and practice. A gap remains between the promise and reality of children's rights in and through education. Closing these gaps would be of much benefit to the citizen child and thereby to the promotion and maintenance of democratic societies.

Many schools continue to function in ways that violate children's rights and are antithetical to promoting democratic citizenship values and behaviours. In fact, schools do not simply pose a challenge to the implementation of rights-based citizenship education; sometimes they are themselves an obstacle to learning. Back in 1964, John Holt argued that it is most adaptive in schools for students not to attempt to understand or think. Little has changed. In fact, critics have drawn comparisons between military ideology and schools – there are three ways to do everything: the right way, the wrong way, and the army (school) way. If you do what you are told without question, you will do well (Scardamalia & Bereiter, 1996). Like the military, schools are designed with an emphasis on conformity, respect, and obedience (Ludbrook, 1996). Scardamalia and Bereiter (1996) described school practices that are anathema to learning. One is product orientation. Rather than being challenged to critically examine their beliefs or attempt to gain understanding of an issue, students are given very specific – and endless – tasks to be completed within some specified time. The task, for example, may be writing a three-page paper using four sources or completing three pages in a workbook; to encourage students towards completion of the task, students who quickly finish their task are often rewarded with some free time during which they may choose to read a book, play on a computer, or day-dream. A second obstacle to learning is the lack of opportunity provided for reflection. As well as encouraging the speedy completion of written tasks, typically teachers want responses to verbal questions quickly. Students who do not take time to think are favoured, and reflective strategies become increasingly non-adaptive. A third obstacle is the emphasis on rote-learning and memorization. Texts are full of facts to be memorized, and blackboards are full of notes to be copied. Recall is valued over understanding, and reproduction is valued over interpretation. But, as Allan Collins (1996) pointed out, a focus on memorization does not teach students how to apply knowledge; it is unmotivating and rarely useful. The approach is also one in which there is no teaching of the broad picture, only components. It is like teaching children the serve, forehand and backhand, for tennis without letting them know that there is a game. It is, of course, also like teaching specific components of citizenship, without letting students know that they are citizens with concomitant rights and responsibilities.

The emphases on speedy completion of tasks and rote-learning reflect the overarching value on performance, testing, and the achievement of certain standards within certain time frames (Grundy, 2002; Henry, 1991; Katz, Earl, & Olson, 2001; Majhanovich, 2002; Rudduck & Flutter, 2000). Strong critic of testing, Alfie Kohn aptly described the current emphasis on standards and testing as 'these dark days of test-driven instruction' (2003, p. 108). Competence continues to be understood as possession of facts, and the focus on testing and grades continues to overshadow the importance of content and learning. Schools need to allow time and patience for learning to occur; they must stop being 'factories of learning where tailored knowledge is conveyed' (Rathenow & Weber, 1998, p. 97). The sense of urgency to impart information may well stem from school curricula guidelines for achievement. Nevertheless, its negative impact on the classroom is unquestionable. Teachers feel they must teach for testing rather than learning. In our current pilot-testing of the Grade 12 rights-based citizenship curriculum, we received the following comment from one of the teachers that was reflective of the attitudes of many, 'My biggest problem is *time*. The discovery approach and cooperative learning are sound methods of putting concepts across to students, but the results take too much time to achieve.' In their current form, schools do not allow students time to learn. The current emphases certainly do not allow students agency through participation in their own learning. There is a real need for schools to shift to a pedagogical norm, based on cooperative learning and critical reflection, that is more likely to engage students and result in real learning and that is consistent with the U.N. Convention on the Rights of the Child and the goals of citizenship education. Article 29 of the Convention requires that education be 'directed to the development of the child's personality, talents and mental and physical abilities to their fullest potential.' An emphasis on testing may be more likely to meet government objectives rather than the child's development.

School policies and procedures are generally inconsistent with the Convention and with the aims of citizenship education. There are, of course, exceptions from which we can learn. In Sweden, for example, it is widely accepted that one task of the school is to actively encourage children to value democracy. To achieve this, students are allowed meaningful participation in the development of policy and management in schools (Ruxton, 1996). In Austria, the details of student participation in schools are in legislation (Kisser, 1996). However, in most European and North American schools, there is little respect for children's participation or other Convention rights. In the U.K. and Italy for example, there is little attention to minority languages or freedom of religion. In France, it is illegal for students to wear religious symbols such as Muslim headcovers (Ruxton, 1996). Schools in Northern Ireland not only prescribe school uniform, but also stipulate acceptable styles of shoes and bags (Walmsley, 2001). Similar violations of children's Convention rights are observed in Australian schools where, like schools in most of the industrialized world, participation opportunities diminish rather than increase with the age of the student (Lewis, 1999). Schools regularly ban political expression in the form of lapel pins, stickers, and T-shirts, and it is generally believed that schools should impose dress codes and uniforms as part of discipline (Ludbrook, 1996).

Sitch and McCoubrey (2001) described an appalling litany of rights violations in Canadian schools. These include the denial of rights information and drug and other searches that are in violatation of privacy rights. The following is an example illustrating the extent to which children's basic human and citizenship rights are violated in Canadian schools. In December 1998, twenty high school students from the province of Ontario were required to submit to a strip search after some money was reported missing. The students were actually required to remove their clothing (including their underwear) in front of their peers and teacher. This was a highly intrusive and disturbing violation of these students' right to privacy and their right to be treated with dignity. It simply would not have happened with adults. And yes, it turned out that the money had been lost, not stolen. Other cases have involved disciplinary action taken against a student who sang a banned song (*Let's Talk about Sex*) while off school property during a lunch hour and a refusal to allow a homosexual student to take his partner to his high school graduation party.

It is not unusual for school discipline to violate children's rights. Again, we can learn from Austria, where what is acceptable is specified: corporal punishment, collective punishments, and insulting remarks are officially banned (Kisser, 1996). Nonetheless, we must be cautious in assuming that they never occur. The situation in Alexandria, Egypt, is informative. Corporal punishment was officially banned in Egyptian schools in 1971. Nonetheless, in a survey of schools in 1998, extensive use of corporal punishment was found: 80 per cent of boys and 62 per cent of girls reported experiencing corporal punishment at the hands of their teacher, some of which resulted in serious injury including loss of consciousness and concussion (Youssef, Attia, & Kamel, 1998). Other jurisdictions continue to allow teachers to use corporal punishment (for example, private schools in Australia, Tasmania, and New South Wales) or a 'reasonable chastisement' exception to the law of assault to defend against criminal prosecution or civil claims for damages (for example, Australia and Canada).

The intent here is not to provide an exhaustive account of the ways in which schools function counter to children's rights and citizenship status. The intent is to underscore the need for rights-respecting and democratic schools for effective citizenship education. Schools that deny children's rights, and their citizenship status, and schools that disallow children's democratic participation in age-appropriate ways cannot teach rights-based citizenship. The gap between what students experience and what they are being told would be too great.

The final challenge to be addressed in this section is the content of curriculum. There are two concerns here. One is the lack of status accorded citizenship education. Despite global consensus on the need for effective citizenship education to deal with the ongoing and emerging issues of democratic structures, citizenship education has very low status in the curriculum (Carrington & Short, 1997; Torney-Purta et al., 1999). Education for global democratic citizenship continues to be perceived as less important than education for global economic competitiveness and technological expertise (Anour, 2002; Knutsson, 1997; Majhanovich, 2002; Priestly, 2002). Moreover, there continues to be an aura of suspicion around citizenship education – especially if it is rights-based – and a lingering belief that it is too value-laden and too political for schools. The second concern is the lack of curricular coherence with regard to article 29. As described in Chapter 4, and noted earlier in this chapter, article 29 of the U.N. Convention on the Rights of the Child sets out the goals of education. These have not yet been taken seriously and used to guide school curricula. A complete examination of what is taught and why it is taught is needed. Many subjects in schools are taught because they always have been. Their continued relevance remains unexamined (Collins, 1996). Were the goals of education articulated in accordance with those described in article 29 of the Convention, rights-based citizenship education would be a priority and an organizing principle for the rest of the school curricula.

It is obvious that school reform is needed. It is equally obvious that this will not happen quickly or on a wholesale basis, nor should it. Incremental changes are usually the most effective and sustainable. Moreover, benefits of rights-based curricula are obtained when they are taught within a traditional school environment (as described in the previous chapter). A long-term strategy is needed. Education reform must involve partnerships among education researchers, practitioners, child rights experts, and students. Cross-cultural and cross-national partnerships are also necessary. What has not yet been acknowledged is that the Convention describes a global consensus on the content and pedagogy of schooling. To date, the focus of education globally has been on the design of infrastructure and the collection of enrollment statistics, with relatively little attention paid to the content or process of teaching (Knutsson, 1997). The paradox, of course, is that the best means of overcoming resistance to school reform that is guided by and consistent with children's rights is through the provision of children's rights education. Yet, there will be no systematic inclusion of children's rights education until educators understand the Convention.

Symbolic Support for the Rights of the Child

There is a great deal of difference between support and commitment. Citizens and governments may express support for the achievement of some principle or policy goal, but they may not have genuine commitment to the realization of the principle or goal. For example, a government may express abstract support for the principle of equality of opportunity for persons with disabilities and for a policy of promoting it through such affirmative measures as requiring access ramps to buildings for persons with wheelchairs, but lack concrete commitment to the actual achievement of the principle. Lack of commitment may be due to several reasons. It may be because of a shortage of financial resources required for the achievement of the objective. Or it may be that there are misgivings about the long-term implications of policy implementation, such as raising public expectations in other areas. Or perhaps the government is not under sufficient pressure to follow through on a course of action or is under pressure from opposition groups to not follow through. These groups may be opposed for principled reasons such as the view that equality of opportunity should be achieved simply through anti-discrimination laws rather than affirmative action measures. Or they may be opposed for reasons of material self-interest, and be pressuring government to direct resources their way rather than in support of equality of opportunity for persons with disabilities.

Regardless of the particular reason, the government adopts a policy of symbolic support for equality of opportunity rather than one of commitment to its realization. To satisfy persons with disabilities, equality-seeking organizations, and citizens with a sense of fairness, the government expresses support for a policy of promoting equality. But to accommodate opposition groups, or because it is not under sufficient pressure to do so, it chooses to not implement or to not implement fully this policy. Such are the politics and policies of symbolism (Edelman, 1985). Through a policy of symbolic support, the government sends out a message that it cares about persons with disabilities and about the issue of equal opportunity. At the same time, to allay the concerns of opponents and critics, or because of misgivings about long-term implications or concerns about the financial costs of the policy, the government fails to implement or delays the implementation of the policy.

In implementing the U.N. Convention on the Rights of the Child, the international record suggests that countries have adopted policies of symbolism rather than commitment to full-scale implementation. This is especially pronounced in the area of children's rights education. On the one hand, by signing the Convention, countries have shown their concern for the welfare of children and their official support for the principle of the rights of the child. In doing so, they have endorsed the principle that children have basic rights, including the participation rights of the child citizen, and not the principle that children simply have needs or interests that require protection. By ratifying the Convention, countries have shown their official support for a policy of implementing the rights of the child as therein described, not simply for recognizing these rights. They have agreed to make their laws, policies, and practices consistent with the Convention and to put the Convention into effect over time, if not immediately. Furthermore, by agreeing to implement articles 42, 29, and 12 of the U.N. Convention on the Rights of the Child, countries have shown their official support for children's rights education. They have agreed to a duty of ensuring the 'appropriate and active' education of children in their rights under the Convention.

On the other hand, as discussed in Chapter 2 and as noted by the U.N. Committee on the Rights of the Child, generally states have failed to fulfil their obligation to provide children's rights education. With few exceptions, they have failed to incorporate children's rights education into the regular school curricula and into programs of citizenship education. They have not provided for appropriate and active education on the Convention, as is required under article 42, and for the systematic and comprehensive teaching of children's rights in schools, as urged by the U.N. Committee. This failure to take children's rights education seriously is indicative of a failure to take children's rights seriously. The enjoyment of rights and the exercise of rights assume that people know and understand that they have rights. This is especially important for child citizens, given their 'evolving capacities' and more limited knowledge and experience. Child citizens need to be educated about their rights and responsibilities in order to practice their democratic citizenship in an age-appropriate manner. But the failure to implement children's rights education, effectively keeping children in the dark about their basic rights, is indicative of a lack of genuine commitment not only to children's rights education but also to the principle of children's rights.

Some of the reasons for such policies of symbolism have already been discussed. In light of growing worldwide concern about children and growing consciousness of the importance of children's rights, governments officially have shown support for the principle of children's rights and children's rights education. But governments have failed to embrace and to implement the principle for a variety of reasons, singly or in combination. Among these is the persistence of traditional views of children. Many citizens – including many parents, school trustees, educators, and politicians – still see children either as parental property, or as incapable and incompetent not-yets, or as innocent creatures who should not be politicized, or as unruly creatures unfit for the rights and responsibilities of citizenship. Another reason, as previously discussed, is an inhospitable educational environment because of teacher difficulties associated with educating children about their rights and traditional school practices being at odds with children's rights-based citizenship education. Such a difficult and unwelcoming environment makes governments pause at deciding to incorporate children's rights education into the school curricula.

There are other reasons as well. To begin with, governments are not under sufficient pressure to implement programs of children's rights education. For example, they are not under pressure from children and youth because children and youth do not have the right to vote and, thus, do not have much direct political influence and power. In addition, because of their limited financial resources, children and youth do not have a great deal of economic power to organize and apply political pressure, as many adults do. But even if they did have voting rights and more economic power, children do not generally know that they have basic rights under the Convention on the Rights of the Child and that governments have an obligation to implement the Convention and to provide for children's rights education. Children do not know, of course, because they have not been educated to know. Thus, they do not apply pressure. Similarly, adults do not apply pressure on behalf of child citizens because adults, too, have generally not been educated about the Convention. Or, those who do have some awareness of the issue of children's rights may not apply pressure because they are ambivalent or have misgivings about granting rights to children. Behind these misgivings is the influence of traditional views of children as property or incompetent not-yets or unruly beings unfit for rights.

Child advocacy organizations, which are made up largely of sympathetic adults who lobby governments on behalf of children, do apply pressure. But there are several problems with their application of political pressure. First, they are but one group among many – with a limited membership – who are trying to influence government. Second, they are internally divided in terms of goals. Some, such as UNICEF, are committed to the principle of children's rights and to pressuring governments into the full-scale implementation of the Convention and of children's rights education (Willemot, 1997). Other child advocacy groups, however, are opposed to or are reluctant to endorse the concept of the *rights* of children, preferring to champion the *welfare* of children instead. In the child protectionist tradition, and with a regard for the welfare and paternalistic treatment of children, they are suspicious of the rights approach and especially of the participation rights of the child (Lansdown, 1995a, b). Their goal is to improve the welfare of children, not to pursue their rights. Third, resources are a problem. Some child advocacy groups lack the financial resources to be effective lobbyists on an ongoing basis; others, who depend on some or much of their funding from government, do not lobby vigorously for fear of offending the hand that feeds them. This is not an uncommon situation for social advocacy groups who depend on government for financial support. Finally, it is difficult to gain public support in order to apply significant pressure on government. For government to act on an issue on the basis of public opinion, the opinion would have to be strong on one side of the issue. But because the public is uneducated about the Convention, and because some members of the public are ambivalent or resistant to the concept of children's rights, it is very difficult for child advocacy groups to mobilize public opinion into a force for pressuring government.

The reluctance of governments to implement children's rights education is due not only to the absence of strong public pressure to do so but also to pressure in the other direction. Governments are quite aware of vocal opposition to the principle of children's rights and children's rights education. Groups holding traditional beliefs about children – family values organizations, parents rights groups, and conservative educators and politicians – are not reluctant to express to political authorities their opposition to children's rights. Furthermore, they do not hesitate to inform authorities that, although countries may have signed and ratified the Convention, they are not really obligated to comply with it because it is not a piece of law enforceable in the courts. Governments realize that such vocal and strong opposition is not representative of a majority of their citizens. But they also realize that these groups may be capable of mobilizing wider public support, given the ambivalence of many adults to granting rights to children. Thus, out of fear of the political costs, it is safer for governments not to proceed with strong programs of children's rights education.

Another reason for the symbolic policy is that governments are reluctant to commit resources to implementing children's rights education.

This applies especially to countries in the developing world, where the resources required for their tremendous social and economic problems such as poverty, inadequate health care, inadequate basic education, and inadequate services and supports for children and families are indeed scarce (Mulinge, 2002; Plantilla, 2002). Given these tremendous difficulties, together with others such as civil war and social unrest, it is not unexpected that governments would choose to not devote limited resources to special curriculum materials and teacher training required for children's rights education. This reluctance to commit resources also applies to countries in the developed world, although to a much lesser degree. Given the desire to reduce budgetary deficits and public debts, and given public resistance to increased taxation to pay for social programs, many governments have chosen to limit or cut education spending, as well as other social spending, especially in areas not deemed to be priority concerns. Where educational programs in the areas of science and technology are often given priority in competition for limited resources, children's rights education has a lower status and is less likely to be given support. Compounding the problem is bureaucratic and cross-sectoral competition for scarce resources among government agencies and departments, even in the area of children's rights (David, 2002). The broad range and interdependence of rights in the U.N. Convention on the Rights of the Child requires bureaucratic and cross-sectoral cooperation and coordination among agencies in implementing rights. But mutual jealousies and turf wars undermine such cooperation. Education departments and their budgets are not immune from the effects of such conflict.

Another reason that governments have not been committed to the implementation of children's rights education is the danger that education would raise public awareness about problems of children's rights, invite criticism of the government, and raise public expectations higher than possibly could be met. This is especially the case in countries of the developing world where violations of children's rights are an ongoing reality and, in some cases, a growing reality (Mulinge, 2002). In these countries, violations of the rights of children continue to be a problem over a wide range of areas, including child labour and economic exploitation, limited access to education and health care, physical abuse and neglect, and the 'global growth industry' of child prostitution and pornography (Mulinge, 2002). Under the Convention, relatively poor countries do have some room to defend themselves from criticism, in reference to the provision under article 4 that they implement the rights of children 'to the maximum extent of their available resources and, where needed, within the framework of international cooperation.' They can, thus, point to the lack of resources and adequate foreign aid as the source of the problem rather than themselves. But the language of rights is a very demanding and uncompromising language, calling for strong and immediate action in remedying a violation of rights (Ignatieff, 2000). When children and adults are made aware that children do have basic rights, and when they observe the contradictions – and sometimes gross contradictions – of this principle, they are more likely to be critical of the responsible authorities, apart from any latitude allowed under the Convention. Thus, governments in the developing world have reason to be wary of children's rights education. However, although not to the same degree, governments in the developed world also have reason to be wary of children's rights education. As the sense of deprivation is relative rather than absolute, there is the danger that such education would make child and adult citizens more aware of any gaps between the principle and reality of children's rights and, thus, more critical of the responsible authorities.

Finally, another reason that governments have adopted a symbolic policy approach to implementing the Convention is that they can do so without negative repercussions, at least in the short term. Unlike constitutional law, or unlike many laws within a country, the Convention is not justiciable or capable of enforcement through the courts. While it may be regarded as part of domestic law in a few countries, for example, Belgium, and while in many countries it may be regarded as a guide to judicial interpretation, generally, the convention cannot be used as a means of holding governments strictly accountable for failing to comply with the law. Governments do have an obligation for making their laws, policies, and practices consistent with the Convention, which is a legally binding piece of international law, but they are not generally accountable to the courts for failing to do so. Enforcement is based not on the work of law enforcement officials and the judicial decisions of the courts, but on a system of five-year country reports to the U.N. Committee on the Rights of the Child and on pressure to comply with the law through the force of domestic and international opinion. If governments fail to comply with certain provisions of the Convention, or if they stall in implementing certain children's rights, they may face criticism by the Committee and by child advocacy organizations, or even a certain degree of political embarrassment. But this typically lasts only for a short period, usually only when Committee or child advocacy reports are released every five years. Governments are not answerable to the courts for failing to provide for the rights of the child but to the episodically expressed opinions of child advocates.

Governments are quite aware that they are not strictly or immediately accountable. This awareness is corroborated by the fact that, to varying degrees, the provisions of many international treaties and conventions – not only the U.N. Convention on the Rights of the Child – are not implemented or are implemented very slowly. Thus, when governments fail to provide for appropriate and active programs of children's rights education (articles 42 and 29), and when they fail to provide for the participation rights of child citizens (article 12), they are aware that they are able to do so without much political cost. Given a situation where children and youth do not vote, where child advocacy communities are not a strong and unified force, where there are financial costs and perhaps longer-term political costs associated with awareness of children's rights, and where many adults are hesitant about granting rights to children, it is understandable that governments would choose not to give serious attention to children's rights education. Symbolic support for children is a more understandable choice.

Prospects for Change

The show of symbolic support for children's rights education is a very positive step. By signing and ratifying the U.N. Convention on the Rights of the Child, by agreeing to the principle of educating child citizens in their rights, and by taking a few steps – small though they be – in the direction of implementing children's rights education, countries have demonstrated a certain degree of political will in support of children and child citizenship. But they have not demonstrated political will in the form of commitment to children, as would be evident in their implementation of strong and comprehensive programs of children's rights education. Our final question is this: What are the prospects that there will be a change from symbolic support to political will that demonstrates commitment to the implementation of children's rights and of education that empowers child citizens with the knowledge that they have rights and value?

We are cautiously optimistic that significant progress will occur over the longer term. Historical developments have shown that symbolic support for values and principles can be an important basis and resource for promoting positive change. For example, over the past two centuries, on the basis of early symbolic support for the values of democracy, equality, and human rights, much progress has been made in achieving these values and principles. Although major problems remain, significant advances have been made in the direction of inclusive citizenship, the expansion of voting rights, the incorporation of human rights into national and international law, and greater equality for women, members of minorities, persons with disabilities, and gays and lesbians, among others. And on the basis of an expanding children's rights consciousness, as part of a wider human rights consciousness, important advances also have been made on behalf of the interests and rights of children. It was not that long ago that children were formally regarded as objects, either in the form of vulnerable little not-yets requiring the protection of society or of parental property, rather than as subjects, persons, and citizens with rights. But on the basis of an emerging worldwide consciousness and consensus that children are persons with basic rights, domestic laws have been developed, and the Convention has been signed and ratified, with the intention of implementing the rights of the child and programs of children's rights education.

As in the past symbolic concern for women and minorities became a force for substantive policy and legal change, the present symbolic support and concern for children's rights can be a force to build pressure and commitment to the fuller implementation of children's rights and children's rights education. Child advocates can help this process along in several ways. First, it is important to appreciate that it is – in all likelihood – an incremental process. Children's rights education is not likely to be implemented overnight, on the basis of a sudden commitment by political and educational authorities. Rather, on the basis of the patience, prodding, and determined energies of child advocates, it is more likely that it will be implemented teacher by teacher, school by school, and jurisdiction by jurisdiction. Successful practice in one jurisdiction or school district can be an effective model for implementation in another jurisdiction or district. Progress is best sustained when done in positive steps.

Second, the process can be helped along through reminding political and educational authorities that the implementation of children's rights and children's rights education is an obligation and official policy of governments that have ratified the U.N. Convention on the Rights of the Child. Regardless of whether a minority of parents or teachers or other adults is ambivalent or hesitant about the principle of children's rights, it is a duty of government to develop appropriate and active programs of children's rights education. At the same time, pointing to gaps between the principle and practice of children's rights can help the process along. In communications with authorities, as well as in advocacy reports to governments, the U.N. Committee on the Rights of the Child, and the media, it can be helpful to point to the discrepancy between articles of the Convention and educational directives by the U.N. Committee, on the one hand, and the actual absence of education for children's rights, on the other. It can be particularly helpful to construct a measure of children's awareness of their basic rights and of the Convention to periodically survey children to assess their degree of awareness over time and then to report the results to the media and to government and educational authorities. Authorities ultimately want to project an image of supporting the rights of the child and of honouring their commitments. That they do not want to face embarrassment is a means by which child advocates can apply pressure.

Third, the process can be helped along by exposing the myths, fictions, and regressive ideas put forward by critics of children's rights. The view that children are the property and responsibility of their parents, and that children do not require rights because parents act in their best interests, can be challenged by exposing it as regressive and oppressive, analogous to the traditional view of women. Like women, children are not property but persons in their own right. And like women in relation to husbands, children cannot always depend on the good will of parents to look after their best interests, as evident in the caseloads of child protection agencies. The view that children are incompetent not-yets, incapable of participation, can be challenged by exposing it as a simplistic characterization and myth. The participation rights of children are to be exercised in relation to their age and maturity. Many older children are quite capable of providing valuable input into decision-making while some adults are much less capable. Participation is about input, not self-determination. The view that childhood should be preserved as a carefree happy period, where children are free from rights and responsibilities, can also be exposed as a myth. Many children live under desperate or difficult circumstances that include poverty, abuse, neglect, or exploitation. What they require is not freedom from politicization but political measures that provide them with the rights of citizenship such as the right to protect their interests. Knowing their basic rights can be a force in this direction. Finally, the view that children are unruly beings unfit for rights can be exposed as a regressive stereotype and fiction. Most children are law-abiding citizens who benefit by being treated with respect and who benefit both themselves and society when they are given age-appropriate opportunities for exercising the rights and responsibilities of citizenship.

Fourth, making clear the reasonableness of the objectives of children's rights education can help the process along. What needs to be emphasized is that, contrary to the half-truths sometimes conveyed through the media, the rights of the child do not centre on unrestrained freedom or the rights of young offenders. Rather, they deal with issues that most reasonable people can agree with. They deal with protection rights (protection from abuse, neglect, exploitation), provision rights (provision of health care, education, basic material needs), and participation rights (which refer not to self-determination but age-appropriate input). What also needs to be emphasized is that when children are learning about their rights, they are also learning about their responsibilities. The goal is not to teach personal rights but universal rights and accompanying social responsibilities. It also needs to be emphasized that the goal is not to rescue children as an oppressed group from parents and adults who deny and violate their rights on a regular basis. Rather, the goal is to provide for children's wider protection and interests. Children are not an oppressed group requiring liberation in the same way as women and minorities were in the past. But children's interests are advanced when their basic rights are recognized and implemented and when they are empowered through knowledge of their rights.

Finally, the process can be helped along by characterizing children's rights education as a vehicle for democratic citizenship. Children's rights education is necessary not only because it is an international obligation of states. It is important also because it is a foundation for citizenship education and for the practice of citizenship. As children are learning their basic rights, they are also learning the rights of others and the value of respecting the rights of others. In doing so, they are learning the knowledge, values, and behaviours that are necessary to promote and sustain democracy and human rights. Through children's rights education, children learn and exercise their rights and social responsibilities as being-citizens. This early exercise of rights and responsibilities and practice of citizen participation is an important foundation for their becoming citizens, their effective participation as adult citizens. Children can, and do, become empowered global citizens through children's rights education. As evidenced in the poem below, children understand the importance of children's rights education.

Rights Conversation

One long Wednesday night, I told my Dad about what I
did at school.
'I did literacy, maths and Oh Yeah, a topic that we're
doing about Children's rights.'
'Children's rights! That's a bit heavy an't it?'

'Don't you know about it Dad? It's important, we're the
only ones in school learning about it!'
'Children have enough rights.'
'It's our right to play in a safe place and to have a good
education and to be safe from drugs!'
'Suppose ... pass the remote.'
'Dad – you must listen – if we didn't have these rights
we might have to go to the army and fight, even me. It
also says all adults and children should know about their
rights from the United Nations Convention on the Rights
of The Child – you have a responsibility to learn them too.'
'It's up to you to teach me then ...'
'Don't worry Dad, I will.'

Jasmin Spanswick, aged 10 years
Knights Enham Junior School,
Andover, England

The United Nations Convention on the Rights of the Child

Preamble

The States Parties to the Present Convention

Considering that, in accordance with the principles proclaimed in the Charter of the United Nations, recognition of the inherent dignity and of the equal and inalienable rights of all members of the human family is the foundation of freedom, justice and peace in the world,

Bearing in mind that the peoples of the United Nations have, in the Charter, reaffirmed their faith in fundamental human rights and in the dignity and worth of the human person, and have determined to promote social progress and better standards of life in larger freedom,

Recognizing that the United Nations has, in the Universal Declaration of Human Rights and in the International Covenants on Human Rights, proclaimed and agreed that everyone is entitled to all the rights and freedoms set forth therein, without distinction of any kind, such as race, colour, sex, language, religion, political or other opinion, national or social origin, property, birth or other status,

Recalling that, in the Universal Declaration of Human Rights, the United Nations has proclaimed that childhood is entitled to special care and assistance,

Convinced that the family, as the fundamental group of society and the natural environment for the growth and well-being of all its members and particularly children, should be afforded the necessary protection and assistance so that it can fully assume its responsibilities within the community,

Recognizing that the child, for the full and harmonious development of his or her personality, should grow up in a family environment, in an atmosphere of happiness, love and understanding,

Considering that the child should be fully prepared to live an individual life in society, and brought up in the spirit of the ideals proclaimed in the Charter of the United Nations, and in particular in the spirit of peace, dignity, tolerance, freedom, equality and solidarity,

Bearing in mind that the need to extend particular care to the child has been stated in the Geneva Declaration of the Rights of the Child of 1924 and in the Declaration of the Rights of the Child adopted by the General Assembly on 20 November 1959 and recognized in the Universal Declaration of Human Rights, in the International Covenant on Civil and Political Rights (in particular in articles 23 and 24), in the International Covenant on Economic, Social and Cultural Rights (in particular in article 10) and in the statutes and relevant instruments of specialized agencies and international organizations concerned with the welfare of children,

Bearing in mind that, as indicated in the Declaration of the Rights of the Child, 'the child, by reason of his physical and mental immaturity, needs special safeguards and care, including appropriate legal protection, before as well as after birth',

Recalling the provisions of the Declaration on Social and Legal Principles relating to the Protection and Welfare of Children, with Special Reference to Foster Placement and Adoption Nationally and Internationally; the United Nations Standard Minimum Rules for the Administration of Juvenile Justice (The Beijing Rules); and the Declaration on the Protection of Women and Children in Emergency and Armed Conflict,

Recognizing that, in all countries in the world, there are children living in exceptionally difficult conditions, and that such children need special consideration,

Taking due account of the importance of the traditions and cultural values of each people for the protection and harmonious development of the child,

Recognizing the importance of international cooperation for improving the living conditions of children in every country, in particular in the developing countries,

Have agreed as follows:

Part I

Article 1

For the purposes of the present Convention, a child means every human being below the age of eighteen years unless, under the law applicable to the child, majority is attained earlier.

Article 2

1 States Parties shall respect and ensure the rights set forth in the present Convention to each child within their jurisdiction without discrimination of any kind, irrespective of the child's or his or her parent's or legal guardian's race, colour, sex, language, religion, political or other opinion, national, ethnic or social origin, property, disability, birth or other status.
2 States Parties shall take all appropriate measures to ensure that the child is protected against all forms of discrimination or punishment on the basis of the status, activities, expressed opinions, or beliefs of the child's parents, legal guardians, or family members.

Article 3

1 In all actions concerning children, whether undertaken by public or private social welfare institutions, courts of law, administrative authorities or legislative bodies, the best interests of the child shall be a primary consideration.
2 States Parties undertake to ensure the child such protection and care as is necessary for his or her well-being, taking into account the rights and duties of his or her parents, legal guardians, or other individuals legally responsible for him or her, and, to this end, shall take all appropriate legislative and administrative measures.
3 States Parties shall ensure that the institutions, services and facilities responsible for the care or protection of children shall conform with the standards established by competent authorities, particularly in the areas of safety, health, in the number and suitability of their staff, as well as competent supervision.

Article 4

States Parties shall undertake all appropriate legislative, administrative, and other measures for the implementation of the rights recognized in the present Convention. With regard to economic, social and cultural rights, States Parties shall undertake such measures to the maximum extent of their available resources and, where needed, within the framework of international co-operation.

Article 5

States Parties shall respect the responsibilities, rights and duties of parents or, where applicable, the members of the extended family or community as provided for by local custom, legal guardians or other persons legally responsible for the child, to provide, in a manner consistent with the evolving capacities of the child, appropriate direction and guidance in the exercise by the child of the rights recognized in the present Convention.

Article 6

1 States Parties recognize that every child has the inherent right to life.
2 States Parties shall ensure to the maximum extent possible the survival and development of the child.

Article 7

1 The child shall be registered immediately after birth and shall have the right from birth to a name, the right to acquire a nationality and, as far as possible, the right to know and be cared for by his or her parents.
2 States Parties shall ensure the implementation of these rights in accordance with their national law and their obligations under the relevant international instruments in this field, in particular where the child would otherwise be stateless.

Article 8

1 States Parties undertake to respect the right of the child to preserve his or her identity, including nationality, name and family relations as recognized by law without unlawful interference.
2 Where a child is illegally deprived of some or all of the elements of his or her identity, States Parties shall provide appropriate assistance and protection, with a view to speedily re-establishing his or her identity.

Article 9

1 States Parties shall ensure that a child shall not be separated from his or her parents against their will, except when competent authorities subject to judicial review determine, in accordance with applicable law and procedures, that such separation is necessary for the best

interests of the child. Such determination may be necessary in a particular case such as one involving abuse or neglect of the child by the parents, or one where the parents are living separately and a decision must be made as to the child's place of residence.

2 In any proceedings pursuant to paragraph 1 of the present article, all interested parties shall be given an opportunity to participate in the proceedings and make their views known.

3 States Parties shall respect the right of the child who is separated from one or both parents to maintain personal relations and direct contact with both parents on a regular basis, except if it is contrary to the child's best interests.

4 Where such separation results from any action initiated by a State Party, such as the detention, imprisonment, exile, deportation or death (including death arising from any cause while the person is in the custody of the State) of one or both parents or of the child, that State Party shall, upon request, provide the parents, the child or, if appropriate, another member of the family with the essential information concerning the whereabouts of the absent member(s) of the family unless the provision of the information would be detrimental to the well-being of the child. States Parties shall further ensure that the submission of such a request shall of itself entail no adverse consequences for the person(s) concerned.

Article 10

1 In accordance with the obligation of States Parties under article 9, paragraph 1, applications by a child or his or her parents to enter or leave a State Party for the purpose of family reunification shall be dealt with by States Parties in a positive, humane and expeditious manner. States Parties shall further ensure that the submission of such a request shall entail no adverse consequences for the applicants and for the members of their family.

2 A child whose parents reside in different States shall have the right to maintain on a regular basis, save in exceptional circumstances, personal relations and direct contacts with both parents. Towards that end and in accordance with the obligation of States Parties under article 9, paragraph 2, States Parties shall respect the right of the child and his or her parents to leave any country, including their own, and to enter their own country. The right to leave any country shall be subject only to such restrictions as are prescribed by law and which are necessary to

protect the national security, public order (*ordre public*), public health
or morals or the rights and freedoms of others and are consistent with
the other rights recognized in the present Convention.

Article 11

1 States Parties shall take measures to combat the illicit transfer and
  non-return of children abroad.
2 To this end, States Parties shall promote the conclusion of bilateral or
  multilateral agreements or accession to existing agreements.

Article 12

1 States Parties shall assure to the child who is capable of forming his or
  her own views the right to express those views freely in all matters
  affecting the child, the views of the child being given due weight in
  accordance with the age and maturity of the child.
2 For this purpose, the child shall in particular be provided the opportunity to be heard in any judicial and administrative proceedings
  affecting the child, either directly, or through a representative or an
  appropriate body, in a manner consistent with the procedural rules of
  national law.

Article 13

1 The child shall have the right to freedom of expression; this right
  shall include freedom to seek, receive and impart information and
  ideas of all kinds, regardless of frontiers, either orally, in writing or in
  print, in the form of art, or through any other media of the child's
  choice.
2 The exercise of this right may be subject to certain restrictions, but
  these shall only be such as are provided by law and are necessary:
  (*a*) For respect of the rights or reputations of others; or
  (*b*) For the protection of national security or of public order (*ordre
  public*), or of public health or morals.

Article 14

1 States Parties shall respect the right of the child to freedom of
  thought, conscience and religion.

2 States Parties shall respect the rights and duties of the parents and, when applicable, legal guardians, to provide direction to the child in the exercise of his or her right in a manner consistent with the evolving capacities of the child.

3 Freedom to manifest one's religion or beliefs may be subject only to such limitations as are prescribed by law and are necessary to protect public safety, order, health or morals, or the fundamental rights and freedoms of others.

Article 15

1 States Parties recognize the rights of the child to freedom of association and to freedom of peaceful-assembly.

2 No restrictions may be placed on the exercise of these rights other than those imposed in conformity with the law and which are necessary in a democratic society in the interests of national security or public safety, public order (*ordre public*), the protection of public health or morals or the protection of the rights and freedoms of others.

Article 16

1 No child shall be subjected to arbitrary or unlawful interference with his or her privacy, family, home or correspondence, nor to unlawful attacks on his or her honour and reputation.

2 The child has the right to the protection of the law against such interference or attacks.

Article 17

States Parties recognize the important function performed by the mass media and shall ensure that the child has access to information and material from a diversity of national and international sources, especially those aimed at the promotion of his or her social, spiritual and moral well-being and physical and mental health. To this end, States Parties shall:

(*a*) Encourage the mass media to disseminate information and material of social and cultural benefit to the child and in accordance with the spirit of article 29;

(*b*) Encourage international co-operation in the production, exchange and dissemination of such information and material from a diversity of cultural, national and international sources;

(*c*) Encourage the production and dissemination of children's books;

(*d*) Encourage the mass media to have particular regard to the linguistic needs of the child who belongs to a minority group or who is indigenous;

(*e*) Encourage the development of appropriate guidelines for the protection of the child from information and material injurious to his or her well-being, bearing in mind the provisions of articles 13 and 18.

Article 18

1 States Parties shall use their best efforts to ensure recognition of the principle that both parents have common responsibilities for the upbringing and development of the child. Parents or, as the case may be, legal guardians, have the primary responsibility for the upbringing and development of the child. The best interests of the child will be their basic concern.

2 For the purpose of guaranteeing and promoting the rights set forth in the present Convention, States Parties shall render appropriate assistance to parents and legal guardians in the performance of their child-rearing responsibilities and shall ensure the development of institutions, facilities and services for the care of children.

3 States Parties shall take all appropriate measures to ensure that children of working parents have the right to benefit from child-care services and facilities for which they are eligible.

Article 19

1 States Parties shall take all appropriate legislative, administrative, social and educational measures to protect the child from all forms of physical or mental violence, injury or abuse, neglect or negligent treatment, maltreatment or exploitation, including sexual abuse, while in the care of parent(s), legal guardians(s) or any other person who has the care of the child.

2 Such protective measures should, as appropriate, include effective procedures for the establishment of social programmes to provide necessary support for the child and for those who have the care of the child, as well as for other forms of prevention and for identification, reporting, referral, investigation, treatment, and follow-up of instances of child maltreatment described heretofore, and, as appropriate, for judicial involvement.

Article 20

1 A child temporarily or permanently deprived of his or her family environment, or in whose own best interests cannot be allowed to remain
   in that environment, shall be entitled to special protection and assistance provided by the State.
2 States Parties shall in accordance with their national laws ensure alternative care for such a child.
3 Such care could include, *inter alia*, foster placement, *kafalah* of Islamic
   law, adoption or if necessary placement in suitable institutions for the
   care of children. When considering solutions, due regard shall be
   paid to the desirability of continuity in a child's upbringing and to the
   child's ethnic, religious, cultural and linguistic background.

Article 21

States Parties that recognize and/or permit the system of adoption shall
ensure that the best interests of the child shall be the paramount consideration and they shall:
  (*a*) Ensure that the adoption of a child is authorized only by compe-
       tent authorities who determine, in accordance with applicable law
       and procedures and on the basis of all pertinent and reliable
       information, that the adoption is permissible in view of the child's
       status concerning parents, relatives and legal guardians and that,
       if required, the persons concerned have given their informed con-
       sent to the adoption on the basis of such counselling as may be
       necessary;
  (*b*) Recognize that inter-country adoption may be considered as an
       alternative means of child's care, if the child cannot be placed in
       a foster or an adoptive family or cannot in any suitable manner be
       cared for in the child's country of origin;
  (*c*) Ensure that the child concerned by inter-country adoption enjoys
       safeguards and standards equivalent to those existing in the case
       of national adoption;
  (*d*) Take all appropriate measures to ensure that, in inter-country
       adoption, the placement does not result in improper financial
       gain for those involved in it;
  (*e*) Promote, where appropriate, the objectives of the present article by
       concluding bilateral or multilateral arrangements or agreements,
       and endeavour, within this framework, to ensure that the place-

ment of the child in another country is carried out by competent authorities or organs.

Article 22

1 States Parties shall take appropriate measures to ensure that a child who is seeking refugee status or who is considered a refugee in accordance with applicable international or domestic law and procedures shall, whether unaccompanied or accompanied by his or her parents or by any other person, receive appropriate protection and humanitarian assistance in the enjoyment of applicable rights set forth in the present Convention and in other international human rights or humanitarian instruments to which the said States are Parties.

2 For this purpose, States Parties shall provide, as they consider appropriate, co-operation in any efforts by the United Nations and other competent intergovernmental organizations or non-governmental organizations co-operating with the United Nations to protect and assist such a child and to trace the parents or other members of the family of any refugee child in order to obtain information necessary for reunification with his or her family. In cases where no parents or other members of the family can be found, the child shall be accorded the same protection as any other child permanently or temporarily deprived of his or her family environment for any reason, as set forth in the present Convention.

Article 23

1 States Parties recognize that a mentally or physically disabled child should enjoy a full and decent life, in conditions which ensure dignity, promote self-reliance and facilitate the child's active participation in the community.

2 States Parties recognize the right of the disabled child to special care and shall encourage and ensure the extension, subject to available resources, to the eligible child and those responsible for his or her care, of assistance for which application is made and which is appropriate to the child's condition and to the circumstances of the parents or others caring for the child.

3 Recognizing the special needs of a disabled child, assistance extended in accordance with paragraph 2 of the present article shall be provided free of charge, whenever possible, taking into account the

financial resources of the parents or others caring for the child, and shall be designed to ensure that the disabled child has effective access to and receives education, training, health care services, rehabilitation services, preparation for employment and recreation opportunities in a manner conducive to the child's achieving the fullest possible social integration and individual development, including his or her cultural and spiritual development.

4 States Parties shall promote, in the spirit of international co-operation, the exchange of appropriate information in the field of preventive health care and of medical, psychological and functional treatment of disabled children, including dissemination of and access to information concerning methods of rehabilitation, education and vocational services, with the aim of enabling States Parties to improve their capabilities and skills and to widen their experience in these areas. In this regard, particular account shall be taken of the needs of developing countries.

Article 24

1 States Parties recognize the right of the child to the enjoyment of the highest attainable standard of health and to facilities for the treatment of illness and rehabilitation of health. States Parties shall strive to ensure that no child is deprived of his or her right of access to such health care services.

2 States Parties shall pursue full implementation of this right and, in particular, shall take appropriate measures:
   (*a*) To diminish infant and child mortality;
   (*b*) To ensure the provision of necessary medical assistance and health care to all children with emphasis on the development of primary health care;
   (*c*) To combat disease and malnutrition, including within the framework of primary health care, through, *inter alia*, the application of readily available technology and through the provision of adequate nutritious foods and clean drinking water, taking into consideration the dangers and risks of environmental pollution;
   (*d*) To ensure appropriate pre-natal and post-natal health care for mothers;
   (*e*) To ensure that all segments of society, in particular parents and children, are informed, have access to education and are supported in the use of basic knowledge of child health and nutrition,

the advantages of breast-feeding, hygiene and environmental sanitation and the prevention of accidents;

(*f*) To develop preventive health care, guidance for parents and family planning education and services.

3 States Parties shall take all effective and appropriate measures with a view to abolishing traditional practices prejudicial to the health of children.

4 States Parties undertake to promote and encourage international co-operation with a view to achieving progressively the full realization of the right recognized in the present article. In this regard, particular account shall be taken of the needs of developing countries.

Article 25

States Parties recognize the right of a child who has been placed by the competent authorities for the purposes of care, protection or treatment of his or her physical or mental health, to a periodic review of the treatment provided to the child and all other circumstances relevant to his or her placement.

Article 26

1 States Parties shall recognize for every child the right to benefit from social security, including social insurance, and shall take the necessary measures to achieve the full realization of this right in accordance with their national law.

2 The benefits should, where appropriate, be granted, taking into account the resources and the circumstances of the child and persons having responsibility for the maintenance of the child, as well as any other consideration relevant to an application for benefits made by or on behalf of the child.

Article 27

1 States Parties recognize the right of every child to a standard of living adequate for the child's physical, mental, spiritual, moral and social development.

2 The parent(s) or others responsible for the child have the primary responsibility to secure, within their abilities and financial capacities, the conditions of living necessary for the child's development.

3 States Parties, in accordance with national conditions and within their means, shall take appropriate measures to assist parents and others responsible for the child to implement this right and shall in case of need provide material assistance and support programmes, particularly with regard to nutrition, clothing and housing.

4 States Parties shall take all appropriate measures to secure the recovery of maintenance for the child from the parents or other persons having financial responsibility for the child, both within the State Party and from abroad. In particular, where the person having financial responsibility for the child lives in a State different from that of the child, States Parties shall promote the accession to international agreements or the conclusion of such agreements, as well as the making of other appropriate arrangements.

Article 28

1 States Parties recognize the right of the child to education, and with a view to achieving this right progressively and on the basis of equal opportunity, they shall, in particular:
   (*a*) Make primary education compulsory and available free to all;
   (*b*) Encourage the development of different forms of secondary education, including general and vocational education, make them available and accessible to every child, and take appropriate measures such as the introduction of free education and offering financial assistance in case of need;
   (*c*) Make higher education accessible to all on the basis of capacity by every appropriate means;
   (*d*) Make educational and vocational information and guidance available and accessible to all children;
   (*e*) Take measures to encourage regular attendance at schools and the reduction of drop-out rates.

2 States Parties shall take all appropriate measures to ensure that school discipline is administered in a manner consistent with the child's human dignity and in conformity with the present Convention.

3 States Parties shall promote and encourage international co-operation in matters relating to education, in particular with a view to contributing to the elimination of ignorance and illiteracy throughout the world and facilitating access to scientific and technical knowledge and modem teaching methods. In this regard, particular account shall be taken of the needs of developing countries.

Article 29

1 States Parties agree that the education of the child shall be directed
to:

(*a*) The development of the child's personality, talents and mental
and physical abilities to their fullest potential;

(*b*) The development of respect for human rights and fundamental
freedoms, and for the principles enshrined in the Charter of the
United Nations;

(*c*) The development of respect for the child's parents, his or her
own cultural identity, language and values, for the national values
of the country in which the child is living, the country from which
he or she may originate, and for civilizations different from his or
her own;

(*d*) The preparation of the child for responsible life in a free society,
in the spirit of understanding, peace, tolerance, equality of sexes,
and friendship among all peoples, ethnic, national and religious
groups and persons of indigenous origin;

(*e*) The development of respect for the natural environment.

2 No part of the present article or Article 28 shall be construed as to
interfere with the liberty of individuals and bodies to establish and
direct educational institutions, subject always to the observance of the
principles set forth in paragraph I of the present article and to the
requirements that the education given in such institutions shall conform to such minimum standards as may be laid down by the State.

Article 30

In those States in which ethnic, religious or linguistic minorities or persons of indigenous origin exist, a child belonging to such a minority or
who is indigenous shall not be denied the right, in community with other
members of his or her group, to enjoy his or her own culture, to profess
and practise his or her own religion, or to use his or her own language.

Article 31

1 States Parties recognize the right of the child to rest and leisure, to
engage in play and recreational activities appropriate to the age of the
child and to participate freely in cultural life and the arts.

2 States Parties shall respect and promote the right of the child to

participate fully in cultural and artistic life and shall encourage the provision of appropriate and equal opportunities for cultural, artistic, recreational and leisure activity.

Article 32

1 States Parties recognize the right of the child to be protected from economic exploitation and from performing any work that is likely to be hazardous or to interfere with the child's education, or to be harmful to the child's health or physical, mental, spiritual, moral or social development.
2 States Parties shall take legislative, administrative, social and educational measures to ensure the implementation of the present article. To this end, and having regard to the relevant provisions of other international instruments, States Parties shall in particular:
   (a) Provide for a minimum age or minimum ages for admission to employment;
   (b) Provide for appropriate regulation of the hours and conditions of employment;
   (c) Provide for appropriate penalties or other sanctions to ensure the effective enforcement of the present article.

Article 33

States Parties shall take all appropriate measures, including legislative, administrative, social and educational measures, to protect children from the illicit use of narcotic drugs and psychotropic substances as defined in the relevant international treaties, and to prevent the use of children in the illicit production and trafficking of such substances.

Article 34

States Parties undertake to protect the child from all forms of sexual exploitation and sexual abuse. For these purposes, States Parties shall in particular take all appropriate national, bilateral and multilateral measures to prevent:
   (a) The inducement or coercion of a child to engage in any unlawful sexual activity;
   (b) The exploitative use of children in prostitution or other unlawful sexual practices;

(*c*) The explorative use of children in pornographic performances and materials.

Article 35

States Parties shall take all appropriate national, bilateral and multilateral measures to prevent the abduction of, the sale of or traffic in children for any purpose or in any form.

Article 36

States Parties shall protect the child against all other forms of exploitation prejudicial to any aspects of the child's welfare.

Article 37

States Parties shall ensure that:

(*a*) No child shall be subjected to torture or other cruel, inhuman or degrading treatment or punishment. Neither capital punishment nor life imprisonment without possibility of release shall be imposed for offences committed by persons below eighteen years of age;

(*b*) No child shall be deprived of his or her liberty unlawfully or arbitrarily. The arrest, detention or imprisonment of a child shall be in conformity with the law and shall be used only as a measure of last resort and for the shortest appropriate period of time;

(*c*) Every child deprived of liberty shall be treated with humanity and respect for the inherent dignity of the human person, and in a manner which takes into account the needs of persons of his or her age. In particular, every child deprived of liberty shall be separated from adults unless it is considered in the child's best interests not to do so and shall have the right to remain contact with his or her family through correspondence and visits, save in exceptional circumstances;

(*d*) Every child deprived of his or her liberty shall have the right to prompt access to legal and other appropriate assistance, as well as the right to challenge the legality of the deprivation of his or her liberty before a court or other competent, independent and impartial authority, and to a prompt decision on any such action.

Article 38

1 States Parties undertake to respect and to ensure respect for rules of international humanitarian law applicable to them in armed conflicts which are relevant to the child.
2 States Parties shall take all feasible measures to ensure that persons who have not attained the age of fifteen years do not take a direct part in hostilities.
3 States Parties shall refrain from recruiting any person who has not attained the age of fifteen years into their armed forces. In recruiting among those persons who have attained the age of fifteen years but who have not attained the age of eighteen years, States Parties shall endeavour to give priority to those who are oldest.
4 In accordance with their obligations under international humanitarian law to protect the civilian population in armed conflicts, States Parties shall take all feasible measures to ensure protection and care of children who are affected by an armed conflict.

Article 39

States Parties shall take all appropriate measures to promote physical and psychological recovery and social reintegration of a child victim of: any form of neglect, exploitation, or abuse; torture or any other form of cruel, inhuman or degrading treatment or punishment; or armed conflicts. Such recovery and reintegration shall take place in an environment which fosters the health, self-respect and dignity of the child.

Article 40

1 States Parties recognize the right of every child alleged as, accused of, or recognized as having infringed the penal law to be treated in a manner consistent with the promotion of the child's sense of dignity and worth, which reinforces the child's respect for the human rights and fundamental freedoms of others and which takes into account the child's age and the desirability of promoting the child's reintegration and the child's assuming a constructive role in society.
2 To this end, and having regard to the relevant provisions of international instruments, States Parties shall, in particular, ensure that:
(*a*) No child shall be alleged as be accused of, or recognized as hav-

ing infringed the penal law by reason of, acts or omissions that were not prohibited by national or international law at the time they were committed;

(b) Every child alleged as or accused of having infringed the penal law has at least the following guarantees:

(i) To be presumed innocent until proven guilty according to law;

(ii) To be informed promptly and directly of the charges against him or her, and, if appropriate, through his or her parents or legal guardians, and to have legal or other appropriate assistance in the preparation and presentation of his or her defence;

(iii) To have the matter determined without delay by a competent, independent and impartial authority or judicial body in a fair hearing according to law, in the presence of legal or other appropriate assistance and, unless it is considered not to be in the best interest of the child, in particular, taking into account his or her age or situation, his or her parents or legal guardians;

(iv) Not to be compelled to give testimony or to confess guilt; to examine or have examined adverse witnesses and to obtain the participation and examination of witnesses on his or her behalf under conditions of equality;

(v) If considered to have infringed the penal law, to have this decision and any measures imposed in consequence thereof reviewed by a higher competent, independent and impartial authority or judicial body according to law;

(vi) To have the free assistance of an interpreter if the child cannot understand or speak the language used;

(vii) To have his or her privacy fully respected at all stages of the proceedings.

3 States Parties shall seek to promote the establishment of laws, procedures, authorities and institutions specifically applicable to children alleged as, accused of, or recognized as having infringed the penal law, and, in particular:

(a) The establishment of a minimum age below which children shall he presumed not to have the capacity to infringe the penal law;

(b) Whenever appropriate and desirable, measures for dealing with such children without resorting to judicial proceedings, providing that human rights and legal safeguards are fully respected.

4 A variety of dispositions, such as care, guidance and supervision orders; counselling; probation; foster care; education and vocational training programmes and other alternatives to institutional care shall be available to ensure that children are dealt with in a manner appropriate to their well-being and proportionate both to their circumstances and the offence.

Article 41

Nothing in the present Convention shall affect any provisions which are more conducive to the realization of the rights of the child and which may be contained in:

(*a*) The law of a State Party; or

(*b*) International law in force for that State.

Part II

Article 42

States Parties undertake to make the principles and provisions of the Convention widely known, by appropriate and active means, to adults and children alike.

Article 43

1 For the purpose of examining the progress made by States Parties in achieving the realization of the obligations undertaken in the present Convention, there shall be established a Committee on the Rights of the Child, which shall carry out the functions herein-after provided.

2 The Committee shall consist of ten experts of high moral standing and recognized competence in the field covered by this Convention. The members of the Committee shall be elected by States Parties from among their nationals and shall serve in their personal capacity, consideration being given to equitable geographical distribution, as well as to the principal legal systems.

3 The members of the Committee shall be elected by secret ballot from a list of persons nominated by States Parties. Each State Party may nominate one person from among its own nationals.

4 The initial election to the Committee shall be held no later than six months after the date of the entry into force of the present Convention

and thereafter every second year. At least four months before the date of each election, the Secretary-General of the United Nations shall address a letter to States Parties inviting them to submit their nominations within two months. The Secretary-General shall subsequently prepare a list in alphabetical order of all persons thus nominated, indicating States Parties which have nominated them, and shall submit it to the States Parties to the present Convention.

5 The elections shall be held at meetings of States Parties convened by the Secretary-General at United Nations Headquarters. At those meetings, for which two-thirds of States Parties shall constitute a quorum, the persons elected to the Committee shall be those who obtain the largest number of votes and an absolute majority of the votes of the representatives of States Parties present and voting.

6 The members of the Committee shall be elected for a term of four years. They shall be eligible for re-election if renominated. The term of five of the members elected at the first election shall expire at the end of two years; immediately after the first election, the names of these five members shall be chosen by lot by the Chairman of the meeting.

7 If a member of the Committee dies or resigns or declares that for any other cause he or she can no longer perform the duties of the Committee, the State Party which nominated the member shall appoint another expert from among its nationals to serve for the remainder of the term, subject to the approval of the Committee.

8 The Committee shall establish its own rules of procedure.

9 The Committee shall elect its officers for a period of two years.

10 The meetings of the Committee shall normally be held at United Nations Headquarters or at any other convenient place as determined by the Committee. The Committee shall normally meet annually. The duration of the meetings of the Committee shall be determined, and reviewed, if necessary, by a meeting of the States Parties to the present Convention, subject to the approval of the General Assembly.

11 The Secretary-General of the United Nations shall provide the necessary staff and facilities for the effective performance of the functions of the Committee under the present Convention.

12 With the approval of the General Assembly, the members of the Committee established under the present Convention shall receive emoluments from United Nations resources on such terms and conditions as the Assembly may decide.

Article 44

1 States Parties undertake to submit to the Committee, through the Secretary-General of the United Nations, reports on the measures they
have adopted which give effect to the rights recognized herein and on
the progress made on the enjoyment of those rights:
  (*a*) Within two years of the entry into force of the Convention for the
    State Party concerned;
  (*b*) Thereafter every five years.
2 Reports made under the present article shall indicate factors and difficulties, if any, affecting the degree of fulfilment of the obligations
under the present Convention. Reports shall also contain sufficient
information to provide the Committee with a comprehensive understanding of the implementation of the Convention in the country
concerned.
3 A State Party which has submitted a comprehensive initial report to the
Committee need not, in its subsequent reports submitted in accordance with paragraph I (*b*) of the present article, repeat basic information previously provided.
4 The Committee may request from States Parties further information
relevant to the implementation of the Convention.
5 The Committee shall submit to the General Assembly, through the
Economic and Social Council, every two years, reports on its activities.
6 States Parties shall make their reports widely available to the public in
their own countries.

Article 45

In order to foster the effective implementation of the Convention and
to encourage international co-operation in the field covered by the
Convention:
  (*a*) The specialized agencies, the United Nations Children's Fund,
    and other United Nations organs shall be entitled to be repre-
    sented at the consideration of the implementation of such provi-
    sions of the present Convention as fall within the scope of their
    mandate. The Committee may invite the specialized agencies, the
    United Nations Children's Fund and other competent bodies as
    it may consider appropriate to provide expert advice on the
    implementation of the Convention in areas falling within the
    scope of their respective mandates. The Committee may invite

the specialized agencies, the United Nations Children's Fund, and other United Nations organs to submit reports on the implementation of the Convention in areas falling within the scope of their activities;

(*b*) The Committee shall transmit, as it may consider appropriate, to the specialized agencies, the United Nations Children's Fund and other competent bodies, any reports from States Parties that contain a request, or indicate a need, for technical advice or assistance, along with the Committee's observations and suggestions, if any, on these requests or indications;

(*b*) The Committee may recommend to the General Assembly to request the Secretary-General to undertake on its behalf studies on specific issues relating to the rights of the child;

(*c*) The Committee may make suggestions and general recommendations based on information received pursuant to articles 44 and 45 of the present Convention. Such suggestions and general recommendations shall be transmitted to any State Party concerned and reported to the General Assembly, together with comments, if any, from States Parties.

Part III

Article 46

The present Convention shall be open for signature by all States.

Article 47

The present Convention is subject to ratification. Instruments of ratification shall be deposited with the Secretary-General of the United Nations.

Article 48

The present Convention shall remain open for accession by any State. The instruments of accession shall be deposited with the Secretary-General of the United Nations.

Article 49

1 The present Convention shall enter into force on the thirtieth day fol-

lowing the date of deposit with the Secretary-General of the United Nations of the twentieth instrument of ratification or accession.

2 For each State ratifying or acceding to the Convention after the deposit of the twentieth instrument of ratification or accession, the Convention shall enter into force on the thirtieth day after the deposit by such State of its instrument of ratification or accession.

Article 50

1 A State Party may propose an amendment and file it with the Secretary-General of the United Nations. The Secretary-General shall thereupon communicate the proposed amendment to States Parties, with a request that they indicate whether they favour a conference of States Parties for the purpose of considering and voting upon the proposals. In the event that, within four months from the date of such communication, at least one-third of the States Parties favour such a conference, the Secretary-General shall convene the conference under the auspices of the United Nations. Any amendment adopted by a majority of States Parties present and voting at the conference shall be submitted to the General Assembly for approval.

2 An amendment adopted in accordance with paragraph 1 of the present article shall enter into force when it has been approved by the General Assembly of the United Nations and accepted by a two-thirds majority of States Parties.

3 When an amendment enters into force, it shall be binding on those States Parties which have accepted it, other States Parties still being bound by the provisions of the present Convention and any earlier amendments which they have accepted.

Article 51

1 The Secretary-General of the United Nations shall receive and circulate to all States the text of reservations made by States at the time of ratification or accession.

2 A reservation incompatible with the object and purpose of the present Convention shall not be permitted.

3 Reservations may be withdrawn at any time by notification to that effect addressed to the Secretary-General of the United Nations, who shall then inform all States. Such notification shall take effect on the date on which it is received by the Secretary-General.

Article 52

A State Party may denounce the present Convention by written notification to the Secretary-General of the United Nations. Denunciation becomes effective one year after the date of receipt of the notification by the Secretary-General.

Article 53

The Secretary-General of the United Nations is designated as the depositary of the present Convention.

Article 54

The original of the present Convention, of which the Arabic, Chinese, English, French, Russian, and Spanish texts are equally authentic, shall be deposited with the Secretary-General of the United Nations.
In witness thereof the undersigned plenipotentiaries, being duly authorized thereto by their respective Governments, have signed the present Convention.

References

Abdallah-Pretceille, M. (1989). *Human rights education in pre-primary schools.* Report of the Fortieth Council of Europe Teachers' Seminar, Donaueschingen, 20–25 June. Strasbourg: Council of Europe.

Alderson, P. (1992). The rights of children and young people. In A. Coote (Ed.)., *The welfare of citizens: Developing new social rights* (pp. 153–180). London: Institute for Public Policy Research.

Alderson, P. (1999). Human rights and democracy in schools – Do they mean more than 'Picking up litter and not killing whales'? *International Journal of Children's Rights, 7,* 85–205.

Alderson, P. (2000). School students' views on school councils and daily life at school. *Children and Society, 14,* 121–134

Alderson, P., & Arnold, S. (1999). *School students' views on schools, councils and daily life at school.* London: Institute of Education, University of London.

Andreopoulos, G. (1997). Human rights education in the post-cold war context. In G. Andreopoulos & R. Claude (Eds.), *Human rights education for the twenty-first century* (pp. 9–20). Philadelphia: University of Pennsylvania Press.

Anour, M. (2002). Educating for coexistence after 9/11. *Education Digest, 68* (1), 4–8.

Apple, M.W., & Beane, J.A. (1995). *Democratic schools.* Alexandria, VA: Association for Supervision and Curriculum Development.

Archard, D. (1993). *Children: Rights and childhood* (pp. 1–12). London: Routledge.

Arendt, H. (1961). *Between past and future: Six exercises in political thought.* New York: Viking.

Arnett, J.J. (2002). The psychology of globalization. *American Psychologist, 57* (10), 774–783.

Arnot, M., Arujo, H., Deliyanni-Konintze, K., Rowe, G., & Tome, A. (1996).

Teachers, gender and discourses of citizenship. *International Studies in the Sociology of Education, 6* (1), 3–35.

Aronson, E., Blaney, N., Sikes, J., Stephan, C., & Snapp, M. (1975). Busing and racial tension: The Jigsaw route to learning and liking. *Psychology Today, 8,* 43–50.

Aronson, E., Stephan, C., Sikes, J., Blaney, N., & Snapp, M. (1978). *The Jigsaw Classroom.* Beverly Hills, CA: Sage.

Ashton, P., & Webb, R. (1986). *Making a difference: Teachers' sense of efficacy and student achievement.* New York: Longman.

Audigier, F. (1996). *Teaching about society, passing on values: Elementary law in civic education.* Strasbourg: Council of Europe.

Ba, H., & Hawkins, J. (1996). *Resolving conflict creatively: Program evaluation project.* New York: Education Development Center.

Bala, N., Hornick, J., Snyder, H., & Paetsch, J. (2002). *Juvenile justice systems: An international comparison of problems and solutions.* Toronto: Thompson Educational.

Barbidge, B. (1981). Facing history and ourselves: Tracing development through analysis of student journals. *Moral Education Forum, 6,* 42–48.

Barbidge, B. (1988). Things so finely human: Moral sensibilities at risk in adolescence. In C. Gilligan, J. Ward, J.M. Taylor, & B. Barbidge (Eds.), *Mapping the moral domain: A contribution of women's thinking to psychological theory and education* (pp. 87–110). Cambridge, MA: Harvard University Press.

Barrett, R. (1999). Middle schooling: A challenge for policy and curriculum. *Education Horizons, 5* (3), 6–9.

Barry, M., Fiehn, J., & Miller, A. (1992). *Industry and the environment – friend or foe?* Warwick, England: SCIP/MESP Schools Curriculum Industry Partnership/Mini-Enterprise in Schools Project.

Batson, C.D., Polyarpou, M., Harmon-Jones, E., Imhoff, H., Mitchner, E., Bednar, L., Klein, T., & Highberger, L. (1997). Empathy and attitudes: Can feeling for a member of a stigmatized group improve feelings toward the group? *Journal of Personality and Social Psychology, 71* (1), 105–118.

Battistich, V., Schaps, E., Solomon, D., & Watson, M. (1991). The role of the school in prosocial development. In H.E. Fitzgerald (Ed.), *Theory and research in behavioral pediatrics* (pp. 89–127). New York: Plenum.

Battistich, V., Watson, M., Solomon, D., Lewis, C., & Schaps, E. (1999). Beyond the 3Rs: A broader agenda for school reform. *Elementary School Journal, 99* (5), 415–32.

Baumeister, R.F., & Muraven, M. (1996). Identity as adaptation to social, cultural and historical context. *Journal of Adolescence, 19,* 405–16.

Beane, J. (1990). *Affect in the curriculum: Towards democracy, dignity and diversity.* New York: Teachers College Press.

Benavot, A. (2002). A critical analysis of comparative research. *Prospects*, XXX11 (1), 51–73.

Benninga, J.S (1988, February). An emerging synthesis in moral education. *Phi Delta Kappan*, February, 415–418.

Benninga, J.S. (1997). Schools, character development and citizenship. In A. Molnar (Ed.)., *The construction of children's character* (pp. 77–96). Chicago: University of Chicago Press.

Berman, P., & McLaughlin, M. (1978). *Federal programs supporting educational Change, vol. 8, Implementing and sustaining innovations*. Santa Monica: Rand.

Berman, S. (1997). *Children's social consciousness and the development of social responsibility*. Albany: SUNY Press.

Berndt, T. (1987). The distinctive features of conversations between friends: Theories, research, and implications for sociomoral development. In W. Kurtines & J. Gewirtz (Eds.)., *Moral development through social interaction* (pp. 281–300). New York: Wiley.

Berreth, D., & Berman, S. (1997). The moral dimensions of schools. *Educational Leadership, 54* (8) 24–27.

Best, F. (1991). Human rights education and teacher training. In H. Starkey (Ed.), *The challenge of human rights education* (pp. 120–129). London: Cassell.

Bickmore, K. (1999). Teaching conflict and conflict resolution in the school: (Extra-) Curricular considerations. In A. Raviv, L. Oppenheimer, & D. Bar-Tal (Eds.), *How children understand war and peace* (pp. 233–259). San Francisco: Jossey-Bass.

Bickmore, K. (2002). Good training is not enough: Research on peer mediation program implementation. *Social Alternatives, 21* (1), 33–38.

Booth, M. (2002). Arab adolescents facing the future: Enduring ideals and pressures for change. In B.B. Brown, R. Larson, & T.S. Saraswathi (Eds.), *The world's youth: Adolescence in eight regions of the globe* (pp. 207–242). New York: Cambridge University Press.

Bourne, R., Gundara, J., Ratsoma, N., & Rukanda, M. (1997). *School-based understanding of human rights in four countries: A commonwealth study*. Education research paper, no. 22, Department of International Development, Commonwealth Secretariat.

Boyt, H.C., & Skelton, N. (1997, February). The legacy of public work: Educating for citizenship. *Educational Leadership*, 12–17.

Brabeck, M.M., & Rogers, L. (2000). Human rights as a moral issue: Lessons for moral educators from human rights work. *Journal of Moral Education, 29* (2), 167–183.

Bridgeman, D.L. (1981). Enhanced role-taking through cooperative interdependence: A field study. *Child Development, 52,* 1231–1238.

Brown, M., & Davies, I. (1998). The Holocaust and education for citizenship:

The teaching of history, religion and human rights. *Educational Review, 50,* 75–84.

Burns, R.J., & Aspelagh, R. (1996). Peace education and the comparative study of education. In R.J. Burns & R. Aspelagh (Eds.), *Three Decades of Peace Education around the World* (pp. 3–23). New York: Garland.

Burr, R. (2002). Global and local approaches to children's rights in Vietnam. *Childhood, 9,* 49–61.

Burwood, L., & Wyeth, R. (1998). Should schools promote toleration? *Journal of Moral Education, 27* (4), 465–473.

Byfield, L. (1999). Vote for rights. *Alberta Report, 26* (37), 2.

Callan, E. (2001). Self-defeating political education. In R.U. Beiner & W. Norman (Eds.), *Canadian political philosophy* (pp. 91–104). Toronto: Oxford University Press.

Campbell, K.M., & Covell, K. (2001). Children's rights education at the university level: An effective means of promoting rights knowledge and rights-based attitudes. *International Journal of Children's Rights, 9,* 123–135.

Cantwell, N. (1992). The origins, development and significance of the United Nations Convention on the Rights of the Child. In S. Detrick (Ed.), *The United Nations Convention on the Rights of the Child* (pp. 19–30). Dordrecht: Martinus Nijhoff.

Carrington, B., & Short, G. (1997). Holocaust education, anti-racism and citizenship. *Educational Review, 49,* 271–283.

Carter, C. (2002). Conflict resolution at school: Building compassionate communities. *Social Alternatives, 21* (1), 49–55.

Cesarani, D. (1997, January). Why we must outlaw these race lies. *Guardian, 30,* 19.

Cherney, I., & Perry, N.W. (1996). Children's attitudes toward their rights. In E. Verhellen (Ed.), *Monitoring children's rights* (pp. 241–250).The Hague: Marvinus Nijhoff.

Chisholm, L. (2001). Critical discussion: From the margins – the darker side of empowerment. In H. Helve & C. Wallace (Eds.), *Youth, citizenship and empowerment* (pp. 129–138). Aldershot: Ashgate Publishing.

Colby, A., & Damon, W. (1992). *Some do care: Contemporary lives of moral commitment.* New York: Free Press.

Cole, P., & Farris, T. (1979). Building a just community at the elementary school level. *Moral Education Forum, 4* (2), 12–19.

Coles, B. (1995). *Youth and social policy: Youth citizenship and young careers.* London: ULC Press.

Collins, A. (1996). Design issues for learning environments. In S. Vosniadou, E. DeCorte, R. Glaser, & H. Mandl (Eds.), *International perspectives on the design of technology-supported learning environments* (pp. 347–361). Mahwah, NJ: Lawrence Erlbaum.

Covell, K., & Howe, R.B. (1999). The impact of children's rights education: A Canadian study. *International Journal of Children's Rights, 7,* 171–183.

Covell, K., & Howe, R.B. (2000). Children's rights education: Implementing article 42. In A.B. Smith, M. Gollop, K. Marshall, & K. Nairn (Eds.), *Advocating for children: International perspectives on children's rights* (pp. 42–50). Otago, N.Z.: University of Otago Press.

Covell, K., & Howe, R.B. (2001a). *The challenge of children's rights for Canada.* Waterloo: Wilfrid Laurier University Press.

Covell, K., & Howe, R.B (2001b). Moral education through the 3 Rs: Rights, respect and responsibility. *Journal of Moral Education, 30,* 31–42.

Covell, K., O'Leary, J.L., & Howe, R.B. (2002). Introducing a new grade 8 curriculum in children's rights. *Alberta Journal of Educational Research, 48* (4), 302–313.

Crick, B. (1998). *Education for citizenship and the teaching of democracy in schools.* Final Report of the Advisory Group on Citizenship. London: Qualifications and Curriculum Authority.

Crick, B. (2000). *Essays on citizenship.* London: Continuum.

Crick, N.R., & Grotpeter, J.K. (1995). Relational aggression, gender and social-psychological adjustment. *Child Development, 54,* 1386–1399.

Cunningham, J. (1991). The human rights secondary school. In H. Starkey (Ed.), *The challenge of human rights education* (pp. 90–103). London: Cassell.

Damon, W., & Gregory, A. (1997). The youth charter: Towards the formation of adolescent moral identity. *Journal of Moral Education, 26* (2), 117–131.

David, P. (2002). Implementing the rights of the child: Six reasons why the human rights of children remain a constant challenge. *International Review of Education, 48* (3–4), 259–263.

Davies, P., Howie, H., Mangan, J., & Telhaj, S. (2002). Economic aspects of citizenship education: An investigation of students' understanding. *Curriculum Journal, 13* (2), 201–223.

Day, J.M. (1991). Role-taking revisited: Narrative and cognitive developmental interpretations of moral growth. *Journal of Moral Education, 20* (3), 305–316.

Decoene, J., & De Cock, R. (1996). The children's rights project in the primary school 'De vrijdagmarkt' in Bruges. In E. Verhellen (Ed.), *Monitoring children's rights.* (pp. 627–636). The Hague: Martinus Nijhoff.

Delors, J. (1996). *Learning: The treasure within. Report of the International Commission on Education for the 21st Century.* Paris: UNESCO.

Demaray, M.K., & Malecki, C.K. (2002). Critical levels of perceived social support associated with student adjustment. *School Psychology Quarterly, 17* (3), 213–241.

Dewey, J. (1916/ reprint 1966). *Democracy and education.* New York: Free Press.

Dewey, J. (1933). *How we think: Restatement of the relation of reflective thinking to the educative process.* Lexington, MA: D.C. Heath

Dias, C. (1997). Human rights education as a strategy for development. In G. Andreopoulos & R. Claude (Eds.), *Human rights education for the twenty-first century* (pp. 51–63). Philadelphia: University of Pennsylvania Press.

Doek, J. (1992). The current status of the United Nations Convention on the Rights of the Child. In S. Detrick (Ed.), *The United Nations Convention on the Rights of the Child* (pp. 632–640). Dordrecht: Martinus Nijhoff.

Dunn, S., Putallaz, M., Sheppard, B., & Lindstrom, R. (1987). Social support and adjustment in gifted adolescents. *Journal of Educational Psychology, 79,* 467–473.

Dye, P. (1991). Active learning for human rights in intermediate and high schools. In H. Starkey (Ed.), *The challenge of human rights education* (pp. 105–119). London: Cassell.

East, P., & Rook, K. (1992). Compensatory patterns of support among children's peer relationships: A test using school friends, non-school friends and siblings. *Developmental Psychology, 28,* 163–172.

Eccles, J.S., Midgley, C., Wigfield, A., Buchanan, C.M., Reuman, D., Flanagan, C., & MacIver, D. (1993). Development during adolescence: The impact of stage-environment fit theory on young adolescents' experiences in schools and in families. *American Psychologist, 48* (2), 90–101.

Edelman, M. (1964/1985). *The symbolic uses of politics.* Urbana: University of Illinois Press.

Eisner, E.W. (2000). Those who ignore the past: 12 'easy' lessons for the next millennium. *Journal of Curriculum Studies, 32,* 343–357.

Elkind, D., & Hetzel, D.C. (1977). *Readings in human development: Contemporary perspectives.* New York: Harper and Row.

Erikson, E. (1968). *Identity: Youth and crisis.* New York: W.W. Norton.

Evers, W.J.G., Brouwers, A., & Tomic, W. (2002). Burnout and self-efficacy: A study on teachers' beliefs when implementing an innovative educational system in the Netherlands. *British Journal of Educational Psychology, 72,* 227–243.

Federle, K. (1994). Rights flow downhill. *International Journal of Children's Rights, 2,* 343–368.

Feinberg, J. (1970). The nature and value of rights. *Journal of Value Inquiry, 4* (4), 55–97.

Feinberg, J. (1973). *Social Philosophy.* Englewood Cliffs, NJ: Prentice-Hall.

Flanagan, C., Bowes, J.M., Jonsson, B., Csapo, B., & Sheblanova, E. (1998). Ties that bind: Correlates of adolescents' civic commitments in seven countries. *Journal of Social Issues, 54* (3), 457–475.

Flekkoy, M., & Kaufman, N. (1997). *The participation rights of the child: Rights and responsibilities in family and society.* London: Jessica Kingsley.

Franklin, A., & Franklin, B. (1996). Growing pains: The developing children's rights movement in the U.K. In J. Pilcher & S. Wagg (Eds.), *Thatcher's children? Politics, childhood, and society in the 1980s and 1990s* (pp. 94–113). London: Falmer.

Franklin, B. (1996). Children's right to participate in decision making. In E. Verhellen (Ed.), *Monitoring children's rights* (pp. 317–326). The Hague: Marvinus Nijhoff.

Freeman, M. (1983). *The rights and wrongs of children.* London: Frances Pinter.

Freeman, M. (1996). Introduction: Children as persons. In M. Freeman (Ed.), *Children's rights: A comparative perspective* (pp. 2–3). Aldershot: Dartmouth Publishing.

Friedman, I.A. (1996). Multiple pathways to burnout: Cognitive and emotional scenarios in teacher burnout. *Anxiety, Stress and Coping: An International Journal, 9* (3), 245–259.

Frimannsson, G. (2001). Civil education and the good. *Studies in Philosophy and Education, 20,* 310–12.

Fullan, M. (1991). *The new meaning of educational change.* New York: Teachers College Press.

Fuller, B., Wood, K., Rapoport, T., & Dornsbusch, S. (1982). The organizational context of individual efficacy. *Review of Educational Research, 52,* 7–30.

Gabriel, C. (2001). Citizens and citizenship. In J. Brodie (Ed.), *Critical concepts* (pp. 261–276). Toronto: Prentice-Hall.

Gallatin, J., & Adelson, J. (1970). Individual rights and the public good: A cross-national study of adolescents. *Comparative Political Studies, 3* (2), 226–242.

Galston, W. (1991). *Liberal purposes: Goods, virtues, and duties in the liberal state.* Cambridge: Cambridge University Press.

Garbarino, J. (1995). *Raising children in a socially toxic environment.* San Francisco: Jossey-Bass.

Geffner, R.A. (1978). The effects of interdependent learning on self-esteem, inter-ethnic relations and intra-ethnic attitudes of elementary school children: A field experiment. Doctoral thesis, University of California at Santa Cruz.

Gilbert, L. (1998). *United Nations Convention on the Rights of the Child – Report Article 42 Consultation Project.* Wellington, N.Z.: Ministry of Youth Affairs and Office of the Commissioner for Children.

Glaser, R., Ferguson, E.L., & Vosniadou, S. (1996). Cognition and the design of learning environments. In S. Vosniadou, E. DeCorte, R. Glaser, & H. Mandl (Eds.), *International Perspectives on the Design of Technology-Supported Learning Environments* (pp. 1–9). Mahwah, NJ: Lawrence Erlbaum.

Glazer, N. (1983). *Ethnic dilemmas.* Cambridge, MA: Harvard University Press.

Glynn, M.T., Bock, G., & Cohn, K.C. (1982). *American youth and the Holocaust: A study of four major Holocaust curricula.* New York: National Jewish Center.

Goldfarb, E.S., & McCaffree, K. (2000). Toward a more effective pedagogy for sexuality education: The establishment of democratic classrooms. *Journal of Sex Education and Therapy, 25* (2–3), 147–156.

Goodman, D. (2000). Motivating people from privileged groups to support social justice. *Teachers College Record, 102* (6), 1061–1086.

Gordon, T., Holland, J., & Lahelma, E. (2000). *Making spaces: Citizenship and differences in schools.* New York: St Martin's Press.

Griffiths, M., & Davies, L. (1995). *In fairness to children: Working for social justice in the primary school.* London: David Fulton.

Grundy, S. (2002). Is large-scale educational reform possible? *Journal of Educational Change, 3,* 55–62.

Grusec, J. (1991). Socializing concern for others in the home. *Developmental Psychology, 27,* 338–342.

Guskey, T. (1987). Context measures that affect measures of teacher efficacy. *Journal of Educational Research, 81,* 41–47.

Haan, N., Aerts, E., & Cooper, B. (1985). *On moral grounds: The search for practical morality.* New York: New York University Press.

Hahn, C. (1998). *Becoming political: Comparative perspectives on citizenship education.* Albany: SUNY Press.

Hahn, C.L. (2002). Implications of September 11 for political socialization research. *Theory and Research in Social Education, 30* (1), 158–162.

Hamm, M., & Adams, D. (2002). Collaborative inquiry: Working toward shared goals. *Kappa Delta Pi Record, 38* (3), 115–118.

Hammarberg, T. (1990). The U.N. Convention on the Rights of the Child – and how to make it work. *Human Rights Quarterly, 12,* 97–105.

Hammarberg, T. (1997). *A school for children with rights.* Innocenti Lectures. Florence: UNICEF.

Hancock, R., & Mansfield, M. (2002). The literacy hour: A case for listening to children. *Curriculum Journal, 13* (2), 183–200.

Handle, C., Oesterreich, D., & Trommer, L. (1999). Concepts of civic education in Germany based on a survey of expert opinion. In J. Torney-Purta, J. Schwille, & J. Amadeo (Eds.), *Civic Education across countries: Twenty-four national case studies from the IEA Civic Education Project* (pp. 257–284). Wellington, N.Z.: Becky Bliss Design and Production.

Harris, I. (2002). Challenges for peace educators at the beginning of the 21st century. *Social Alternatives, 21* (1), 28–31.

Hart, R. (1992). *Children's Participation: From Tokenism to Citizenship.* Innocenti Essays, No. 4. Florence: UNICEF.

Hart, S.N. (1991). From property to person status: Historical perspective on children's rights. *American Psychologist, 46* (1) 53–59.

Hart, S.N., & Pavlovic, Z. (1991). Children's rights in education: An historical perspective. *Social Psychology Review, 20* (3), 345–358.

Harter, S. (1988). The construction and conservation of the self: James and Cooley revisited. In D.K. Lapsley and F.C. Power (Eds.), *Self, Ego and Identity: Integrated Approaches* (pp. 44–70). New York: Springer-Verlag.

Hartsell, T., & Ricker, A. (2002). What teachers think: Intellectual, social and physical changes in students since 1993. *educational Horizons, 81* (1), 45–52.

Harwood, D. (1995). The pedagogy of the world studies 8–13 project: The influence of the presence/absence of the teacher upon children's collaborative groupwork. *British Educational Research Journal, 21* (5), 587–611.

Harwood, D. (1997). Teacher roles in World Studies democratic pedagogy. *Evaluation and Research in Education, 11* (2), 65–90.

Hauser, S.T., & Bowlds, M.K. (1990). Stress, coping and adaptation. In S.S. Feldman & G.R. Elliott (Eds.), *At the threshold: The developing adolescent* (pp. 388–413). Cambridge, MA: Harvard University Press.

Heater, D. (1990). *Citizenship: The civic ideal in world history, politics and education.* London: Longman.

Heater, D. (1993). Political education for global citizenship. In J. Lynch, C. Modgil, & S. Modgil (Eds.), *Cultural diversity and the schools: Human rights, education, and global responsibilities* (pp. 189–204). London: Falmer.

Heater, D. (2001).The history of citizenship education in England. *Curriculum Journal, 12* (1), 103–123.

Heater, D. (2002). The history of citizenship education: A comparative outline. *Parliamentary Affairs, 55,* 457–474.

Hebert, Y. (2002). *Citizenship in transformation in Canada.* Toronto: University of Toronto Press.

Heiman, G. (1966). The nineteenth-century legacy: Nationalism or patriotism? In P. Russell (Ed.), *Nationalism in Canada* (pp. 323–340). Toronto: McGraw-Hill.

Held, D. (1995). *Democracy and the global order.* London: Polity.

Helwig, C. (1997). The role of agent and social context in judgments of freedom of speech and religion. *Child Development, 68,* 484–495.

Henrich, C.C., Brown, J.L., & Aber, J.L. (1999). Evaluating the effectiveness of school-based violence prevention: Developmental approaches. *Social Policy Report, 13* (3), 1–16.

Henry, C.P. (1991). Educating for human rights. *Human Rights Quarterly, 13,* 420–423.

Hess, D. (2002). Teaching controversial public issues discussions in secondary social studies classrooms: Learning from skilled teachers. *Theory and Research in Social Education, 30* (1), 10–41.

Higgins, A. (1991). The just community approach to moral education: Evolution of the idea and recent findings. In W. Kurtines & J. Gerwitz (Eds), *Handbook of moral behavior and development,* vol. 3, *Application* (pp. 111–141). Hillsdale, NJ: Lawrence Erlbaum.

Hilden, T. (2001). Skinheads – masculinity and violent action. In H. Helve & C. Wallace (Eds.). *Youth, citizenship and empowerment* (pp. 139–47). Aldershot: Ashgate Publishing.

Hodgkin, R., & Newell, P. (1998). *Implementation handbook for the Convention on the Rights of the Child.* New York: UNICEF.

Hodgson, D. (1996). The international human right to education and education concerning human rights. *International Journal of Children's Rights, 4,* 237–262.

Hoffman, M.L. (1984). Empathy, its limitations, and its role in a comprehensive moral theory. In W. Kurtines & J. Gewirtz (Eds.), *Morality, moral behavior and moral development,* vol. 3, *Application* (pp. 283–302). New York: Wiley.

Holden, C. (1998). Keen at 11, cynical at 18? Encouraging pupil participation in school and community. In C. Holden & N. Clough. (Eds.), *Children as citizens: Education for participation* (pp. 46–62). London: Jessica Kingsley.

Holden, C., & Clough, N. (1998). *Children as citizens: Education for participation.* London: Jessica Kingsley.

Holt, J. (1964). *How children fail.* New York: Pitman.

Hornberg, S. (2002). Human rights education as an integral part of general education. *International Review of Education, 48* (3–4), 187–198.

Howe, R.B. (2001). Do parents have fundamental rights? *Journal of Canadian Studies, 36* (3), 61–78.

Howe, R.B., & Covell, K. (1998). Teaching children's rights: Considerations and strategies. *Education and Law Journal, 9,* 97–113.

Howe, R.B., & Covell, K. (2001). Youth justice reform and the rights of the child. *Canadian Journal of Community Mental Health, 20* (2), 91–106.

Hughes, A., & Filer, H. (June, 2003). *The Rights of the child: The impact of teaching in a year 6 class.* Andover, England: Knights Enham Junior School.

Humphrey, J. (1987). Epilogue. In N. Tarrow (Ed.), *Human rights and education* (pp. 235–236). Oxford: Pergamon.

Ignatieff, M. (2000). *The rights revolution.* Toronto: Anansi.

Irving, K. (2001). Australian students' perceptions of the importance and existence of their rights. *School Psychology International, 22* (2), 224–240.

Jeary, J. (2001). *Character Education Report.* Calgary: Board of Education.

John, M. (1996). Voicing: Research and practice with the 'silenced.' In M. John (Ed.), *Children in charge: The child's right to a fair hearing* (pp. 3–24). London: Jessica Kingsley.

Johnson, D.W., Johnson, R.T., & Holubec, E. (2001). Cooperative learning. *Newsletter of the Cooperative Learning Institute, 16* (1), 1–2.

Joseph, Y. (1995). Child protection rights. In C. Cloke & M. Davies (Eds.), *Participation and empowerment in child protection* (pp. 1–18). London: Pitanm.

Kaplan, W. (1993). Who belongs? Changing concepts of citizenship and nationality. In William Kaplan (Ed.), *Belonging* (pp. 245–264). Montreal: McGill-Queen's University Press.

Katz, S. (April, 1981). Curriculum innovation: Teacher commitment, training and support. Paper presented at the annual conference of the American Educational Research Association, Los Angeles. ERIC Document Reproduction Service No. ED200546.

Katz, S., Earl, L., & Olson, D. (2001). The paradox of classroom assessment: A challenge for the 21st century. *McGill Journal of Education, 36* (1), 13–26.

Keighley-James, D. (2002). Student participation and voices in curriculum redevelopment: The view from a curriculum development agency. *Curriculum Perspectives, 22* (1), 1–7.

Kerr, D., McCarthy, S., & Smith, A. (2002). Citizenship education in England, Ireland, and Northern Ireland. *European Journal of Education, 37,* (2) 180–191.

Kielburger, C. (1998). *Free the Children.* Toronto: McClelland and Stewart.

Kielsmeier, J.C. (2000). A time to serve, a time to learn: Service-learning and the promise of democracy. *Phi Delta Kappan, 81* (9), 652–657.

Kisser, C. (1996). Children exercise children's rights: Participation of pupils in Austrian schools. *International Journal of Children's Rights, 4,* 407–414.

Knutsson, K.E. (1997). *Children: Noble causes or worthy citizens?* Florence: UNICEF.

Kohlberg, L. (1980). High school democracy and educating for a just society. In R. Mosher (Ed.), *Moral education: A first generation of research and development* (pp. 20–57). New York: Praeger.

Kohlberg, L. (1985). The just community approach to moral education in theory and in practise. In M. Berkowitz & F. Oser (Eds.), *Moral education: Theory and application* (pp. 27–87). Hillsdale, NJ: Lawrence Erlbaum.

Kohn, A. (1997, February). How not to teach values: A critical look at character education. *Phi Delta Kappan,* 429–439.

Kohn, A. (2003). Professors who profess: Making a difference as scholar activists. *Kappa Delta Pi Record, 39* (3), 108–113.

Kulynych, J. (2001). No playing in the public sphere: Democratic theory and the exclusion of children. *Social Theory and Practice, 27* (2), 231–264.

Kymlicka, W. (2001). *Politics in the vernacular: Nationalism, multiculturalism, and citizenship.* Oxford: Oxford University Press.

Kymlicka, W. & Norman, W. (1995). Return of the citizen: A survey of recent work on citizenship theory. In R. Beiner (Ed.), *Theorizing citizenship* (pp. 283–322). Albany: SUNY Press.

Lagerpetz, K.M., Bjorkquist, K., & Peltonen, T. (1988). Is indirect aggression more typical of females? *Aggressive Behavior, 14,* 403–414.

Lanotte, J.V., & Goedertier, G. (1996). Monitoring human rights: Formal and procedural aspects. In E. Verhellen (Ed.), (pp. 73–111). *Monitoring children's rights.* The Hague: Martinus Nijhoff.

Lansdown, G. (1995a). The children's rights development unit. In B. Franklin (Ed.), *The handbook of children's rights comparative policy and practice* (pp. 107–118). London: Routledge.

Lansdown, G. (1995b). Children's rights to participation and protection. In C. Cloke & M. Davies (Eds.), *Participation and empowerment in child protection* (pp. 19–37). London: Pitman.

Lawson, H. (2001). Active citizenship in schools and the community. *Curriculum Journal, 12,* (2), 163–178.

Leat, D., & Higgins, S. (2002). The role of powerful pedagogical strategies in curriculum development. *Curriculum Journal, 13* (1), 71–85.

Lebedev, O., Maiorov, A., & Zolotukhina, V. (2002). The rights of children. *Russian Education and Society, 44* (8), 6–34.

LeBlanc, L.J. (1995). *The Convention on the Rights of the Child: U.N. lawmaking on human rights.* Lincoln, NE: University of Nebraska Press.

Lee, J. (2000). Teacher receptivity to curriculum change in the implementation stage: The case of environmental education in Hong Kong. *Journal of Curriculum Studies, 32,* 95–115.

Legislationline. (2004). Citizenship France, citizenship Germany. http://legislationline.org/index Retrieved 14 Sept. 2004.

Leming, J.S. (1997). Research and practice in character education: A historical perspective. In A. Molnar (Ed.), *The construction of children's character* (pp. 31–44). Chicago: University of Chicago Press.

Leming, J.S. (1981). Curriculum effectiveness in moral/values education: A review of the research. *Journal of Moral Education, 10* (3), 147–164.

LeRoux, J. (2001). Re-examining global education's relevance beyond 2000. *Research in Education, 65,* 70–81.

Levine, H. (2000). Book review of *Children's rights education curriculum resource.* *International Journal of Children's Rights, 8,* 391–394.

Lewis, R. (1999). Preparing students for democratic citizenship: Codes of conduct in Victoria's 'Schools of the Future.' *Educational Research and Evaluation, 5* (1), 41–61.

Lickona, T. (1997a). Educating for character: The school's highest calling. Atlanta, GA: Humanities Council Lecture.

Lickona, T. (1997b). Educating for character: A comprehensive approach. In A. Molnar (Ed.), *The construction of children's character* (pp. 45–62). Chicago: University of Chicago Press.

Lickona, T. (1991a). *Educating for character.* New York: Bantam.

Lickona, T. (1991b). Moral development in the elementary school classroom. In W.M. Kurtines & J.L. Gewirtz (Eds.), *Handbook of moral behavior and development,* vol. 3, *Application* (pp. 143–161). Hillsdale, NJ: Lawrence Erlbaum.

Lickona, T. (1993). The return of character education. *Educational Leadership, 51* (3), 6–11.

Lieberman, A., Falk, B., & Alexander, L. (1995). A culture in the making: Leadership in learner-centered schools. In J. Oakes & K. Hunter Quartz (Eds.), *Creating New Educational Communities* (pp. 108–29). Chicago: University of Chicago Press.

Lieberman, M. (1981). Facing history and ourselves: A project evaluation. *Moral Education Forum, 6,* 349–378.

Lieberman, M. (1986). *Evaluation Report 78680D to the Joint Dissemination Review Panel.* Brookline, MA: Facing History and Ourselves Resource Center.

Lieberman, M. (1991). *Facing history and ourselves: Evaluation report 1990.* Wellesley, MA: Responsive Methodology.

LifeSite Daily News. (9 Nov. 1999). http://www.lifesite.net

Lohrenscheit, C. (2002). International approaches in human rights education. *International Review of Education, 48* (3–4), 173–185.

Lucker, G.W., Rosenfield, D., Sikes, J., & Aronson, E. (1977). Performance in the interdependent classroom: A field study. *American Educational Research Journal, 13,* 115–123.

Ludbrook, R. (1996). Children's rights in school education. In K. Funder (Ed.), *Citizen child: Australian law and children's rights* (pp. 84–112). Melbourne: Australian Institute of Family Studies.

Luff, I. (2000). I've been in the Reichstag: Rethinking roleplay. *Teaching History, 100,* 8–18.

Mabry, L., & Ettinger, L. (1999). Supporting community-oriented educational change. *Education Policy Analysis Archives, 7* (14), 1–17.

Magendzo, A. (1994). Tensions and dilemmas about education in human rights in democracy. *Journal of Moral Education, 23,* 251–260.

Majhanovich, S. (2002). Conflicting visions, competing expectations: Control and de-skilling of education. *McGill Journal of Education, 37*(2), 159–176.

Mann, S., & Patrick, J. (Eds). (2000). *Education for civic engagement in democracy.* Bloomington, IN: ERIC Clearinghouse.

Manzer, R. (1994). *Public schools and political ideas: Canadian educational policy in historical perspective.* Toronto: University of Toronto Press.

Marks, S. (1997). Human rights education in U.N. Peace Building. In G. Andreopoulos & R. Claude (Eds.), *Human rights education for the twenty-first century* (pp. 35–50). Philadelphia: University of Pennsylvania Press.

Marquette, H., & Mineshima, D. (2002). Civic education in the United States: Lessons for the U.K. *Parliamentary Affairs, 55*, 542–545.

Marshall, K. (1997). *Children's rights in the balance: The participation-protection debate.* Edinburgh: Stationery Office.

Marshall, T.H. (1950). *Citizenship and Social Class.* Cambridge: Cambridge University Press.

McCoy, E. (1988). Childhood through the ages. In K. Finsterbusch (Ed.), *Sociology 88/89* (pp. 44–47). Guilford, CT: Dushkin.

McLoyd, V.C. (1998). Socioeconomic disadvantage and child development. *American Psychologist, 53* (2), 185–204.

McNeely, C.A., Nonnemaker, J.M., & Blum, R.W. (2002). Promoting school connectedness: Evidence from the National Longitudinal Study of Adolescent Health. *Journal of School Health, 72* (4), 138–146.

McQueen, C. (2001). Teaching to win. *Kappa Delta Pi Record, 38* (1), 12–15.

Mead, L. (1986). *Beyond entitlement: The social obligations of citizenship.* New York: Free Press.

Meintjes, G. (1997). Human rights education as empowerment. In G. Andreopoulos & R. Claude (Eds.), *Human rights education for the twenty-first century* (pp. 64–79). Philadelphia: University of Pennsylvania Press.

Melchior, A. (1999, Fall). Impact on youth and communities. *State Education Leader,* 6.

Melton, G. (1996). The child's rights to a family environment. *American Psychologist, 51* (12), 1234–1238.

Melton, G. (2002). Starting a new generation of research. In B. Bottoms, M. Kovera, & B. McAulifff (Eds.), *Children, social science and the law* (pp. 449–453). Cambridge: Cambridge University Press.

Melton, G., & Limber, S. (1992). What children's rights mean to children: Children's own views. In M. Freeman and P. Veerman (Eds.), *The ideologies of children's rights* (pp. 167–187). Dordrecht: Kluwer Academic Publishers.

Menezes, I., Xavier, E., Cibele, C., Amaro, G., & Campos, P. (1999). Civic education issues and the intended curricula in basic education in Portugal. In J. Torney-Purta, J. Schwille, & J. Amadeo (Eds.), *Civic education across countries: Twenty-four national case studies from the IEA Civic Education Project* (pp. 483–504). Wellington, N.Z.: Becky Bliss Design and Production.

Miljeteig-Olssen, P. (1992). Children's participation: Giving children the opportunity to develop into active and responsible members of society. *Social Education, 56* (4), 216.

Mortimore, P. (2001). Globalization, effectiveness and improvement. *School Effectiveness and School Improvement, 12* (1), 229–249.

Mulgan, G. (1991). Citizens and responsibilities. In G. Andrews (Ed.), *Citizenship* (pp. 37–49). London: Lawrence and Wishart.

Mulinge, M.M. (2002). Implementing the 1989 United Nations Convention on the Rights of the Child in Sub-Saharan Africa: The overlooked socioeconomic and political dilemmas. *Child Abuse and Neglect, 26,* 1117–1130.

Murray, E. (1999). Exploring children's emerging conceptions of their participation rights and responsibilities. Doctoral Dissertation, University of Victoria, Victoria, B.C.

Murray, E. (2002). Impact of children's rights education on primary-level children. Paper, Mount Royal College, Calgary, Alberta.

Muscroft, S. (1999). *Children's rights: Reality or rhetoric?* London: International Save the Children Alliance.

Nagel, N. (2001). Empowering young students to become active citizens through real-world problem-solving. *Democracy and Education, 14* (2), 6–9.

Nakkula, M., & Selman, R.L. (1991). How people 'treat' each other: Pair therapy as a context for the development of interpersonal ethics. In W. Kurtines & J. Gerwitz (Eds.), *Handbook of Moral Behavior and Development,* vol. 3, *Application* (pp. 179–211). Hillsdale, NJ: Lawrence Erlbaum.

Narvaez, D. (2002). Does reading moral stories build character? *Educational Psychology Review, 14* (2), 155–171.

Naval, C., Print, M., & Veldhuis, R. (2002). Education for democratic citizenship in the new Europe: Context and reform. *European Journal of Education, 37* (2), 107–128.

Neacsu-Hendry, L., Turek, I., Kviecinska, J., Kati, K., & Orlin, T. (1997). Implementing human rights education in three transitional democracies. In G. Andreopoulos & R. Claude (Eds.), *Human rights education in the twenty-first century* (pp. 414–516). Philadelphia: University of Pennsylvania Press.

Neimark, E.D. (1982). Adolescent thought: Transition to formal operations. In B.B. Wolman (Ed.), *Handbook of developmental psychology* (pp. 486–502). Englewood Cliffs, NJ: Prentice-Hall.

Nisan, M. (1996). Personal identity and education for the desirable. *Journal of Moral Education, 25* (1), 75–84.

Noddings, N. (1997). Character education and community. In A. Molnar (Ed.), *The construction of children's character* (pp. 1–16). Chicago: University of Chicago Press.

Nordland, E. (1996). Think and teach globally, act locally. In R.J. Burns & R. Aspeslagh (Eds.), *Three decades of peace education around the world* (pp. 291–305). New York: Garland.

Nucci, L.P. (2001). *Education in the moral domain.* Cambridge: Cambridge University Press.

Ochaita, E., & Espinosa, M. (1997). Children's participation in family and school life: A psychological and development approach. *International Journal of Children's Rights, 5,* 279–297.

O'Moore, A.M., & Hillery, B. (1991). What do teachers need to know? In *Bullying: A practical guide for coping in schools*. Harlow: Longman.

Onheiber, M.D. (1997). Toward a reorientation of values and practice in child welfare. *Child Psychiatry and Human Development, 27* (3), 151–164.

Osborne, K. (1991). *Teaching for democratic citizenship*. Toronto: Our Schools / Our Selves Education Foundation.

Osborne, K. (2000). Public schooling and citizenship education in Canada. *Canadian Ethnic Studies, 32* (1), 8–37.

Osler, A., & Starkey, H. (2002). Education for citizenship: Mainstreaming the fight against racism. *European Journal of Education, 37* (2), 143–159.

Parker, W.C. (1996). Curriculum for democracy. In R. Soder (Ed.), *Democracy, education and the schools* (pp. 182–210). San Francisco: Jossey-Bass.

Pateman, C. (1970). *Participation and democratic theory*. Cambridge: Cambridge University Press.

Pateman, C. (1989). The patriarchal welfare state. In C. Pateman (Ed.), *The disorder of women* (pp. 179–209). Stanford: Stanford University Press.

Payne, P. (2000). Identity and environmental education. *Environmental Education Research, 7* (1), 67–88.

Pellegrini, A.D. (1998). Bullies and victims in school: A review and call for research. *Journal of Applied Developmental Psychology, 19* (2), 165–176.

Piaget, J. (1952). *The origins of intelligence in children*. New York: International Universities Press.

Pike, G. (2000). A tapestry in the making: The strands of global education. In T. Goldstein & D. Selby (Eds.), *Weaving connections: Educating for peace, social and environmental justice* (pp. 218–41). Toronto: Sumach.

Pike, G., & Selby, D. (1991). *Global teacher, global learner*. Toronto: Hodder and Stoughton.

Pike, G., & Selby, D. (1997). *Human rights: An activity file*. Nepean, ON: Bacon and Hughes.

Pike, G., & Selby, D. (1999). *In the global classroom*, vol. 1. Toronto: Pippin.

Pike, G., & Selby, D. (2000). *In the global classroom*, vol. 2. Toronto: Pippin.

Plantilla, J.R. (2002). Consultation and training for human rights education. *International Review of Education, 48* (3–4), 281–282.

Pocock, J.G. (1995). The ideal of citizenship since classical times. In Ronald Beiner (Ed.), *Theorizing Citizenship* (pp. 29–52). Albany: SUNY Press.

Pollock, P. (1983). *Forgotten children: Parent-child relations from 1500 to 1900*. Cambridge: Cambridge University Press.

Porter, J. (1999). *Reschooling and the global future: Politics, economics and the English experience*. Oxford: Symposium Books.

Posch, P. (1999). The ecologisation of schools and its implications for educational policy. *Cambridge Journal of Education, 29* (3), 340–348.

Power, F.C. (1997, March). Understanding the character in character education. Paper presented at the meeting of the American Educational Research Association, Chicago.

Power, F.C., Higgins, A., & Kohlberg, L. (1989). *Lawrence Kohlberg's approach to moral education.* New York: Columbia University Press.

Price, C. (1996). Monitoring the United Nations Convention on the Rights of the Child in a non-party state. In E. Verhellen (Ed.), *Monitoring children's rights* (pp. 486–488). The Hague: Martinus Nijhoff.

Priestly, M. (2002). Global discourses and the national reconstruction: The impact of globalization on curriculum policy. *Curriculum Journal, 13* (1), 121–138.

Print, M., Ornstrom, S., & Nielsen, H.S. (2002). Education for democratic processes in schools and classrooms. *European Journal of Education, 37* (2), 193–210.

Purdy, L. (1992). *In their best interest.* Ithaca: Cornell University Press.

Puurula, A., Neill, S., Vasileiou, L., Husbands, C., Lang, P., Katz, Y., Romi, S., Menezes, I., & Vriens, L. (2001). Teacher and student attitudes to affective education: A European collaborative research project. *Compare, 31* (2), 165–186.

Raadi-Azarakhchi, S. (1997). The United Nations decade for human rights education. In E. Verhellen (Ed.), *Understanding children's rights* (pp. 1–7). Ghent: University of Ghent Children's Rights Centre.

Rathenow, H.F., & Weber, N.H. (1998). Education after Auschwitz: A task for human rights education. In C. Holden & N. Clough (Eds.), *Children as citizens: Education for participation* (pp. 95–112). London: Jessica Kingsley.

Raths, L.E., Harmin, M., & Simon, B. (1966). *Values and teaching.* Columbus, OH: Charles E. Merrill.

Rauch, F. (2002). The potential of education for sustainable development for reform in schools. *Environmental Education Research, 8* (1), 43–51.

Rawls, J. (1971). *A theory of justice.* Cambridge, MA: Harvard University Press.

Rawls, J. (1993). *Political liberalism.* New York: Columbia University Press.

Reardon, B.A. (1988). *Comprehensive peace education: Educating for global responsibility.* New York: Teachers College, Columbia University.

Reimer, J., Paolitto, D.P., & Hersh, R.H. (1983). *Promoting moral growth.* New York: Longman.

Richardson, R. (1988). Changing the curriculum. In D. Hicks (Ed.), *Education for peace* (pp. 231–244). London: Routledge.

Robinson, J.P., & Gorrel, J. (1994). Predictors of efficacy of teachers during implementation of a new curriculum model. *Journal of Vocational Home Economics Education, 12* (2), 25–35.

Roche, J. (1999). Children: Rights, participation and citizenship. *Childhood, 6* (4), 475–93.

Rodgers, C.R. (2002). Voices inside schools: Seeing student learning – teacher change and the role of reflection. *Harvard Educational Review, 72* (2), 230–253.

Rouissi, M. (2002). Learning to live together: An integral part of citizenship education. *Prospects, 32* (1), 83–86.

Ruck, M., Keating, D., Abramovitch, R., & Koegl, C. (1998). Adolescents' and children's knowledge about rights: Some evidence for how young people view rights in their own lives. *Journal of Adolescence, 21,* 275–289.

Rudduck, J., & Flutter, J. (2000). Pupil participation and pupil perspective: Carving a new order of experience. *Cambridge Journal of Education, 30* (1), 75–90.

Ruxton, S. (1996). *Children in Europe,* London: NCH Action for Children.

Ryan, A.M. (2000). Peer groups as a context for the socialization of adolescents. *Educational Psychologist, 35* (2), 101–112.

Ryan, A.M. (2001). The classroom social environment and changes in adolescents' motivation and engagement during middle school. *American Educational Research Journal, 38* (2), 437–460.

Salomon, G. (2002). The nature of peace education: Not all programs are created equal. In G. Salomon & B. Nevo (Eds.). *Peace education: The concept, principles and practices around the world* (pp. 2–14). Mahwah, NJ: Lawrence Erlbaum.

Salomon, G. (2003). *Does peace education make a difference?* Haifa: University of Haifa, Center for Research on Peace Education.

Salomon, G. (2004). A narrative-based view of coexistence education. *Journal of Social Issues, 60* (2), 273–288.

Sarason, S. (1990). *The predictable failure of educational reform.* San Francisco: Jossey-Bass.

Scardamalia, M., & Bereiter, C. (1996). Adaptation and understanding: A case for new cultures of schooling. In S. Vosniadou, E. DeCorte, R. Glasser, & H. Mandl (Eds.), *International perspectives on the design of technology-supported learning environments* (pp. 149–163). Mahwah, NJ: Lawrence Erlbaum.

Schmidt, M., & Reppucci, N.D. (2002). Children's rights and capacities. In B. Bottoms, M. Kovera, & B. McAuliff (Eds.), *Children, social science, and the law* (pp. 76–105). Cambridge: Cambridge University Press.

Schmidt-Sinns, D. (1980). How can we teach human rights? *International Journal of Political Education, 3,* 177–185.

Schnack, K. (1998). Why focus on conflicting interests in environmental education? In M. Ahlberg & W.L. Filho (Eds.), *Environmental education for sustainability: Good environment, good life* (pp. 83–96). New York: Peter Lang.

Schubert, W.H. (1997). Character education from four perspectives on curriculum. In A. Molnar (Ed.), *The construction of children's character* (pp. 17–30). Chicago: University of Chicago Press.

Schultz, L.H., Barr, D.J., & Selman, R.L. (2001). The value of a developmental approach to evaluating character development programmes: An outcome study of Facing History and Ourselves. *Journal of Moral Education, 30* (1), 3–27.

Schwille, J., & Amadeo, J. (2002). The paradoxical situation of civic education in school: Ubiquitous and yet elusive. In G. Steiner-Khamasi, J. Torney-Purta, & J. Schwille (Eds.), *New paradigms and recurring paradoxes in education for citizenship* (pp. 105–136). Amsterdam: Elsevier.

Scott, W., & Oulton, C. (1998). Environmental values education: An exploration of its role in the school curriculum. *Journal of Moral Education, 27* (2), 209–224.

Seaford, H. (2001). Children and childhood: Perceptions and realities. *Political Quarterly, 72* (4), 454–466.

Sears, A., Clarke, G., & Hughes, A. (1999). Canadian citizenship education: The pluralist ideal and citizenship education for a post-modern state. In J. Torney-Purta, J. Schwille, & J. Amadeo (Eds.), *Civic education across countries* (pp. 111–135). Amsterdam: International Association for the Evaluation of Educational Achievement.

Sears, A.M., & Hughes, A.S. (1996). Citizenship education and current educational reform. *Canadian Journal of Education, 21* (2), 123–142.

Seaton, A. (2002). Reforming the hidden curriculum: The key abilities model and four curricular forms. *Curriculum Perspectives, 22* (1), 9–15.

Selman, R.L. (1980). *The growth of interpersonal understanding: Development and clinical analysis.* New York: Academic Press.

Shafer, N. (1992). Human rights education: Alternative conceptions. In J. Lynch, C. Modgil, & S. Modgil (Eds.), *Human rights education and global Responsibility,* vol. 4, *Cultural diversity and schools* (pp. 21–50). London: Falmer.

Shetty, A., & Ratna, K. (2002). Knowing rights from wrongs in India. *Childrens' Rights Information Network Newsletter, 16* (October), 31–32.

Shue, H. (1980). *Basic rights.* Princeton: Princeton University Press.

Sitch, G., & McCoubrey, S. (2001). Stay in your seat: The impact of judicial subordination of students' rights on effective rights education. *Education and Law Journal, 11,* 173–202.

Slavin, R. (1983). When does cooperative learning increase student achievement? *Psychological Bulletin, 94,* 429–445.

Slavin, R. (1995). *Cooperative learning: Theory, research and practice.* Boston: Allyn and Bacon.

Small, M., & Limber, S. (2002). Advocacy for children's rights. In B. Bottoms, M. Kovera, & B. McAulifff (Eds.), *Children, social science and the law* (pp. 64–72). Cambridge: Cambridge University Press.

Smith, T. (2002). How citizenship got on to the political agenda. *Parliamentary Affairs, 55,* 475–487.

Sprinthall, N.A., Hall, J.S., & Gerler, E. (1992). Peer counseling for middle school students. *Elementary School Guidance and Counselling, 26,* 279–294.

Sprinthall, N.A., & Scott, J. (1989). Promoting psychological development, math achievement, and success attributions of female students through deliberative psychological education. *Journal of Counseling Psychology, 36,* 440–446.

Starkey, H. (1991). The Council of Europe recommendation on the teaching and learning of human rights in schools. In H. Starkey (Ed.), *The challenge of human rights education* (pp. 21–38). London: Cassell.

Stasiulis, D. (2002). The active child citizen: Lessons from Canadian policy and the children's movement. *Citizenship Studies, 6* (4), 507–538.

Steel, K. (1999). One child, one vote: UNICEF and Elections Canada team up to enthuse kids on their 'rights.' *B.C. Report,* 9 Aug. 9, 28–31.

Stewart, F. (1991). Citizens of planet earth. In G. Andrews (Ed.), *Citizenship* (pp. 65–75). London: Lawrence and Wishart.

Stone, L. (1977). *The family, sex and marriage in England.* New York: Harper and Row.

Strom, M.S., & Parsons, W.S. (1982). *Facing history and ourselves: Holocaust and human behavior.* Brookline, MA: Facing History and Ourselves Foundation.

Stuhlman, M.W., Hamare, B., & Planta, R. (2002). Advancing the teen/teacher connection. *Education Digest, 68* (3), 15–20.

Sutherland, M. (2002). Educating citizens in Europe: Conflicting trends. *European Education, 34* (3), 77–97.

Synott, J. (2000). The emergence of a global paradigm in education. *New Horizons in Education, 102,* 1–10.

Tapp, P. (1997). Children's views on children's rights: You don't have rights, you only have privileges. *Children's Issues, 30* (1), 23–30.

Tarrow, N. (1992). Human rights education: Alternative conceptions. In J. Lynch, C. Modgil, & S. Modgil (Eds.), *Human rights education and global responsibility,* vol. 4, *Cultural diversity and schools* (pp. 21–50). London: Falmer.

Taylor, N., Smith, A.B., & Nairn, K. (2001). Rights important to young people: Secondary student and staff perspectives. *International Journal of Children's Rights, 9,* 137–156.

Terren, E. (2002). Post-modern attitudes: A challenge to democratic education. *European Journal of Education, 37* (2), 162–177.

Thies-Sprinthall, L., & Sprinthall, N.A. (1987). Experienced teachers: Agents for revitalization and renewal as mentors and teacher educators. *Journal of Education, 169,* 65–79.

Tiana, A. (2002). Are our young people prepared? *Prospects, 31* (1), 39–50.

Tibbits, F. (1997). *An annotated primer for selecting democratic and human rights education teaching materials.* Amsterdam: Open Society Institute / Human Rights Education Associates.

Tibbits, F. (2002). Understanding what we do: Emerging models for human rights education. International Review of Education. Special Issue on Education and Human Rights, 48 (3–4), 159–171.

Toope, S. (1996). The Convention on the Rights of the Child: Implications for Canada. In M. Freeman (Ed.), *Children's rights: A comparative perspective* (pp. 33–64). Aldershot: Dartmouth Publishing.

Torney-Purta, J. (1982). Socialization and human rights research: Implications for teachers. In M.S. Branson & J. Torney-Purta (Eds), *International human rights, society and the schools* (pp. 35–48). Washington, D.C.: National Council for Social Studies.

Torney-Purta, J. (1984). Human rights. In N.J. Graves, O.J. Dunlop, & J. Torney-Purta (Eds.), *Teaching for international understanding, peace, and human rights* (pp. 59–84). Paris: UNESCO.

Torney-Purta, J. (2002). Patterns in the civic knowledge, engagement and attitudes of European adolescents: The IEA Civic Education Study. *European Journal of Education, 37* (2), 129–141.

Torney-Purta, J., Lehmann, R., Oswald, H., & Schultz, W. (2001). *Citizenship and education in twenty-eight Countries: Civic knowledge and engagement at age fourteen.* Amsterdam: The International Association for the Evaluation of Educational Achievement.

Torney-Purta, J., Schwille, J., & Amadeo, J. (Eds.). (1999). *Civic education across Countries: Twenty-four national case studies from the IEA Civic Education Project.* Wellington, N.Z.: Becky Bliss Design and Production.

Travers, C.J., & Cooper, C.L. (1993). Mental health, job satisfaction and occupational stress among U.K. teachers. *Work and stress, 7* (3), 203–219.

U.N. Committee on the Rights of the Child (2003). *Country Reports.* New York: author.

Canada. (2001). CRC/C/83/Add.6

Costa Rica. (1998). CRC/C/65/Add.7

Czech Republic. (2002). CRC/C/83/Add.4

Denmark. (2000). CRC/C/70/Add.6

Egypt. (1999). CRC/C/65/Add.9

Ethiopia. (2000). CRC/C/70/Add.7

Honduras. (1998). CRC/C/65/Add.2

Iceland. (2003). CRC/C/83/Add.5

Poland. (2002). CRC/C/70/Add.12

Russian Federation. (1998). CRC/C/65/Add.5

Sweden. (1998). CRC/C/65/Add.3

Ukraine. (2201). CRC/C/70/Add.11

– (1999). *Concluding observations of the Committee on the Rights of the Child* New York: author. Includes the following Country Reports:

Austria. (1999). CRC/C/15/Add.98.

Costa Rica. (1993). CRC/C/15/Add.11

France. (1994). CRC/C/15/Add.20

Iceland. (1996). CRC/C/15/Add.50

Norway. (1994). CRC/C/15/Add.23

Poland. (1995). CRC/C/15/Add.31

Sweden. (1993). CRC/C/15/Add.2

United Kingdom. (1995). CRC/C/SR.205

– (1996). Report of the Committee on the Rights of the Child Supplement No. 41 (A/51/41). New York: author.

– (30 Oct. 1991). *General guidelines regarding the form and content of initial reports.* CRC/C/5. New York: author.

UNCED. (1992). *Earth Summit 1992: The United Nations Conference on Environment and Development Agenda 21.* London: Regency.

UNESCO. (1974). Council of Europe Committee of Ministers. *Recommendation No. R. (85)7: On teaching and learning about human rights in schools.* Paris: author.

UNICEF. (1992). *Education for development.* New York: author.

Van Bueren, G. (1995). *The international law on the rights of the child.* Dordrecht: Martinus Nijhoff.

Veenman, S., Kenter, B., & Post, K. (2000). Cooperative learning in Dutch primary classrooms. *Educational Studies, 26* (3), 281–303.

Verhagen, F.C. (2002). The Earth Community School (ECS) model of secondary education: Contributing to sustainable societies and thriving civilizations. *Social Alternatives, 21* (1), 11–17.

Verhellen, E. (1993). Children's rights and education. *School Psychology International, 14* (3), 199–208.

Verhellen, E. (1994). *Convention on the Rights of the Child.* Kessel-Lo, Belgium: Garant.

Verhellen, E. (1999). Facilitating children's rights in education. *Prospects, 29* (2), 224–231.

Wade, R.C. (1994). Conceptual change in elementary social studies: A case study of fourth graders' understanding of human rights. *Theory and Research in Social Education, 22* (1), 74–95.

Wall, D., Moll, M., & Froese-Germaine, G. (2000). *Contemporary approaches to citizenship education.* Ottawa: Canadian Teachers Federation.

Wall, J., Covell, K., & MacIntyre, P. (1999). Implications of social supports for adolescents' education and career aspirations. *Canadian Journal of Behavioural Science, 31* (2), 63–71.

Walmsley, A. (2001). Teaching in Belfast. *Kappa Delta Pi Record, 38* (1), 35–36.

Welti, C. (2002). Adolescents in Latin America: Facing the future with skepticism. In B.B. Brown, R. Larson, & T.S. Saraswathi (Eds.), *The world's youth: Adolescence in eight regions of the globe.* (pp. 276–306). New York: Cambridge University Press.

Willemot, Y. (1997). *UNICEF and child rights education.* In E. Verhellen (Ed.), *Understanding children's rights* (pp. 725–732). Ghent: University of Ghent, Children's Rights Centre.

Willinsky, J. (2002). Democracy and education: The missing link may be ours. *Harvard Educational Review, 72* (3), 367–392.

Woll, L. (2000). *The Convention on the Rights of the Child Impact Study.* Sweden: Save the Children.

Wraga, W.G. (2001). Lessons from progressives. *Democracy and Education, 14* (2), 29–32.

Wringe, C. (1999). Being good and living well: Three attempts to resolve an ambiguity. *Journal of Philosophy of Education, 33,* 287–293.

Wronka, J. (1994). Human rights and social policy in the United States: An educational agenda for the 21st century. *Journal of Moral Education, 23,* 261–272.

Wyse, D. (2001). Felt-tip pens and school councils: Children's participation rights in four English schools. *Children and Society, 15* (4), 209–218.

Young, I. (1989). Polity and group difference: A critique of the ideal of universal citizenship. *Ethics, 99,* 250–274.

Young, I. (1997). Difference as a resource for democratic communication. In J. Bohman & W. Rehg (Eds.), *Deliberative democracy: Essays on reason and politics* (pp. 383–406). Cambridge, MA: MIT Press.

Youniss, J. (1980). *Parents and peers in social development.* Chicago: University of Chicago Press.

Youssef, R.M., Attia, M., & Kamel, M. (1998). Children experience violence 11: Prevalence and determinants of corporal punishment in schools. *Child Abuse and Neglect, 22* (10), 975–984.

Zsuzsa, M. (1999). In transit: Civic education in Hungary. In J. Torney-Purta, J. Schwille, & J. Amadeo (Eds.), *Civic education across countries: Twenty-four national case studies from the IEA Civic Education Project* (pp. 341–370). Wellington, N.Z.: Becky Bliss Design and Production.

Index